COURTS AND TRIALS

A Reference Handbook

Other Titles in ABC-CLIO's
**CONTEMPORARY
WORLD ISSUES**
Series

American Homelessness, Mary Ellen Hombs
Capital Punishment, Michael Kronenwetter
Families in America, Jeffrey Scott Turner
New Slavery, Kevin Bales
Nuclear Power, Harry Henderson
Nuclear Weapons and Nonproliferation, Sarah J. Diehl and James
    Clay Moltz
Police Misconduct in America, Dean J. Champion
Racial Justice in America, David B. Mustard
Rainforests of the World, Kathlyn Gay
Religion and Politics, Glenn H. Utter and John W. Storey
The Religious Right, Glenn Utter and John W. Storey
Tax Reform, James John Jurinski
Tobacco, Harold V. Cordry
U.S. National Security, Cynthia A. Watson
Urban Sprawl, Donald D. Williams
Work and Family in America, Leslie Stebbins
World Population, Geoffrey Gilbert

Books in the Contemporary World Issues series address vital issues in today's society such as genetic engineering, pollution, and biodiversity. Written by professional writers, scholars, and nonacademic experts, these books are authoritative, clearly written, up-to-date, and objective. They provide a good starting point for research by high school and college students, scholars, and general readers as well as by legislators, businesspeople, activists, and others.

Each book, carefully organized and easy to use, contains an overview of the subject, a detailed chronology, biographical sketches, facts and data and/or documents and other primary-source material, a directory of organizations and agencies, annotated lists of print and nonprint resources, and an index.

Readers of books in the Contemporary World Issues series will find the information they need in order to have a better understanding of the social, political, environmental, and economic issues facing the world today.

COURTS AND TRIALS

A Reference Handbook

Christopher E. Smith

**CONTEMPORARY
WORLD ISSUES**

ABC-CLIO

Santa Barbara, California
Denver, Colorado
Oxford, England

Library of Congress Cataloging-in-Publication Data

Smith, Christopher E.
    Courts and trials : a reference handbook / Christopher E. Smith.
        p. cm. (Contemporary world issues)
    Includes index.
    ISBN 1-57607-933-3 (hardcover : alk. paper); 1-57607-934-1 (e-book)
    1. Courts—United States. 2. Trials—United States. 3. Procedure
(Law) I. Title. II. Series.
    KF8719.S552 2003
    347.73'1—dc21   2002155573

06 05 04 03 02   10 9 8 7 6 5 4 3 2 1

This book is also available on the World Wide Web as an e-book.
Visit abc-clio.com for details.

ABC-CLIO, Inc.
130 Cremona Drive, P.O. Box 1911
Santa Barbara, California 93116–1911

This book is printed on acid-free paper ∞.
Manufactured in the United States of America

Contents

Preface, xi

Chapter 1   Introduction, 1
The Image and Legitimacy of Courts, 1
The Distinguishing Characteristics and Functions of
    Courts, 3
    Distinctive Decisionmaking, 3
    Norm Enforcement, 4
    Dispute Processing, 5
    Buffer between Citizens and Government, 6
    Policymaking, 7
The Structure of Courts, 7
    Trial Courts of Limited Jurisdiction, 9
    Trial Courts of General Jurisdiction, 12
    Appellate Courts, 13
Trial Processes and the Role of Rights, 16
    Rights in the Criminal Trial Process, 16
    Criminal Trial Processes, 19
    Civil Trial Processes, 29
Conclusion, 30
References and Further Reading, 31

Chapter 2   Issues and Controversies, 33
Methods for Selecting Judges, 34
    Judicial Elections, 35
    Judicial Appointments, 36
    Merit Selection, 38
The Adversary System versus the Inquisitorial System, 40
    The Adversary System, 41
    The Inquisitorial System, 42
    The Systems Compared, 43
Legal Representation for the Poor, 45
    Appointed Counsel, 47

Contract Counsel, 47
Public Defenders, 48
Another Alternative, 48
The Capacity of Citizen-Jurors to Make Judicial
    Decisions, 49
    The History of Jury Trials, 50
    Jury Trials around the World, 51
    U.S. Jury Trials, 52
    Complex Information and the Jury, 54
Accessibility of Civil Courts for Dispute Resolution, 56
    Small-Claims Court, 57
    Contingency Fees, 58
    European Approaches, 59
    Court Access and Governmental Priorities, 61
Civil Justice Reform, 62
    Tort Reform, 63
    Cyber Court, 64
    Court-Annexed Alternative Dispute Resolution, 65
    Binding Arbitration, 68
Public Access to Information about Court Cases, 68
    Conflicts between Public Access and Other Goals, 69
    Cameras in the Courtroom, 70
    Security Risks and Open Trials, 72
Sentencing Reform, 73
    Mandatory Sentences, 74
    Sentencing Guidelines, 74
Conclusion, 76
References and Further Reading, 76

Chapter 3   Chronology, 79
References and Further Reading, 104

Chapter 4   Biographical Sketches, 107

Chapter 5   Documents and Statistics, 131
Selected Provisions of the U.S. Constitution, 132
    Article III, 132
    Amendment V (1791), 133
    Amendment VI (1791), 133
    Amendment VII (1791), 134
    Amendment VIII (1791), 134

Amendment XIV (1868), 135
Selected Examples of Additional Statutory
and Other Materials, 136
Merit Selection of Judges in Missouri, 136
Judicial Selection in New Mexico, 138
Alternative Dispute Resolution in Florida, 139
Sentencing Guidelines Commission in Minnesota, 139
North Dakota Rules on Cameras in the Courtroom, 140
Michigan's Cyber Court, 142
Juror Note-Taking in Missouri, 142
Eligibility for Legal Assistance: Legal Services
Corporation, 143
Excerpts from the Testimony: President of the
Legal Services Corporation, 144
Key Decisions of the U.S. Supreme Court Affecting
Courts and Trials, 146
Data on Courts and Trials, 169
Court Organization, 169
The Nature of Court Caseloads and the
Prevalence of Trials, 170
Case Processing Time and Duration of Trials, 173
Sentencing Guidelines, 173

Chapter 6   Agencies and Organizations, 177

Chapter 7   Print Resources, 205
Books, 205
Journals, Magazines, and Newsletters, 226
Government Documents and Agency Publications, 230

Chapter 8   Nonprint Resources, 235
Films, 236
Internet Addresses, 242

Glossary, 245
Index, 253
About the Author, 265

Preface

Courts are governmental institutions that serve important functions for society, including dispute processing, policymaking, and the enforcement of rules. Courts have a profound effect on people within their jurisdiction, especially individuals subjected to a civil lawsuit or a criminal prosecution. When legal cases proceed through the court system to reach the trial stage—the most elaborate and expensive court process—average citizens can be involved as litigants, jurors, and consumers of news media coverage. Despite their importance, courts are often shrouded in mystery because their proceedings are controlled by specially trained professionals; much about their operations is not understood by the public. Courts seem familiar to people, especially in the United States, where many TV shows portray dramatic stories of lawyers and judges. However, the public image of courts and trials often fails to capture the details, controversies, and developments that shape the manner in which courts affect people's lives.

Courts are not static institutions. They evolve and change as officials make new decisions about how judicial institutions and processes can be reformed to fulfill society's needs. These decisions often require difficult choices from among options that emerge during debates about controversial questions. Many of these questions are not easy to evaluate: Are average citizens capable of being good decisionmakers on juries? Should poor people have greater access than they currently have to legal processes and professional representation? Should judges use their own discretion in determining sentences for criminal offenders? Can disputes be handled more effectively through processes, such as mediation and arbitration, that are different than traditional adversarial trials? Debates over the best ways to shape courts and trials are important because of the impact these institutions and processes have on public policy and the lives of individual citizens.

This book provides a comprehensive overview of courts and trial processes, including the functions of courts for society. It also examines important debates about how courts and trials might be improved to better serve people's needs, including coverage of specific court reforms and their effects. In addition, information about the history of courts and trials is given, including people and events that figured prominently in determining the image and impact of judicial proceedings. Finally, several chapters provide resources that may be used in order to obtain additional information about courts and trials. The development of Internet websites, in particular, has made it possible for citizens to obtain an unprecedented wealth of information about courts and trials.

Chapter 1 presents the functions of courts for society and describes the details of trial processes. Chapter 2 discusses eight important issues that generate questions and debates about how courts and trial processes might be refined and improved. A chronology of important events in court history and major trials, presented in Chapter 3, provides perspective on how judicial institutions and processes have developed and affected society. Brief biographical sketches, presented in Chapter 4, highlight important individuals who shaped courts or who used trial processes to impact society. Chapter 5 contains important primary source materials and data on courts and trials. Included within the same chapter are selected provisions of the U.S. Constitution, examples of state statutes about court reforms and trial procedures, and information about the number and kinds of cases processed in the courts. Court organizations and judicial reform groups are profiled in Chapter 6. Chapter 7 contains information on print resources, including books, magazines, and government reports. The coverage of nonprint resources in Chapter 8 focuses on films and Internet websites. In addition, there is a glossary defining many important terms relevant to court organization and trial processes.

1

Introduction

This chapter presents an overview of courts, including their organization and functions. Although courts are components of government, they are mysterious and complicated institutions because they are controlled by officials with special training in law and are not easily accessible to the public. The processes and decisions of courts have significant impacts on people's lives. Court decisions in criminal cases determine which people will be punished for crimes and whether or not they will be sent to prison. Court decisions in civil lawsuits transfer significant sums between businesses and individuals to remedy personal injuries, contract violations, and other matters. Court decisions can also shape public policies concerning various issues like abortion and the environment. Because the organization and processes of courts influence how they produce decisions, citizens of any country have strong reasons to be interested in debates about whether courts are structured to operate in a manner that best fulfills these institutions' functions for society.

The Image and Legitimacy of Courts

When people envision the governing institutions called courts, they usually picture majestic marble buildings containing ornate rooms in which black-robed judges preside from impressive elevated benches. These judges speak with great formality, using words and phrases that are unfamiliar to the layperson. Even in

English-speaking countries, judges employ Latin and French phrases that are incomprehensible to fellow citizens. In several countries, judges wear powdered white wigs reminiscent of those worn by eighteenth-century British aristocrats. Such images convey the message that courts are rooted in ancient traditions and thereby deserve deference and cooperation from a country's people. Indeed, the majesty and formality of courts may make them seem more like respected religious institutions than like fallible agencies of government. In reality, these familiar images are not necessarily accurate for all courts. Low-level courts that handle only traffic offenses or lawsuits for small amounts of money may consist of a single judicial officer dressed in regular street clothes who supervises proceedings in a simple room containing only folding chairs and a modest desk or table. These courts, however, are less visible to the public and are seldom portrayed in TV shows and films. Instead, the familiar imagery of majesty, tradition, and power associated with courts is reinforced in the minds of the public. This imagery supports the power and effectiveness of courts, because people have learned that courts are institutions that must be respected and obeyed. Courts fulfill important functions for a society, and they need cooperation from the public to be effective.

Courts are institutions that produce important decisions on behalf of a country's governing system. The organization, processes, and powers of these institutions vary from country to country. In the United States, courts are exceptionally powerful because the U.S. Constitution provides a basis for decisions by judges that shape controversial public policies. U.S. judges can declare that acts by the president, Congress, and state legislatures violate the Constitution; thereby judges can nullify the decisions made by elected officials at all levels of federal and state governments. Judges in other countries, by contrast, can seldom invalidate actions by national leaders or legislatures. More important, different countries' courts share similarities in the basis for their decisions and in their functions.

The Distinguishing Characteristics and Functions of Courts

Distinctive Decisionmaking

Decisions produced by courts are distinguished from decisions by other governing institutions in two important ways. First, unlike decisions generated by other authoritative institutions within governments, court decisions are guided by law. Decisionmakers within courts, whether they are juries, judges, or other judicial officers, seek to follow the authoritative rules of society as embodied in constitutions, statutes, and court precedents. Although decisionmakers make discretionary judgments and apply personal values in reaching decisions, the application of discretion and values is limited by decisionmakers' efforts to make their decisions fit the boundaries and guidelines imposed by legal rules. By contrast, decisionmakers, such as presidents, prime ministers, legislators, and military officers, within other institutions openly make decisions based on discretionary judgments, policy preferences, and orders from superior officials. Although courts cultivate an image as institutions producing decisions based on neutral principles of justice and the established rules of society, institutions and decisionmakers elsewhere in government are viewed as being guided by political self-interest. Second, court decisions typically must be generated by carefully specified legal processes. Claims presented to the courts must be filed using specific forms and be couched in the language of law. Usually, legal claims must be presented by attorneys who are trained in law rather than by average citizens who lack knowledge about the technical rules of court procedure. The opposing sides in a legal case are generally permitted to submit arguments and evidence intended to persuade the judge or jury about the merits of their respective positions.

In addition, courts use specific rules of evidence to determine what kinds of information can be included in decisions (whether by a judge or a jury) about the guilt of criminal defendants or the winning side in a civil lawsuit. By contrast, decisions in legislatures may be produced through backroom deals and lobbying by interest groups. In executive agencies, unilateral decisions may be made behind closed doors without permitting the public to observe or contribute to the decisionmaking process.

These distinctive aspects of courts reinforce their image as trustworthy institutions guided by principles rather than by politics. Unlike national leaders who command military forces and legislatures that can use taxing and spending policies to ensure compliance with their decisions, judges have no direct capacity to ensure that their decisions are obeyed. Thus courts need to enhance and maintain the revered image of the judicial branch to garner sufficient public respect and compliance to enable courts to fulfill their functions for society.

Norm Enforcement

Courts perform several functions. In criminal cases, courts serve a norm-enforcement function. Societies define certain rules as being of sufficient importance to require that punishments be imposed upon people who violate those rules. These rules, as embodied in the criminal laws, represent important norms, or values, for society. In the effort to enforce rules, courts play an essential role in processing the cases of those accused of criminal violations, including the determination of guilt and the pronouncement of punishment. The use of formal procedures in courts is intended to ensure that determinations of guilt are careful, proper, and consistent with the rules of justice. Moreover, the formal setting and procedures in courts communicate to the public the importance of the laws and social norms being enforced. In some societies, guilt is determined and punishment swiftly imposed through discretionary decisions of military leaders or rulers. Surprise nighttime arrests, swift and secret determinations of guilt, and summary executions provide the most graphic examples of discretionary norm-enforcement processes by authoritarian governments. Such methods are likely to frighten the public and to thereby convey the message that the government regards the criminal laws as an extremely important mechanism for maintaining order and controlling the populace. However, such methods are also likely to breed hostility from the public as well as suspicions that the determinations of guilt are based on political opposition to the government rather than actual criminal acts. By contrast, courts' image as majestic institutions that make decisions according to careful deliberation and principles of law can reassure the public that government enforcement of criminal laws is fair, proper, and worthy of respect and acceptance.

Dispute Processing

Another function served by courts is dispute processing. When individuals have disputes over property, money, contracts, and personal injuries, a society needs mechanisms to process and resolve them. In the absence of official mechanisms to handle disputes, people would address conflicts themselves and thereby produce risks that interpersonal violence would eventually develop when disagreements are sufficiently intense. The use of self-help justice can produce unfair results if the stronger disputant can intimidate an opponent into surrendering despite the legitimacy of the weaker party's claim. Moreover, self-help justice, especially in its violent forms, produces social instability and fear. Without fair and reliable dispute-processing mechanisms, people would be reluctant to buy and sell goods, enter into contracts, and interact in ways that are beneficial to economic growth.

A society can have mechanisms for norm enforcement and dispute processing without using courts. Religious leaders or village elders, for example, could decide the outcomes of disputes or impose punishments based on customs when all of the people in a community share common values, religious beliefs, and respect for traditions. Similarly, a society could have a custom of relying on specific community figures or tribal councils to mediate disputes and define punishments under the authority of a traditional governing system based on a shared religion or culture. However, in a large diverse society in which people do not share common religious beliefs or cultural traditions, governments create laws to address issues of norm enforcement and dispute processing. In such societies, which are characteristic of modern nation-states, courts serve as the institutional entities that fulfill such important functions.

Because courts use law as the basis for decisionmaking, they can apply rules that were well-established and known to citizens as the citizens interact in contracts, sales, and other encounters that can produce disputes. In processing disputes, courts permit both sides in a dispute to present their arguments and evidence, thereby increasing the probability that disputants will feel as if their claims were heard and taken seriously by the decisionmakers. Moreover, because courts use careful legal procedures within a formal setting that conveys an image of importance and respect, their decisions are delivered to the public in a manner that encourages disappointed disputants to accept defeats and comply with court orders (e.g., to pay money to opponents with whom they vehemently disagreed). In addition, the legitimacy of courts as dispute-processing forums often leads executive agencies to use their powers and resources to enforce court orders. For example, in the aftermath of a court judgment in a civil lawsuit, a sheriff may seize property from the losing disputant to pay the debt.

Buffer between Citizens and Government

In some countries, courts also serve as a buffer between individual citizens and the government. Under U.S. law, for example, individuals can file lawsuits against the government for certain personal injuries, property damage, and deprivations of legal rights allegedly caused by governmental actions. If not for the availability of courts as forums to process claims against the government, individuals may feel frustrated and helpless and thereby become hostile to the government. Court proceedings serve to equalize the stature of disputants and convey the idea that each side will receive an equal hearing. Thus an individual has a genuine opportunity to have an authoritative decision-maker order the government to provide compensation, respect civil rights, or otherwise remedy a governmental violation of the law. Under some governing systems, however, courts may be subordinate to other branches of government and thus may lack the authority to consider claims against the government or to order the government to undertake remedial actions for the benefit of individuals.

To perform these functions effectively, courts must possess sufficient power and independence to make decisions and to have those decisions obeyed by citizens and governmental officials alike. If courts purport to fulfill these functions without possessing sufficient power, there is a risk that court proceedings can give the appearance of fair procedures and deliberate judgments, when in fact governmental officials secretly dictate to judges the decisions to be issued in court cases. When there are suspicions that judges' decisions are not produced independently in accordance with the rules of law, courts will lose legitimacy, and people will cease to rely on courts for dispute processing and for redressing claims against the government.

Policymaking

In the United States, more so than in other countries, courts serve one additional function. U.S. courts produce public policy, especially when judges interpret constitutional provisions and statutes. Because U.S. judges possess the authority to invalidate decisions taken by other branches of government, judges effectively determine what government will or will not do with respect to certain policy issues. For example, in its 1973 decision in *Roe v. Wade,* the U.S. Supreme Court determined that a woman's ability to make choices about abortions during the first six months of pregnancy is a protected component of a constitutional right to privacy. As a result, the Court effectively told federal and state governments that they could not create laws that would prevent women from making their own choices about terminating a pregnancy. Other court decisions have shaped public policies concerning such issues as school desegregation, religious activities in public schools, conditions in prisons, and capital punishment. In most other countries, courts can serve dispute-processing and norm-enforcement functions, but they lack the power to shape public policy by overruling the decisions by other branches of government concerning policy issues.

The Structure of Courts

U.S. TV shows and films portray jury trials as typical court proceedings. In dramatized criminal cases, prosecutors and defense attorneys square off in lengthy courtroom battles that involve the presentation of dramatic testimony from witnesses; physical evidence, such as blood, weapons, and fingerprints found at the crime scene; and impassioned arguments intended to persuade the jury about the defendant's guilt or innocence. Portrayals of civil legal actions concerning personal injuries, divorces, and other disputes between individuals are similarly dramatic and dependent on the persuasiveness and showmanship of the attorneys representing each side. And though such dramatics do occur, they are much less common than portrayed in the media. Moreover, the courtroom trial reflects only one type of legal process, and it occurs only in certain courts. In reality, there are different kinds of courts, and the nature of legal proceedings therein depends on the court's function within the legal system.

The United States has an especially complex court system. Unlike countries with national court systems providing common rules and procedures for courts throughout an entire nation, the United States has a *dual court system:* The federal court system is separate from parallel state systems that coexist throughout the country. Both systems have their own trial courts as well as courts to handle appeals. The dual structure reflects the system of *federalism* that characterizes the nature of the government established by the U.S. Constitution. Under federalism, the national government as well as the states are authorized to have their own legislatures, executive agencies, and court systems that create and enforce laws for the territory under their jurisdiction. The U.S. Constitution authorizes the federal government to enact laws and programs concerning specified issues, such as international trade, interstate commerce, the national treasury, and national security. States create and enforce laws affecting the complete range of other issues for people and events within their own borders. Thus, in the context of criminal justice, federal courts hear only cases concerning the limited range of criminal laws that the federal government is authorized to enact and administer. These cases concern criminal laws against smuggling, counterfeiting, tax evasion, espionage, the assassination of federal officials, and other topics related to national security, international trade, and federal taxation powers. By contrast, states define and enforce laws governing the full range of remaining crimes, such as murder, assault, and robbery. The vast majority of criminal cases are processed in state courts because they concern violations of state laws. Similarly, the overwhelming majority of civil cases concerning property ownership, contract disputes, personal injuries, and other noncriminal matters are handled by state courts. Federal civil cases primarily concern issues arising from federal statutes and the U.S. Constitution, such as disputed claims for Social Security benefits, alleged violations of constitutional rights, or discrimination (e.g., in employment or housing). In light of the U.S. system of federalism, it is more accurate to describe the United States as having fifty-one separate court systems, one for each state and one for the federal government.

The complexity of the dual court system in the United States is enhanced by the diversity of court structures and laws within the states. Each state can design its own court system and operate it according to state laws (as long as those laws do not violate the U.S. Constitution). For example, no state can authorize racial discrimination in violation of the Equal Protection Clause contained in the Fourteenth Amendment to the U.S. Constitution. However, states can use their own rules for determining deadlines for filing appeals and for defining punishments applied to criminal offenders, as well as other matters that affect court operations. Although there is great similarity among states' criminal laws, there are some actions, such as gambling, that will be legal in some states but illegal in others. There is even greater diversity in civil laws that address taxation, the environment, and other matters. Because the details are unique to each state, U.S. lawyers cannot easily practice before the courts in multiple states. Usually, they gain expertise in the laws of one particular state. Moreover, because each state controls the licensing of its attorneys, U.S. lawyers cannot practice law throughout the country. They must fulfill the licensing requirements within each state where they will handle cases. In specific cases, out-of-state attorneys may be permitted to practice in another jurisdiction, but usually they must be working with an attorney from that jurisdiction in representing the client.

Individual countries and U.S. states design their own court systems. Typically, one or more levels of a court system are *trial courts* responsible for processing cases and producing an initial decision. In criminal cases, these courts hear evidence and oversee judgments on the guilt of defendants who have been accused of violating criminal laws. Some countries use juries of fellow citizens drawn from the community, but some systems rely exclusively on judges as the decisionmakers. In civil cases, trial courts help determine whether or not a party owes compensation or whether an individual's legal rights have been violated. Often, one or more higher-level courts are responsible for hearing appeals of trial court decisions. In addition, some court systems have specialized courts that handle only specific kinds of cases. A few states have separate appellate courts for civil and criminal cases. The federal system has specialized trial courts for bankruptcy cases and specialized appellate courts for reviewing denials of veterans appeals, issuing search warrants to monitor suspected spies and terrorists, and considering appeals in patent disputes.

Trial Courts of Limited Jurisdiction

At the lowest level of U.S. state court systems are trial courts of limited jurisdiction. These courts handle civil cases involving disputes over small amounts of money or criminal cases concerning traffic offenses and misdemeanors (as compared to felonies). Some states have small-claims courts that process civil lawsuits seeking $2,000 or less in disputes over damaged property or violations of leases. Other states have courts dedicated to processing traffic violations. Trials are relatively rare in limited-jurisdiction courts. People charged with traffic violations and minor criminal offenses usually face light penalties, typically fines or probation. Only a small percentage of offenders face the prospect of a few days or months in jail (e.g., because they committed a misdemeanor assault or are repeat offenders). Prosecutors usually do not wish to devote time and money to conducting trials in minor cases, especially because limited jurisdiction trial courts have significant caseloads. Thus prosecutors usually offer plea agreements intended to induce quick guilty pleas. Plea bargaining feeds the self-interest of most people accused of lesser offenses because they can avoid the risk of receiving the maximum penalty as well as the time and expense of trial preparation. As a result, limited jurisdiction trial courts are often characterized as assembly-line operations in which dozens and dozens of people quickly plead guilty and receive punishments of fines and probation. Similarly, civil lawsuits for small sums of money seldom produce trials because the cost of hiring an attorney would exceed the amount being sought in the proceeding. Litigants present their own cases in quick proceedings before a judicial officer, or they negotiate settlement agreements with opponents.

The federal court system does not have limited jurisdiction trial courts. Its trial courts are general jurisdiction courts that handle a full range of legal matters. U.S. bankruptcy courts are specialized trial courts in the federal system. However, they are considered to be components of general jurisdiction federal trial courts and under the supervision of U.S. district judges rather than separate, limited-jurisdiction courts like small-claims courts and traffic courts in state systems.

In England and Wales, trial courts of limited jurisdiction are known as Magistrate Courts. The decisionmakers in these courts are lay magistrates, that is, people drawn from the community who serve as judges despite a lack of legal training. The selection of magistrates has been criticized because few people from working-class backgrounds or members of racial and ethnic minority groups are selected to serve. On a part-time basis, magistrates, who go by the title justice of the peace, decide cases concerning minor offenses such as assault, traffic violations, and disorderly conduct. The magistrates sit in groups of three in deciding cases, and they cannot sentence offenders to more than one year of incarceration. Decisions of the Magistrate Courts can be appealed to the higher-level Crown Courts, which are overseen by judges who are trained in law (Jason-Lloyd 1997).

In the United States, many states have limited-jurisdiction courts that specialize in specific areas of law. These courts may handle matters that involve significant issues or large sums of money, but they have authority on a limited range of legal matters or a specific category of people. For example, after Illinois became the first state to establish a special juvenile court to handle matters involving children in 1899, other states quickly copied the innovation. As a result, separate courts within each state handle cases concerning criminal offenses and delinquent behavior by juveniles. In addition, many states have expanded the authority of these specialized institutions to create *family courts* that handle juvenile matters as well as matters of divorce, child custody, parental rights, and adoptions. Rather than strictly follow rigid rules and freely impose punishment, these courts often follow informal procedures that seek to restore family ties or rehabilitate wayward youths.

Because of growing concerns about violent crimes committed by youths, states began to create mechanisms to prosecute young offenders as adults in the regular trial courts that hear felony cases. Through these mechanisms, juveniles accused of serious felonies could be *waived* into adult courts. Some states' mandatory waiver statutes required youths above a certain age, say, fourteen, to be automatically placed in the adult criminal justice system if they were accused of specific serious crimes such as murder. Other states give prosecutors the authority to make discretionary determinations about which youths should be prosecuted as adults. Still others give judges the authority to waive juveniles into adult courts. The discretionary decisions by judges and prosecutors were usually based on the nature of the alleged offense and related behavior by the accused offender, such as gang membership or the commission of other violent acts. The increasing tendency of U.S. states to place juvenile offenders into the adult criminal justice system has attracted criticism at home and abroad by those who believe that it is inappropriate to punish youths as severely as adults, thereby foregoing any efforts to rehabilitate troubled youths.

Trial Courts of General Jurisdiction

Trial courts of general jurisdiction are the forums for the adversarial courtroom battles most familiar to viewers of TV shows and films about lawyers. There are dramatic presentations of evidence, arguments between opposing attorneys, and determinations of guilt or liability (or the lack thereof) in extended proceedings before a judge or a jury. Trial courts handle serious criminal charges, or felonies (as compared to misdemeanors), which can produce sentences ranging from one year in prison to the death penalty. Trial courts also process the full range of civil lawsuits for any amounts that exceed the low limits of the aforementioned limited-jurisdiction courts. Thus general jurisdiction trial courts process lawsuits seeking amounts typically ranging from $2,000 to many millions of dollars. Although a few individuals may represent themselves in general jurisdiction trial courts, most people have professional representation. Under the right to counsel contained in the Sixth Amendment to the U.S. Constitution, any defendant facing the possibility of incarceration as a punishment for conviction of a felony or serious misdemeanor in U.S. courts is always entitled to have an attorney provided by the government if he is too poor to afford to hire one. In civil cases, people seldom pursue litigation for large sums unless they have hired an attorney to represent them. Without an attorney's training in law and her experience with technical court procedures, it is difficult to navigate the complicated aspects of court procedures, especially when being vigorously challenged by an opponent's attorney. In the United States, there is no constitutional right to representation by an attorney in civil cases. Thus poor people are often simply unable to pursue valid civil lawsuits (Smith 1991).

In the United States, governments use different names for general jurisdiction trial courts. The federal trial courts are called *U.S. district courts*, whereas states use various names, including circuit courts (e.g., Michigan), superior courts (California), and courts of common pleas (Ohio). Each government, state and federal, creates its rules for its own trial courts. As a result, there are differences in the filing fees required to initiate civil lawsuits, the procedural steps in civil and criminal cases, and the rules concerning evidence that may be presented to prove guilt (criminal cases) or liability (civil cases). For example, some jurisdictions, including federal district courts, require that a grand jury issue an indictment before the prosecutor charges any person with a serious criminal offense. A grand jury is a body of citizens called together to meet in secret to decide whether a prosecutor's initial evidence justifies pursuing criminal charges against an individual. The grand jury's historic purpose was to prevent abusive or unjustified prosecutions by permitting community representatives to block unwarranted prosecutions. By contrast, in most state courts, prosecutors can initiate criminal charges through their own discretionary decisions as long as a judge agrees that sufficient evidence exists to justify the charges if a defendant demands that the initial evidence be presented in a preliminary hearing.

As in limited jurisdiction trial courts, most cases in U.S. trial courts of general jurisdiction are decided through negotiations between the opposing sides. Even in serious criminal cases, negotiated guilty pleas (plea bargains) produce more than 90 percent of the convictions. Except in the most serious cases, such as murder charges that can bring sentences of the death penalty or life in prison without possibility of release, most defendants eventually decide that they are better off pleading guilty and accepting a less-than-maximum sentence rather than risking a harsher result at trial. The plea-bargaining process also serves the interests of prosecutors, defense attorneys, and judges who usually prefer a swift, certain outcome to the lengthy and uncertain processes of trial. Defendants who are sufficiently wealthy to pay a lawyer to complete lengthy trial preparations, or those whose potential punishment is so severe that they might as well proceed to trial and hope for the possibility of acquittal, have strong incentives to go to trial. Most other defendants do not have such motivation, unless they strongly assert that they are actually innocent. Civil cases create similar pressures for negotiated outcomes because both sides often prefer to avoid the costs, delays, and uncertain results from trials.

Appellate Courts

After a trial, the losing side—whether a guilty criminal defendant or a liable civil litigant—can usually file an appeal. Most U.S. court systems have *intermediate appellate courts* that handle the initial appeals after the trial courts have entered their verdicts or judgments. The courts of appeals, or appellate courts, whether at the federal or state level, have very different purposes and procedures compared to trial courts. Appellate courts do not hear evidence, do not hold trials, do not use juries, and do not decide whether or not criminal defendants are guilty. They merely examine specific errors that the losing side claims were made during the trial court proceedings. Thus appellate courts can be asked to decide whether errors by police in collecting evidence should have been corrected by the trial court through the exclusion of evidence. Losing parties may also claim that the trial judge made improper instructions to the jury or that the judge interpreted the law improperly in deciding the case. If the appellate court decides that errors were made by the police, prosecutor, judge, or jury in the trial court proceedings, criminal defendants do not automatically go free, and losing civil litigants do not automatically win their cases. Instead, favorable appellate decisions frequently lead to an order that the trial court begin again and conduct a new trial in the case.

In appellate cases, lawyers submit written arguments, called *appellate briefs*, that review the relevant law and present arguments about the existence of errors in trial court proceedings. In many cases the lawyers will be invited to present oral arguments, but some appellate decisions are based only on written arguments submitted to the court. In U.S. intermediate appellate courts, there may be as many as two dozen judges serving on a single court. However, the judges split into smaller groups to decide cases; thus a court of appeals can hear several cases simultaneously. Decisions are usually made by panels consisting of three judges who hear and discuss a case together and then decide which one of the three will write an opinion expressing the court's decision. The judges do not need to be unanimous in their decision. Many appellate cases are decided by a 2-1 vote. In such cases, the judge who does not agree with the court's decision may issue a *dissenting opinion* to express reasons for the disagreement. In later cases, lawyers and judges may use the reasoning presented in dissenting opinions to formulate new arguments as to why cases with similar issues should be decided differently.

The top level of the U.S. court systems are courts of last resort, which are typically called *supreme courts*. The U.S. Supreme Court, comprised of nine justices, is the court of last resort for the federal court system. Each state has its own top court. State supreme courts usually consist of either five or seven justices. In deciding cases, the justices sit together as an entire group to hear and decide cases. As in other appellate courts, there are no trials, presentations of evidence, or juries. The highest courts of each jurisdiction consider whether there were specific errors of law and procedure in the lower trial and appellate courts that justify granting a request for a new trial. The supreme courts hear appeals from parties who lost in the intermediate courts of appeals. However, unlike intermediate appellate courts that decide a steady flow of appeals, courts of last resort usually have the discretionary authority to pick cases that they want to hear. The U.S. Supreme Court receives more than 6,000 requests each year to accept cases for hearing, but the justices typically give full hearings and decisions to fewer than 85 cases each year. Courts of last resort seek to reserve their time and energy for cases that raise significant questions about the meaning of state constitutions or, in the case of the U.S. Supreme Court, the U.S. Constitution. They also make decisions in cases that will impact a wide range of other cases. For example, if a particular kind of issue repeatedly arises concerning police officers' authority to search automobiles, a state supreme court is likely to decide one of those cases to settle the question and thereby give guidance to police and judges throughout the jurisdiction about how to handle such situations.

In the United States, each state supreme court is the authoritative institution that defines the meaning of its jurisdiction's constitution. By interpreting constitutions, supreme courts shape public policy. The U.S. Constitution, for example, provides a right to be represented by counsel in criminal cases. Lawyers brought cases to the U.S. Supreme Court seeking clarification of the meaning of these provisions. In interpreting the right to counsel, it was the U.S. Supreme Court that decided that poor criminal defendants are entitled to a government-provided defense attorney whenever they face the possibility of serving time in jail or prison upon conviction (*Argersinger v. Hamlin* [1972]). However, there is no similar entitlement to an attorney when the defendant merely faces the possibility of a fine as a criminal punishment (*Scott v. Illinois* [1979]). The words of the Constitution do not make any distinctions between cases concerning incarceration and cases concerning fines, but the Supreme Court justices created that distinction through their interpretation of the Constitution. By producing authoritative interpretations of constitutional provisions, supreme courts establish public policies by telling government officials what they can, cannot, or must do. In the right-to-counsel cases, Supreme Court decisions told government officials when they must provide defense attorneys for poor defendants.

Supreme Court decisions have similar impacts on other issues, such as police officers' authority to conduct searches, citizens' rights to practice their religions and to speak freely, and governmental practices that produce racial or gender discrimination.

Trial Processes and the Role of Rights

Rights in the Criminal Trial Process

The nature of the criminal trial process depends, in part, on the legal rights granted to the accused. The specific rights granted to criminal defendants determine what prosecutors and judges can and cannot do. The nature of rights varies from country to country and produces differences in the processes used in different countries' trials. In the United States, criminal trials are shaped significantly by the rights provided to criminal defendants in the U.S. Constitution. The constitutional provisions most relevant to criminal trials are contained in the Fifth and Sixth Amendments.

Among the rights contained in the Fifth Amendment, two are especially important for criminal trials. The amendment provides that "no person . . . shall be compelled in any criminal case to be a witness against himself." Thus U.S. criminal defendants are permitted to remain silent during their trials, and the prosecutor is not allowed to use that silence as evidence that the defendant is guilty. The prosecutor is responsible for presenting evidence to establish guilt, and no negative inferences can be drawn from the defendant's refusal to testify on his or her own behalf. By contrast, if criminal defendants in France refuse to testify at their own trials, the judges and jury are permitted to consider that silence as evidence that the defendant is attempting to hide relevant information. As a result, most defendants in France testify at their own trials to avoid the prospect of negative inferences (Jacob et al. 1996). By contrast, many U.S. defendants never testify. Moreover, under U.S. rules, defendants with criminal records are discouraged by their attorneys from testifying because rules of evidence usually forbid prosecutors from informing the judge and jury about the defendant's unrelated prior criminal convictions unless the defendant opens the subject for examination by agreeing to testify in the case.

The Fifth Amendment also says "nor shall any person be subject for the same offence to be twice put in jeopardy of life or limb." The underlying purpose of this right is to prevent the prosecution from placing a defendant on trial over and over again after failing to gain a conviction in an initial criminal proceeding. Although the right against *double jeopardy* is generally regarded as limiting the prosecution to one opportunity to convict a defendant at trial, in reality the Supreme Court's interpretation of this constitutional provision permits a number circumstances in which a defendant can be tried more than once. For example, a police officer found not guilty of assaulting a motorist in a state criminal trial may face a second trial in federal court if the federal prosecutor can present proof that the officer was motivated by racial discrimination and therefore violated federal civil rights laws in the same incident. Moreover, if a convicted defendant successfully appeals his or her conviction, there can be a second trial because the successful appeal has, in effect, erased the existence of the first trial. Thus the protection against double jeopardy prohibits a second trial on the same charges in the same jurisdiction when the defendant is acquitted in the first trial.

The Sixth Amendment contains a variety of rights relevant to criminal trials. The amendment says: "In all criminal prosecutions, the accused shall enjoy the right to a speedy and public trial, by an impartial jury of the State and district wherein the crime shall have been committed, which district shall have been previously ascertained by law, and to be informed of the nature and cause of the accusation; to be confronted with the witnesses against him; to have compulsory process for obtaining witnesses in his favor, and to have the Assistance of Counsel for his defence." Despite the opening words "in all criminal prosecutions," the Supreme Court has interpreted some of the Sixth Amendment's rights as applying only to specific kinds of trials. As described in the foregoing section on jury trials, for example, the right to trial by jury applies only when defendants face serious charges punishable by six months or more of incarceration (*Lewis v. United States* [1996]). Similarly, the right to "Assistance of Counsel for his defence" means that the government must provide defense attorneys for poor criminal defendants, but that right does not apply to trials of minor offenses punishable only by fines (*Scott v. Illinois* [1979]) or appeals to courts of last resort (*Ross v. Moffitt* [1974]).

The right to a speedy trial is intended to prevent prosecutors from holding charges indefinitely over the heads of defendants. If the government possesses proof of an individual's guilt, the prosecutor must move forward and bring the defendant to trial. The term *speedy trial* does not, however, guarantee that the trial will occur within any specified time period. The U.S. Supreme Court has declined to place a specific time limit on criminal trials. Instead, the Court requires that the fulfillment of the right be judged by a general assessment of the length of delays, the reasons for delays, and whether the delays caused any disadvantages for the defense attorney's preparation of the case on behalf of the defendant. Thus if a prosecutor caused a lengthy delay and witnesses who would have supported the defendant's version of events died during the delay, then the right to speedy trial might have been violated. However, the Court has approved delays in excess of five years between the charging of a defendant and the initiation of a trial when the delay did not cause any disadvantages for the defendant (*Barker v. Wingo* [1972]). Despite the exceptional circumstances in which long delays may occur prior to trial, the existence of the right to speedy trial creates an incentive for prosecutors to move forward promptly to avoid the risk that a judge might dismiss charges against a defendant by finding that a delay occurred for improper reasons or harmed the defendant's case. Thus nearly all U.S. criminal cases are brought to trial within one year, and many occur within a matter of months after the defendant was arrested. By contrast, not all countries have rules that discourage or prevent long delays. Such circumstances can be especially harsh in countries that do not routinely release defendants on bail while they await their trials.

The right to a public trial is considered to be an important protection against the risk that the U.S. government might convict and punish people improperly in secret trials. When trials are open to the public and to the news media, a democratic government will feel pressure to follow proper procedures and make sure that sufficient evidence is presented to justify a finding of guilt. In exceptional circumstances, U.S. judges may limit access to certain court proceedings, such as some pretrial hearings in sex-offense cases, especially if the information available at the hearing will embarrass or intimidate a child victim. When an actual trial takes place, however, the trial will be open to the public. In Canada and Great Britain, trials are also open to the public, but those countries' laws impose restrictions on the information that can be reported in the news media. The purpose of such laws is to ensure that the accused has a fair trial. There are risks that publicly available information about a crime may make it difficult to find jurors who have not already developed an opinion about the case without having heard any official evidence in court. In the United States, judges issue orders to limit reporting by the news media only on rare occasions, and such orders are often challenged by news organizations and subsequently overturned by appellate courts. Generally, U.S. judges will order a *change of venue*—meaning an order to move a trial to a different location—if they conclude that potential jurors in the local area may have heard too much about or are likely to react too emotionally to a highly publicized crime.

In regular criminal trials, defendants enjoy the right to confront accusers and the right to compulsory process. The right to compulsory process refers to the defense attorneys' ability to gain orders requiring witnesses to appear in court. If defense attorneys had no power to compel the attendance of witnesses, there would be a risk that innocent defendants could be convicted if witnesses with favorable testimony were unwilling to come to court. The right to confrontation is intended to ensure that defendants can hear the accusations and evidence against them. In effect, the right to confrontation gives defendants a right to be present at their own trials. Otherwise, if trials occurred without the defendant, the accused would not know the precise nature and strength of evidence and would not have an adequate opportunity to challenge that evidence. The right to confrontation is not an absolute right to have a face-to-face confrontation with all accusers. The U.S. Supreme Court has permitted child sex-abuse victims to testify at trials via closed-circuit TV so that the defendant can see and hear their testimony; in this way young victims are not retraumatized by being forced to see their victimizer in person (*Maryland v. Craig* [1990]).

Because constitutional rights in the United States define the relationship between the individual and the government, rights are less important as elements in civil litigation involving lawsuits between private individuals or businesses. The Seventh Amendment to the Constitution guarantees a right to trial by jury in civil lawsuits in federal court, but the right does not apply to state courts. The availability of juries in state court civil cases is determined by the laws of each state.

Criminal Trial Processes

The pretrial stage of criminal cases begins with the discovery of a crime, usually through a report to the police by a citizen. Police officers investigate the crime by pursuing the goals of identifying the person or people responsible for the crime and of gathering evidence to prove the culpable individuals' guilt in court. In some countries, such as France and Spain, judges may assume responsibility for directing police investigations. In the United States and elsewhere, police bear primary responsibility for criminal investigations, and they work closely with prosecutors in carrying out such tasks.

In the United States, police must follow specific rules in undertaking investigations to ensure that the evidence obtained is admissible in court. Because the Fourth Amendment to the U.S. Constitution specifies conditions for granting search and arrest warrants and the amendment prohibits "unreasonable searches and seizures," police must follow rules when conducting searches and making arrests. If the police violate the rules established through judges' interpretations of the Fourth Amendment, then the evidence that police obtain may be barred from use against the defendant because of *exclusionary rule*. The exclusionary rule is intended to deter U.S. police from using their own discretion to invade the privacy of people's homes and property when searching for criminal evidence. Even if evidence might clearly establish the guilt of a defendant, it may be excluded from use against that defendant if police officers did not follow proper procedures. Other countries typically do not have such strict rules that force police officers to respect citizens' rights while investigating criminal cases.

Police in the United States must also follow rules when questioning suspects who are in custody. There is nothing to prohibit a police officer from asking someone questions on the street. Judges in this country presume that people know that they are not required to answer questions posed by a police officer. By contrast, when a person has been taken into custody, there are fears that he will be pressured to provide incriminating information about himself in violation of the Fifth Amendment's privilege against compelled self-incrimination. U.S. history is filled with many examples of police officers beating and torturing people to obtain confessions. Such confessions not only violate the principles of the Fifth Amendment; they are also inherently unreliable. If people confess to get police to stop inflicting excruciating pain upon them, then they may be saying what the police want them to say instead of telling the truth. Thus police officers, before questioning a suspect in custody, must inform the person of his or her constitutional right to remain silent and to have a defense attorney present during questioning (*Miranda v. Arizona* [1966]). Many suspects voluntarily agree to talk and subsequently provide incriminating evidence even after being told about their rights.

Statements cannot be obtained through the use of physical force or the threat of physical force, but police officers can use psychological tricks, such as pretending to be sympathetic to the defendant, to obtain voluntary statements. If statements are obtained through the use of threats or physical force or if police officers fail to inform arrested suspects of their rights, then the exclusionary rule will bar the use of those statements as evidence in court, except in a few exceptional circumstances, such as a situation involving an urgent threat to public safety (*New York v. Quarles* [1984]). Many countries have no such rules that limit the circumstances of police interrogations. Every year international human rights organizations harshly criticize many countries around the world for using beatings and torture to extract confessions from suspects and then using those confessions as the sole basis for criminal convictions that produce long prison sentences or the death penalty.

After the police have gathered sufficient evidence to satisfy a judge that the constitutionally required *probable cause* existed to make an arrest, a person may be taken into custody. A judge may approve the existence of probable cause prior to taking the person into custody by issuing an arrest warrant. Alternatively, the arrestee may be brought before a judge within a few days after the arrest so that the police may present preliminary evidence to justify the arrest. If the judge believes that insufficient evidence has been presented to show that it is likely that the arrestee committed the crime, then the person must be released from custody. If police gather additional evidence to establish probable cause, the person can be arrested again.

A bail hearing will be held soon after the arrest to determine whether the suspect will be released from custody while the case is pending. For minor offenses, suspects are released routinely when they promise to appear for their scheduled court dates (released on own recognizance) or when they pay a small amount of money that will be forfeited if they fail to appear. For serious offenses, judges hold bail hearings at which prosecutors make arguments about the amount of money and conditions of release that should be imposed before returning a suspect to the community. In some cases, prosecutors recommend that specific suspects be denied release on bail if they are so wealthy that no amount of bail will deter them from risking forfeiture by fleeing; if they are charged with the most serious offenses that provide them with a great incentive to flee; or if they have committed violent acts that indicate they will pose a danger to the community. People charged with murder are often denied bail and kept in jail. The Eighth Amendment to the U.S. Constitution bars "excessive bail," but it does not provide any right to have bail set. If a judge chooses to set a bail amount, it cannot be excessive.

The prosecutor is a key figure in criminal cases. U.S. prosecutors have broad discretion to determine what charges to impose against a defendant, what bail amounts to recommend, and what strategies to use in plea negotiations and trial preparations. Prosecutors often charge suspects with multiple offenses to pressure them into pleading guilty on some count. The prosecutor offers to drop some of the charges if the defendant agrees to plead guilty to the remaining charge(s). Even if the defense attorney does not believe that the prosecutor possesses sufficient evidence to prove the defendant's guilt on all charges, the attorney may be fearful of taking the risk that a jury might find the defendant guilty of multiple offenses and thereby produce a significant sentence of punishment. Thus defense attorneys often encourage their clients to plead guilty to one charge if the plea will lead the prosecutor to drop the other charges. U.S. prosecutors have complete discretion to drop charges because there is typically no higher authority to prevent them from exercising such discretion. Most U.S. prosecutors are elected officials in individual counties throughout the country. They operate independently and make decisions that can lead to jarringly different results from similar cases in other jurisdictions. By contrast, federal prosecutors (e.g., U.S. attorneys and assistant U.S. attorneys) are appointed to office and work under the oversight of the U.S. Attorney General and the Department of Justice. Because most state and local prosecutors are elected and must please voters to gain reelection, there are risks that political considerations will affect decisions about whom to prosecute and what charges to pursue. In some communities, for example, the children of politically connected wealthy families are much less likely to be prosecuted to the full extent of the law for drug and other offenses than are young people whose families lack political influence. In many other countries, prosecution is a civil-service career so that prosecutors are less susceptible to employing political considerations in their decisions. Prosecutors in countries such as Germany do not enjoy the same discretionary authority to engage in plea negotiations and recommend sentences as their U.S. counterparts.

At the *arraignment,* the judge reads the formal charges to the defendant, and the defendant is asked to enter a plea. Most defendants in the United States plead not guilty because their defense attorneys are just beginning the process of examining the evidence, and plea negotiations between the prosecution and defense may have not yet begun. Most of those defendants will later change their pleas to guilty when their attorney has reached an agreement with the prosecutor about the number of charges that are actually provable in court and the sentence that the prosecutor will recommend to the judge. Approximately 90 percent of convictions in U.S. courts are obtained through guilty pleas each year. Only about 10 percent of criminal cases are actually decided through a trial.

If no plea agreement is reached, then both the prosecutor and the defense attorney prepare for trial. Cases may proceed to trial for several reasons. Plea negotiations may fail for serious offenses, such as murder, because the defendant is facing a similarly severe sentence from a guilty plea or a trial conviction. Defendants with prior convictions may wish to contest additional charges that will cause them to be labeled habitual offenders and thereby subject to significantly increased punishments. For example, California's so-called *three-strikes law,* which mandates sentences in excess of twenty years for every offender who is convicted of a third felony, created a strong incentive for defendants to demand trials to avoid additional felony convictions. Middle-class defendants who strongly believe in their innocence and have a degree of faith in the system's ability to validate their innocence may refuse to plead guilty. Affluent defendants who can afford to pay attorneys to fight on their behalf through the entire trial process may also demand trials. By contrast, poor defendants may be more fatalistic and accept quick plea agreements for lesser sentences because they do not believe that the system will reach a proper result—even if they believe that they are not guilty of a crime.

The prosecutor must determine how the defendant's actions and motives can be reconstructed for the judge and jury based on the available physical evidence and witness testimony. A prosecutor in this country must prove the defendant's guilt beyond a reasonable doubt—a high level of proof—to obtain a conviction.

Thus the prosecutor interviews witnesses, reviews documents, and discusses the case with the police in an effort to plan how to make the most effective presentation of evidence and arguments in court.

In both criminal and civil cases, the process through which attorneys examine evidence and prepare for trial is called discovery. In civil cases, there are specific rules about each side sharing requested information with its opponents. In criminal cases, by contrast, the defense attorney is under no obligation to share information with the prosecution, except for notifying the prosecution about which witnesses will be called to present testimony for the defense. This witness list gives the prosecutor prior to trial the opportunity to interview the witnesses and plan how to question them. The defense can keep its discussions and plans secret from the prosecution. Communications between defendants and their attorneys are confidential to protect the defendants' rights and ensure that they receive the benefits of the right to counsel under the adversary system. In the aftermath of the terrorist attacks on the World Trade Center and Pentagon in September 2001, U.S. Attorney General John Ashcroft proposed empowering the federal government to use electronic surveillance, such as wiretaps and secret microphones, to monitor conversations between suspected terrorists and their attorneys. The proposal received widespread criticism because it clashed with a long-standing tradition of protecting lawyer-client relationships and communications.

Under constitutional rules produced through decisions by U.S. judges, prosecutors are obligated to share with the defense any information that tends to support a defendant's claim of innocence (*Brady v. Maryland* [1963]). The rule, known as the Brady rule, is intended to prevent prosecutors from hiding evidence that, if revealed in court by the defense, might have stopped an unjust, erroneous conviction from occurring. The Brady rule can create significant disagreements between prosecutors and defense attorneys about which evidence tends to support a defendant's innocence. These problems are attributable, in part, to the existence of an adversary system in which prosecutors' desire to gain convictions, especially when they want to impress the public with their crime-fighting effectiveness to win reelection, can lead them to emphasize winning rather than truth-seeking. Such problems are often avoided in counties that have open-file systems in which prosecutors give defense attorneys free access to all evidence gathered by the police and prosecutors. The sharing of evidence by prosecutors may exist because of a specific prosecutor's policy or local court rules, but prosecutors are not generally required to share all of their evidence. Thus the discovery process is a source of conflict between prosecution and defense in many locations. By contrast, in inquisitorial systems employed in other countries, the civil-service prosecutor, the investigating judge, and the trial judge all are obligated to seek the truth rather than merely seek convictions, so there is little reason for them to hide any evidence from the defense if they are doing their jobs properly.

For U.S. trials, the clerk of the court summons dozens of citizens to appear as potential jurors. The jury pool is typically produced by randomly selecting names from voter registration lists and other governmental lists, such as holders of drivers' licenses or hunting licenses. In some states, people are excluded from jury eligibility if they have ever been convicted of a felony. People who do not appear when summoned may be fined or jailed for disobeying a court order, but most courts are too busy to pursue and punish citizens who fail to fulfill their civic obligation of serving on juries. Those citizens who appear in court may be questioned by the judge, prosecutor, and defense attorney to determine their fitness and suitability for service as a juror in a specific case.

The process of questioning jurors is called *voir dire*. In many cases, the jurors are asked a few questions about whether they are personally acquainted with any participants in the trial, including the defendant; whether they have ever been personally involved in a criminal case; and whether they have any prior knowledge about the case or defendant. Thus the voir dire process may be relatively quick for lesser offenses. By contrast, when the stakes are higher in cases of serious crimes, voir dire may be a lengthy process. Each attorney may seek to ask detailed questions about the potential jurors' backgrounds and attitudes. The attorneys will employ their *challenges for cause* in asking the judge to excuse specific potential jurors who show overt indications of potential bias. They will also use their *peremptory challenges*, a limited number of exclusions they can use if they suspect that specific jurors will be unsympathetic to their arguments. In murder trials, the voir dire process may take several days, and in highly publicized cases the jury selection process may last more than a week. In bench trials, in which the judge is the sole decisionmaker, there is no voir dire process. Bench trials occur when defendants waive their right to a jury because they believe that they will receive fairer or more sympathetic consideration from a judge, possibly due to the emotionally explosive nature of charges, such as sex offenses, facing the defendant. Bench trials also occur when defendants decline to plead guilty to petty offenses for which there is no right to trial by jury.

The trial begins with opening statements by the prosecutor and the defense attorney. From the moment opening statements begin until the final instructions to the jury are announced by the judge and the verdict is rendered, a court reporter records each and every word spoken in the courtroom to create a complete trial transcript. Opening statements permit each side's attorney to describe the evidence that will be presented and to lay the groundwork for persuading the jurors to be receptive to their version of the facts in the case. The opening statement also permits each attorney to attempt to make a good first impression as a likable, persuasive, and trustworthy advocate. Opening statements do not count as evidence that prove anything about the defendant's possible guilt. Judges instruct jurors that they cannot include any information from the opening statement in their verdict.

The prosecution makes the initial presentation of evidence because the prosecutor carries the burden of proving the defendant's guilt beyond a reasonable doubt. Evidence must be presented according to state or federal rules of evidence, which generally require that witness testimony be based on personal knowledge and that the discovery and testing of other pieces of evidence be described in detail to ensure reliability. Evidence consists of testimony from witnesses, including citizens who observed the criminal event or have knowledge about the defendant's actions, as well as police officers who investigated the case. The prosecutor may also call expert witnesses who can testify about scientific tests conducted on evidence, such as DNA testing on blood or human hair found on the victim or elsewhere at the crime scene. The prosecutor draws out the testimony by asking a planned series of questions to each witness that will portray the criminal event and the defendant's actions in the manner most favorable to the prosecution's theory of the case. Evidence also may include such tangible things as objects and fingerprints found at the crime scene, photographs of the crime scene, and weapons, stolen property, or other items found in possession of the defendant. At the conclusion of the prosecution's questioning of each witness, the defense attorney is permitted to cross-examine each witness by asking questions that may elicit answers that will undercut the witness's credibility or the reliability of the inferences that the prosecutor wants drawn from the testimony. In order to succeed, the defense attorney need not demonstrate that the witness is mistaken. The attorney only needs to cast sufficient doubt on the witness's observations and conclusions to make the decisionmaker believe that reasonable doubts exist as to the defendant's guilt.

Throughout the presentation of evidence, the defense attorney may raise objections to statements made by witnesses and the prosecutor and to the nature of evidence presented. The objections assert that statements or objects have been presented in violation of the rules of evidence or in a manner that is inconsistent with the court's procedural rules. The judge must make a ruling about whether the statements or other evidence were presented properly. If the judge upholds the objection, the judge must instruct the jury to ignore anything that violates legal rules. (There are significant questions about whether jurors are truly capable of ignoring statements that they have heard in court.) Prosecutors can also raise objections when the defense is questioning witnesses or presenting its own evidence. Judges use their discretion in making such rulings and interpreting the relevant legal rules. These rulings often serve as the basis for appeals by the losing side.

After the prosecutor finishes presenting evidence, the defense attorney has the opportunity to present the defendant's version of the case. The defendant's case typically consists of testimony from witnesses who can cast doubt on the prosecution's theory of the case, including testimony supporting the defendant's alibi, such as a claim that the defendant was elsewhere when the crime was committed. Other defense witnesses may be questioned on the theory that a legal defense justifies the defendant's action in committing the action deemed a crime by the prosecution. For example, a defense witness may support a defendant's claim that action was taken in self-defense. Expert witnesses may challenge the scientific conclusions of the prosecution's experts or, if presented by a psychiatrist, support the defense claim that the defendant was insane and therefore immune from criminal culpability when the crime was committed. The prosecutor is permitted to cross-examine each defense witness after the defense attorney has completed the initial witness examination.

Both sides are permitted to present rebuttal witnesses at the conclusion of the presentation of evidence. These witnesses, who are usually people already called to testify either on behalf of the prosecution or the defense, can address questions raised during cross-examination or clarify aspects of previously presented evidence, but they may not present new evidence. After the rebuttal witnesses, both attorneys make their closing statements. Like opening statements, closing statements are not evidence: They provide attorneys the opportunity to interpret and summarize the evidence in the manner most favorable to their side.

At the conclusion of the case, the judge provides instructions to the jury about what evidence they can consider in reaching their verdict and what elements of the crime needed to be proven by the prosecution beyond a reasonable doubt in order to find the defendant guilty. Prior to instructing the jury, the judge receives suggestions from the prosecutor and defense attorney about how the relevant law should be described to the jury. In complex cases, the judge may be required to instruct the jury on so many issues that the delivery of the jury instructions can take several hours. There are significant questions about lay jurors' capacity to understand the details of legal rules; jurors may struggle to remain attentive during the delivery of long, detailed instructions by a judge.

Jury deliberations occur in private. No one is permitted into the jury room, and no one can oversee or observe the jury discussions. Jurors may request to have testimony read to them again from the trial transcript. They may also ask for clarification of the judge's jury instructions. The jurors traditionally elect one member as the foreperson to guide discussions and ultimately announce the jury's verdict inside the courtroom. Because there are no observers of the jury's deliberations or any record of discussions in the jury room, there is no way to guard against individual jurors making prejudicial statements, misinterpreting the judge's instructions, or verbally bullying less confident jurors into agreeing with a particular interpretation of the facts.

The adversary system basically trusts a group of citizens to work together with their shared recollections and understandings of the evidence to reach a correct conclusion about the defendant's guilt or innocence. If some jurors do not understand the judge's instructions, the adversary system presumes that other jurors will instruct them and persuade them about the proper way to understand the law governing the case. Most states require juries to reach a unanimous verdict in order to convict defendants, but a few states permit convictions based on nonunanimous supermajority votes of 11-1, 10-2, or even 9-3. If a jury cannot reach a verdict (whether unanimous or otherwise as required by law), then the case has produced a *hung jury,* and the judge ends the proceedings without a verdict. In such cases, the prosecutor must decide whether to initiate a new trial. If the prosecutor believes that a new jury might come to the same conclusion, the prosecutor may drop or lessen the charges against the defendant and move on to other cases. In cases of murder or other serious crimes, prosecutors may be reluctant to disappoint the public by dropping charges. Thus the prosecutor may retry the cases even if there is uncertainty about whether the available evidence will persuade a jury to make a finding of guilt beyond a reasonable doubt. If the defendant is acquitted, the prosecutor cannot file an appeal or retry the case because of the Fifth Amendment prohibition on double jeopardy. If the defendant is convicted, there may be an appeal to an appellate court asking that court to consider whether any errors by the police, judge, jury, or defense attorney during the investigation and trial would justify granting a new trial.

Civil Trial Processes

Civil trials are different from criminal trials in many important respects. There is no right to counsel, and the entitlement to jury trials is governed by each state's laws. The person initiating a civil lawsuit is called the *plaintiff* and the lawsuit is filed against a *defendant.* The lawsuit must assert that the defendant took an improper action resulting in a harm to the plaintiff that is recognized by law. Civil lawsuits often concern personal injuries, damage to property, or violations of contracts. Civil jury trials employ the same jury-selection procedures as criminal trials. Much like the prosecutor's role in the criminal case, the plaintiff carries the burden of proof and therefore makes the first presentation of evidence. Unlike the difficult standard of proof in criminal cases (beyond a reasonable doubt), a civil plaintiff merely has to show that a preponderance of evidence supports the claim. Thus a plaintiff will prevail by presenting evidence that persuades the jury that it is more likely than not that the defendant committed the alleged actions and caused the asserted harm to a legally protected interest. Unlike criminal cases, which permit appeals only by defendants at the conclusion of a trial because of the right against double jeopardy, any party that loses a civil case may appeal, whether it is the plaintiff or the defendant. Prosecutors generally cannot appeal after losing criminal trials because it would violate the defendant's right against double jeopardy if an appellate court ordered a second trial on the prosecutor's behalf.

Conclusion

Courts are important government institutions that serve essential functions, especially for democratic societies. Courts bear responsibility for norm enforcement by processing criminal cases and dispute processing through civil litigation. In democratic societies, courts mediate between the government and individuals by upholding constitutional rights and other legal protections. U.S. courts possess unique authority to shape public policy because of the power of judicial review, which permits judges to overrule actions by legislatures and executive-branch officials when their actions are deemed to be in conflict with the constitution.

Courts differ from religious and other institutions that serve norm-enforcement and dispute-processing functions because court decisionmakers aspire to follow principles of law. By using the language of law and looking to constitutions, statutes, and case precedents for guidance in making decisions, judges convey the message that they are not creating rules for decisions or using political considerations to decide important issues. In democracies, courts rely on the development and maintenance of an image of legitimacy and neutrality to gain the public's respect for and obedience to its decisions. The formal atmosphere and reverential settings in which courts operate mask the discretionary decisions made by judges, prosecutors, and lawyers based on their attitudes and values. Courts are imperfect institutions operated by fallible human decisionmakers. The rules of evidence and court procedure are designed to enhance the reliability of judicial decisions and case outcomes, but they do not ensure accuracy and consistency in decisions by prosecutors, juries, and judges. Despite courts' aspiration to rely on neutral principles of law for decisions, individuals who are drawn into the judicial process will not necessarily experience the same processes and outcomes as others facing comparable cases.

Each country establishes its own legal rules and designs its own court processes. In the United States, constitutional rights as defined by interpretations of state supreme courts and the U.S. Supreme Court are important factors that define rules for how judicial proceedings must occur, especially in criminal cases. Courts in the United States and several other former British colonies use jury trials in an adversarial process that presumes that the truth will be revealed through the clash of skilled opposing attorneys. By contrast, many other countries use an inquisitorial system in which judges play an active role in overseeing the investigation of criminal cases and in ensuring that the court processes reveal as much as information as possible—even if that information is favorable to a criminal defendant. Individual actors differ within countries' court systems. For example, state and local prosecutors in the United States are usually elected local officials who possess nearly unrestrained discretion for determining criminal charges to be pursued and plea agreements to be accepted (as well as sentence recommendations and trial strategies). By contrast, German prosecutors are career civil-service officials who have much less discretionary authority and are secondary to judges in shaping outcomes in Germany's inquisitorial system (Jacob et al. 1996).

The inherently imperfect nature of decisionmaking in human institutions, including courts, and the examples of alternative court institutions and processes in countries around the world raise the question about whether court processes might be improved. There are frequent debates about proposed court reforms that might enhance the accuracy and reliability of decisions as well as improve the consistency of equal outcomes for all people. Courts are not static institutions that are immune to change. Because the organization of courts and the rules of court procedure are designed by statutes enacted by legislatures, there are opportunities to consider useful reforms. Spain and Russia, for example, significantly altered their court processes by introducing juries as decisionmakers in trials during the 1990s (Doran and Jackson 2000). Other court systems might also be reformed in ways that will better enable them to fulfill their functions and serve societal needs.

References and Further Reading

Baum, Lawrence. 1998. *U.S. Courts: Process and Policy,* 4th ed. Boston, MA: Houghton Mifflin.

Carp, Robert A., and Ronald Stidham. 1998. *Judicial Process in America,* 4th ed. Washington, DC: Congressional Quarterly Press.

Doran, Sean, and John Jackson, eds. 2000. *The Judicial Role in Criminal Proceedings.* Oxford, UK: Hart Publishing.

Jacob, Herbert, et al. 1996. *Courts, Law, and Politics in Comparative Perspective.* New Haven, CT: Yale University Press.

Jason-Lloyd, Leonard. 1997. *The Framework of the English Legal System.* London: Frank Cass.

Smith, Christopher E. 1997. *Courts, Politics, and the Judicial Process,* 2nd ed. Chicago: Nelson-Hall.

———. 1991. *Courts and the Poor.* Chicago: Nelson-Hall.

Cases Cited

Argersinger v. Hamlin, 407 U.S. 25 (1972)

Barker v. Wingo, 407 U.S. 514 (1972)

Brady v. Maryland, 373 U.S. 83 (1963)

Lewis v. United States, 518 U.S. 322 (1996)

Maryland v. Craig, 497 U.S. 836 (1990)

Miranda v. Arizona, 384 U.S. 436 (1966)

New York v. Quarles, 467 U.S. 649 (1984)

Roe v. Wade, 410 U.S. 113 (1973)

Ross v. Moffitt, 417 U.S. 600 (1974)

Scott v. Illinois, 440 U.S. 367 (1979)

2

Issues and Controversies

Courts serve important functions and must do so while maintaining their image as forums for neutral and fair decisionmaking. As human institutions, courts are inherently imperfect. Innocent people are sometimes wrongly convicted of crimes. Guilty people are sometimes set free. Similarly situated people can be treated differently in civil as well as criminal cases. Thus governments frequently consider how to reform court organizations and procedures to improve the quality of decisionmaking and the fairness of case outcomes.

Because various countries' court systems differ in structures and processes, governments look for ideas to improve their own court systems. In considering potential reforms, however, governments must consider how court reforms affect the public perception of courts as well as the courts' ability to fulfill the judicial functions essential to government systems. Because courts' public image and legitimacy often rest, in part, on conveying the idea that law is steeped in important traditions and the accumulated wisdom of society, sudden or drastic changes can threaten the public faith in judicial processes.

This chapter focuses on eight issues and controversies that remain perpetually important in discussions of court reform:

- Methods for selecting judges;
- The adversary system versus the inquisitorial system;
- Legal representation for the poor;
- The capacity of citizen-jurors to make judicial decisions;
- Accessibility of civil courts for dispute resolution;
- Civil justice reform;

• Public access to information about court cases; and
• Sentencing reform.

For each topic, this chapter summarizes the nature of the issue and describes key positions in debates about proposed court reforms. Comparisons of practices in various countries as well as U.S. states will provide examples of the consequences of specific reforms. The chapter's overall purpose is to introduce readers to important issues facing court systems in the United States and elsewhere in the world.

Methods for Selecting Judges

If you asked people "What qualities should we seek in a person who will be a judge?" the responses are likely to be predictable and demonstrate a high degree of consensus about desirable qualifications. People would list such qualities as being fair, knowledgeable about the law, experienced in court procedures, wise, thoughtful, and intelligent. However, if you asked people to take the next step and actually identify specific individuals who possess such qualities, then the apparent consensus is likely to disappear. In the United States, it is common for people to see individuals from their own political party as the ones who are wise, intelligent, and thoughtful. Not surprisingly, people identify wisdom and good judgment in others who share their values and policy preferences. Other people may see desirable qualities as primarily or even exclusively possessed by men, members of a specific religion, or people from a particular racial or ethnic group. It is easy to think of generic qualities for a judge, but it is much more difficult to actually agree about which individuals possess those qualities.

The methods used to select judges are intimately related to the issue of qualifications because the choice of methods will influence which kinds of people are selected for office. If judges are appointed to office, they are likely to reflect the biases and value preferences of the people making the appointments. If the appointers are from a particular ethnic group, social class, or political party, then it would not be surprising if the appointed judges came from the same groups. Because courts typically try to maintain an image of independence, nonpartisanship, and fairness, the methods for selecting judges must be carefully considered to avoid the risk that judges will simply be viewed as politicians in black robes whose decisions flow from politics rather than from law. The effectiveness of courts, especially in democracies, is affected by the extent to which the public respects and instantly obeys judicial decisions. In nondemocracies, the courts' image may be less important because judicial decisions are often overseen by a country's military or other authoritarian leadership and because those decisions are subsequently enforced by military power.

Judicial Elections

The United States is unique for electing judges in many state court systems. Twelve states use partisan elections in which candidates from two or more parties vie for judgeships. An additional seventeen states use nonpartisan elections in which voters choose judges in periodic elections (however, the ballots do not inform voters of the candidates' political affiliations). Many nonpartisan judicial elections are strongly influenced by political parties because the parties endorse candidates and provide support for the election campaigns (Smith 1997).

The arguments favoring the use of elections for choosing judges focus on the desirability of holding public officials accountable in a democracy. Elections permit voters to choose the decisionmakers for their courts and then hold those decisionmakers accountable by deciding whether or not to retain them in subsequent elections. The emphasis on accountability recognizes that judicial decisions are not directly determined by law, but rather by judges' interpretation and application of the law. In the process of interpretation, judges inevitably rely on their own values and policy preferences. They do not have unrestrained authority to decide cases however they wish. Their decisions are guided and restrained by governing statutes, constitutions, and prior judicial decisions. Yet they possess discretionary authority to interpret, refine, and adapt existing legal rules in deciding cases. Judicial elections permit the public to make sure that judges' interpretations and values are consistent with those of the community. Judges whose decisions are out of step with community values risk losing their positions when they come up for reelection. Although the election system creates uncertainty about the qualifications that judicial candidates will possess when they gain election, advocates of the election system do not believe this uncertainty will cause problems. These advocates assert that political leaders have a strong incentive to put forward highly qualified candidates to impress the voters and gain support. In addition, advocates of the election system claim that voters in this country cannot reach clear agreement on which individuals are most qualified to be judges; therefore it is better to emphasize accountability so that voters can remove judges who do not satisfy the public. To advocates of the election system, it would be far worse to appoint to a judgeship someone who appeared to be highly qualified but who then turned out to be a lousy judge who could not be easily removed from office.

Lawyers and public officials from other countries often express shock at electing judges. To critics from here and abroad, the use of elections makes courts too connected to partisan politics. As a result, the image of courts as neutral law-based institutions will suffer, and the public may not show sufficient respect for and obedience to judicial decisions. The public may regard court decisions as merely an alternative form of politics and policymaking rather than the embodiment of neutral legal principles. In addition, there are risks that judges worried about reelection may make decisions to please the public rather than to provide a carefully considered judgment. Moreover, the election system may do little to ensure that the most capable and qualified candidates are chosen to be judges. Many political parties select lawyers as candidates for judgeships for reasons unrelated to qualifications. Such candidates are selected as a reward for loyalty to the party, because they have demonstrated a significant capacity for campaign fund-raising, which may help to win and keep the seat for the party, or because they have widespread name recognition, which may gain support from the voters. However, none of these qualifications is related to the ideal qualities of wisdom and knowledge that many people believe judges ought to possess.

Judicial Appointments

Nine states permit the governor or state legislature to select judges. In a similar fashion, the U.S. president nominates judges for the federal bench subject to confirmation by the U.S. Senate. Advocates argue that this process permits the appointing authority to select highly qualified people, even if those individuals would not have had the political connections or fund-raising capacity to gain office under election systems. In reality, however, there is no guarantee that political considerations are not the central element in appointments. Studies of federal appointments indicate that the president as well as senators use the selection process to reward political allies and advance their own policy preferences rather than make objective assessments about nominees' qualifications.

In the federal system for appointing judges, senators are influential in naming U.S. district court judges. If a state's senators are from the same political party as the president, the president usually defers to the senators' recommendations about those who should be nominated. Thus the senators' friends, political supporters, and allies are often nominated for judgeships. In states where senators are not from the president's political party, the highest officials from the party within the state make recommendations to the president. These other officials are usually the governor, members of the U.S. House of Representatives, big-city mayors, or political party leaders. Although senators and other politicians do not want to appoint unqualified or incompetent people to judgeships, they have little incentive to search the state for the most experienced, highly qualified candidate. Judgeships are given to people who are successful and accomplished in business and politics because of their connections to or service on behalf of politicians and political parties. They are not necessarily selected because they have proven themselves to be outstanding judges in state courts or lawyers whose personal qualities indicate that they will make outstanding judges.

When seats are open on federal circuit courts of appeals, the president's advisers solicit recommendations from officeholders, politicians, and political supporters connected to the president's party, but the president asserts greater control over the final decision on the person to be nominated. Appellate appointments also go to people who have actively served the president's party. However, the president may focus more attention on identifying individuals whom the president believes share the kinds of values and policy preferences that the president wishes to see embodied in appellate court decisions.

The politics of judicial appointments becomes more complicated when the U.S. Senate is not controlled by the president's political party. Because the Senate must confirm judicial nominees, the president may be forced to select compromise candidates who are perceived to hold moderate views that will be more palatable to the president's political opponents. For district court judges, senators usually defer to their colleagues' choices (perhaps because they do not want opposition to form when their own favorites are up for nomination). For appointments to U.S. courts of appeals or the U.S. Supreme Court, however, senators look more closely at the individual's record of statements and decisions. If the values, beliefs, and legal philosophy of the president's nominee appear to be too extreme in the eyes of the opposing political party, then the senators from that party may use their majority status in the Senate to block the nomination. Thus partisan politics plays an important role in shaping the composition of the judiciary in the nomination and appointment system used in U.S. federal courts.

European countries attempt to separate the selection of judges from partisan politics through civil service; judges are career civil servants. In France, university graduates in law may take a competitive examination for admission to the national school for judicial studies to pursue eventual careers as judges. After graduation, initial appointments to lower-court judgeships are made on the basis of competitive examinations. Promotions to higher-level judgeships depend on seniority, impressing senior judges with outstanding performance in office, and a willingness to relocate elsewhere in the country. Aspiring judges in Germany must also work their way up from prosecutors' offices and lower-court appointments by seeking promotions within a civil-service system. Experienced attorneys do not become judges. Judging is a separate profession that a person chooses early in a career (Jacob et al. 1996). Judges in these countries have job security and promotion possibilities so they need not worry about reelection or impressing politicians. These judges have greater separation from partisanship than do U.S. judges. However, European judges must impress administrators and senior judges in their own judicial systems; they are not completely independent. These European systems attempt to emphasize qualifications and judicial performance as the basis for promotion to higher-level courts.

Merit Selection

Nearly half of all U.S. states have followed Missouri's lead in creating merit-selection systems that seek to emphasize the qualifications of judicial appointees and separate judges from the reelection pressures that exist in electoral systems. In most merit-selection systems, the governor appoints a selection committee that solicits and screens applicants for judgeships and then recommends a list of finalists to the governor. The governor either chooses the judge from the list of recommended finalists or asks the committee to conduct a new search. After the judge has served a term in office, typically six or eight years, the public has the opportunity to vote in a retention election that will determine whether the judge serves for an additional term. In retention elections, the public simply votes on whether to retain the judge. No judicial candidate runs against the judge in the retention election.

Although merit selection represents an effort by states to emphasize the qualifications of judges and reduce the influence of politics, political considerations can still affect the selection of judges. Governors may seek to advance their own political values and policy preferences by appointing committee members who share the governor's political views or by appointing like-minded judges from the list of finalists. In addition, interest groups and political parties sometimes campaign to convince citizens to vote against the retention of specific judges. These campaigns are not necessarily based on evidence that the judges have performed poorly. Instead, they may be efforts to create new vacancies in courts so that a new governor, who shares the political values of the interest groups and political parties, can appoint new judges whose decisions are more likely to advance the preferences of the organized interests.

In the late 1970s, President Jimmy Carter attempted to employ merit-selection principles within the appointment system for federal judges. Carter created nominating commissions for judicial vacancies on the U.S. circuit courts of appeals. The citizens placed on the nominating commissions were instructed to consider possible nominees based on their qualifications for service as outstanding appellate judges. Carter's effort reduced the heavy reliance on service to political party and personal relationships with politicians as the basis for choosing federal judges. However, because most nominating-commission members were from Carter's political party, it was not surprising that most of the nominees were from Carter's party. These were the lawyers and judges whose values and viewpoints were viewed most favorably by the like-minded members of the commissions. The reforms opened opportunities for some nontraditional candidates, such as distinguished law professors who were not active in partisan politics. However, this form of merit selection did not eliminate politics from the process.

For federal district court vacancies, Carter encouraged U.S. senators to develop merit-selection committees within their home states. Some senators did so, but others did not. Ultimately, the federal experiment in merit selection ended when Ronald Reagan was elected president in 1980. Reagan placed a high priority on appointing federal judges who shared his political philosophy, so he returned control over the process to his staff members in the White House and the U.S. Department of Justice. As a result, the judges appointed during the Reagan administration reflected the traditional qualifications of service to political party, support from politicians, and values and policy preferences that were compatible with those of the president.

Could the United States adopt the European approach for selecting judges by creating a civil service for judges whose selection and promotions would be based on performance? Many observers believe that such a separation of judicial selection from partisan politics is not possible in the United States due to the unique policymaking power of U.S. judges. Because judges here can declare acts of other government officials to be unconstitutional and thereby shape public policy on many controversial issues, organized political interests in the United States do not view courts as merely dispute-processing and norm-enforcing institutions. Instead, courts are viewed—like legislatures and executive agencies—as policymaking forums that political parties seek to influence and control. Thus the existing connections between the selection of judges and partisan politics may be inevitable.

The Adversary System versus the Inquisitorial System

There are many ways to determine criminal guilt or civil liability. One could flip a coin and let the decision be determined by chance. Alternatively, one could place authority in the hands of a specific official and permit that official to use his or her own discretion in making the decision. For example, a village elder or an army general could be given the authority to determine guilt and settle disputes. Are these good methods for making important decisions? The answer to that question depends on the values, beliefs, and goals that underlie the choice of methods. The use of trials is typically based on the desire to make accurate decisions within a framework of fair procedures. In a trial, evidence is presented to and examined by decisionmakers according to an established set of procedures. Depending on the country in which the trial is held, the decisionmaker may be a single judge, a panel of judges, a mixed jury of judges and citizens, or a lay jury of citizens drawn from the community.

In developing trial procedures, each country must decide what rules and procedures are necessary for a fair proceeding and a reliable decision. In the United States, for example, criminal proceedings involve preliminary hearings to ensure that sufficient evidence exists to carry a prosecution forward; a period of time for prosecutors and defense attorneys to prepare the evidence that they will present in court (discovery); and then the actual trial, during which each side presents evidence and arguments in front of a decisionmaker. Although the procedures and rules for trials vary from state to state and country to country, most processes are similar, except as to the roles of lawyers and judges. Most countries that use lawyers and judges in a trial process can be divided into one of two systems: adversary or inquisitorial. The *adversary system* involves battles between opposing attorneys as the judge listens passively to the presentations, whereas the *inquisitorial system* requires the judge to take a more active role in investigating the case and examining the evidence. Many people disagree about which approach produces the most reliable decisions in the trial process.

The Adversary System

In accordance with the tradition of English law, trials in the United States and other former British colonies are conducted by using an adversary system. The adversary system is based on the assumption that the truth is best revealed through head-to-head courtroom combat between two skilled advocates. Thus the lawyers for each side in a legal case make careful preparations by gathering evidence and composing persuasive arguments that are intended to convince the judge or jury that their side is making the most accurate presentation of the relevant facts. For example, when a defendant is charged with murder during a fight at a bar, the prosecution will attempt to show that the defendant planned and carried out the killing. By contrast, the defense attorney may attempt to show that the killing was accidental or that it was done in self-defense when the victim attacked the defendant with a weapon. The outcome of the case will rest on whether the decisionmaker (judge or jury) believes the prosecutor's version of the facts or the defense attorney's version of the facts. Under the adversary system, the judge takes a passive role, similar to that of a referee at a sporting event. The judge listens to the lawyers' presentations and interrupts when a rule of evidence or court procedure has been violated. The judge may instruct the jury to disregard some of the evidence presented or remind the attorneys that certain kinds of statements are not permitted under court rules. The judge does not actively participate in the process of drawing out information from witnesses or attorneys. If one attorney is more skilled and persuasive than the other attorney and the judge recognizes that this attorney's effectiveness is shaping the direction of the case more significantly than the actual facts being presented, the judge does not provide balance by taking actions to assist the opposing attorney. The judge is supposed to sit quietly and permit the attorneys to develop the facts of the case, even when it appears that a more complete presentation of facts would be available if, for example, one of the attorneys asked additional questions of the witnesses. The judge's responsibility to remain relatively passive and silent reflects the prevailing assumption that the battle between the attorneys will reveal the truth without any extra participation by the judge.

The Inquisitorial System

By contrast, many countries in Europe use an inquisitorial system in which judges take a much more active role. In the inquisitorial system, the judge investigates the case and asks questions of the witnesses. In some countries, judges actually take a prosecutorial role in determining when someone should be accused of a crime and then overseeing the process of gathering evidence concerning culpability. Under the inquisitorial system, if a defense attorney or prosecutor is ineffective, the judge's active participation in raising questions and issues may reveal the truth about what happened when the crime occurred and whether the defendant is guilty. In France, for example, a judge known as an examining magistrate oversees the investigation of the crime by ordering witnesses to appear for questioning and authorizing searches. A different chief judge presides at the trial and is one of the decisionmakers along with two other judges and nine citizen-jurors.

The chief judge asks questions of the witnesses, including a court-room interrogation of the accused, and also approves all questions that the lawyers want to ask (Jacob et al. 1996). Because the judge is a central figure in the inquisitorial system, the effectiveness of this process depends on the ability of the individual judge to be thorough and fair. Any deficiencies or biases affecting the judge's performance will also have adverse effects on the quality of the truth-seeking process.

The Systems Compared

The adversary system creates a risk that the outcome will depend on the persuasiveness and effectiveness of the lawyers rather than the actual facts. If one attorney is inexperienced, inarticulate, or otherwise ineffective, the opposing attorney may seem much more persuasive to the decisionmakers, even if an accurate presentation of the facts would have favored the less effective attorney's client. Mismatches between attorneys can be exacerbated when one side has more time and resources. For example, in a criminal case, a team of prosecutors may have the services of an entire police department to help gather and prepare evidence, as well as a budget for hiring expert witnesses to testify about scientific issues. Meanwhile, a lone public defender with a high caseload may be preparing the defense without the assistance of any investigators or expert witnesses and without adequate time to devote to any single case. Although the adversary system presumes that opposing attorneys will bring forward all relevant evidence in the case, the adversary system may create incentives to hide unfavorable information or make misleading characterizations about the evidence being presented. In the adversary system, attorneys' desire to win may override any commitment to revealing the truth. Because most local prosecutors in the United States are elected officials, the political pressure to win cases and please voters may exacerbate the adversary system's tendency to value victory over truth-seeking. Thus attorneys in this country, including prosecutors, criminal defense attorneys, and civil litigation lawyers, have often been caught hiding evidence from the court that might have been favorable to the opposition. In the worst circumstances of such behavior, innocent people have been convicted of crimes, and even sentenced to death, when the prosecutor withheld information that might have cast doubt upon the defendant's guilt.

The inquisitorial system differs from the adversary system because there is less emphasis on the rights of the criminal defendant. Criminal defendants in this country enjoy a variety of constitutional protections that reflect the mistrust of government felt by the country's founders. In the United States, for example, the Fifth Amendment to the U.S. Constitution provides a privilege against compelled self-incrimination. Defendants cannot be required to testify, and their refusal to testify cannot be regarded as evidence of guilt. By contrast, defendants in France normally surrender their opportunity to remain silent in court because the judge may treat their refusal to testify as evidence that they have something to hide (Jacob et al. 1996). Similarly, German criminal defendants do not enjoy the right to be represented by defense attorneys, a right guaranteed to defendants by the Sixth Amendment to the U.S. Constitution. Criminal defendants facing the possibility of incarceration for a crime in the United States must have an attorney appointed to represent them if they are too poor to hire one. There is no such guarantee in Germany. Moreover, even if a defense attorney is provided, as is the case for most German defendants facing very serious charges, the defense attorney shares the prosecutor's obligation to present objective facts and arguments (Jacob et al. 1996). By contrast, defense attorneys here are obligated to represent clients zealously, even if it means presenting plausible but inaccurate theories and arguments to the jury that lead to the acquittal of individuals who are actually guilty of criminal offenses.

The U.S. adversary system reflects a historic mistrust of government and an emphasis on individual rights. These elements have fed a belief that criminal defendants and civil litigants need to be represented by vigorous advocates to have their rights and interests protected. Moreover, most court systems that use jury trials employ the adversary system. Thus they give decisionmaking authority to citizens rather than government officials. By contrast, the inquisitorial system reflects greater trust in the fairness and judgment of governmental decisionmakers. In trials under the inquisitorial system, legal professionals control the process. Prosecutors and defense attorneys cooperate with the judge in illuminating the relevant facts so that the judge or a panel of judges can reach a decision. European countries may place greater trust in their judges in part because judges are selected and promoted through a civil-service process rather than through a partisan political system that may cast doubt on their independence, qualifications, and neutrality.

Which system provides the most accurate decisions about criminal guilt and civil liability? Many observers would argue that the inquisitorial system is structured to focus on truth-seeking without risking that decisionmakers will be fooled or distracted by inflammatory arguments and concealed evidence, as is the case in the adversary system. Still, the adversary system may create greater incentives for attorneys to search for any available evidence, whereas judges and lawyers in the inquisitorial system may overlook evidence because they erroneously presume that they have already gathered all of the facts. Whatever the merits of each method, it would be difficult for countries to switch to a different system. The choice of an inquisitorial system versus an adversary system is based on long-standing traditions, political values, and the methods used for selecting judges.

Legal Representation for the Poor

The Sixth Amendment's right to assistance of counsel is an important protection for defendants in U.S. criminal trials. Because the U.S. system is based on the adversary model, the effectiveness of the trial process depends on the skill of the defense attorney in challenging the evidence presented by the prosecutor. Defendants who are sufficiently affluent must hire their own attorneys. To these defendants, the right simply means that the government cannot prevent them from obtaining professional representation. Although they must dig into their own pockets and pay thousands of dollars, wealthy defendants can choose their own attorneys and attempt to secure the services of the most experienced and effective lawyer available.

For most of U.S. history, poor defendants in state criminal trials were not entitled to representation. The right to counsel merely meant that the government could not stop defendants from hiring an attorney. But poor defendants could not afford to pay attorneys' fees. Therefore most criminal proceedings consisted of a mismatched confrontation between a professional prosecutor supported by the investigative resources of the police department squaring off against a solitary defendant who often had little education or knowledge of criminal law. Not surprisingly, prosecutors obtained very quick and easy convictions in most cases. In 1963, however, the U.S. Supreme Court interpreted the Sixth Amendment's right to counsel as requiring states to provide defense attorneys for defendants who were too poor to hire their own if those defendants were facing serious criminal charges punishable by six months or more of incarceration (*Gideon v. Wainwright* [1963]). Prior to that decision, poor defendants received representation only if the state legislature or supreme court had ordered the appointment of defense counsel in state criminal trials. After 1963, all states were obligated to provide defense attorneys. The states' obligation expanded in 1972 when the Supreme Court required the appointment of defense counsel for all criminal defendants who faced the possibility of incarceration, even for short jail sentences (*Argersinger v. Hamlin* [1972]). The right does not extend, however, to defendants charged with minor offenses who will merely receive small fines if convicted (*Scott v. Illinois* [1979]).

The right to counsel in the Sixth Amendment applies only to criminal trials and to the initial appeal after a criminal trial. There is no right to representation in U.S. civil cases. People must obtain their own attorneys to protect their interests in disputes concerning contracts, personal injuries, property damage, and other matters that enter courts as legal actions between two private parties or actions by individuals against government. This limitation can pose special difficulties for poor people who, as a result, may have little opportunity to make use of courts and trial processes for seeking remedies for civil injuries and disputes.

There is also no right to counsel in criminal appeals beyond the first appeal of right. If offenders seek to contest their convictions in state supreme courts or the U.S. Supreme Court, either through appeals or through the habeas corpus process, they must often attempt to prepare their own cases if they cannot afford an attorney. Habeas corpus is the traditional process through which incarcerated people challenge the legality of the government's action in depriving them of liberty. Under U.S. law, most habeas corpus cases must raise a claim that the police or prosecutor violated the offender's rights in the course of obtaining a criminal conviction. It can be especially difficult and, in fact, futile for uneducated prisoners to attempt to prepare and file their own appeals or habeas corpus petitions. As a result, people in prison with potentially valid habeas corpus claims may have no realistic opportunity to have those claims properly presented to a court for consideration.

Within the one category of cases to which the Sixth Amendment right to counsel applies—criminal prosecutions at the trial level that may lead to incarceration—there are several methods employed by U.S. courts to provide attorneys for defendants. These methods each have drawbacks and pose the risk of inadequate representation.

Appointed Counsel

In theory, the right to counsel fulfills the requirements of the adversary system by ensuring that U.S. criminal defendants receive zealous professional representation when facing the possibility of incarceration. In reality, there are questions about whether defense attorneys for poor defendants always perform effectively and provide proper advocacy on behalf of their clients. Many counties in the United States appoint attorneys from private practice on a case-by-case basis to represent poor criminal defendants. Such attorneys are not necessarily experienced, knowledgeable about criminal law, or interested in their clients' best interests. They may be new attorneys seeking to gain experience or unsuccessful attorneys seeking to pick up some easy money. These attorneys receive small fees from the government to provide this representation. Unfortunately, the fees are often so small that there may be little incentive to battle the prosecutor vigorously and take cases to trial. Instead, it may be more profitable to persuade the defendant to enter a quick guilty plea so that the attorney can move to other cases. Sometimes these plea bargains actually provide a guilty defendant with the best possible outcome. There are risks, however, that attorney's self-interested desire to terminate cases quickly may influence the effort devoted to each case and, in the worst case scenario, lead the attorney to pressure an innocent defendant to plead guilty. Moreover, appointed attorneys often do not receive additional funds to hire investigators and expert witnesses so that they cannot, even if they take a case to trial, match the resources and time being expended by the prosecution.

Contract Counsel

Another method for providing representation for poor defendants in the United States is the use of annual contracts. Attorneys or law firms submit bids to seek a year-long contract under which they would represent all of the poor defendants in a single county. In awarding the contract, the county government saves money by taking the lowest bid, but the defendants' interests may not be well served by attorneys who have an incentive to terminate cases as quickly and inexpensively as possible to maximize their own profits. If the contract attorneys are experienced and dedicated, the system may provide good representation. If not, there are risks that the defendants will not receive the zealous advocacy that the adversary system presumes will best reveal the truth.

Public Defenders

Many observers believe that the best method of providing representation for poor defendants is through the use of public defenders—salaried government employees whose entire job is to handle criminal defenses. Because public defenders have chosen this as their career and work full-time on criminal cases, they often have more knowledge, experience, and dedication than some of the private-practice attorneys who work as appointed counsel or contract lawyers. In addition, public defenders are more likely to receive continuing training about the latest court cases concerning criminal law because they work for an agency with a singular focus on criminal defense. The most significant drawback of relying on public defenders is the risk that they will handle such massive caseloads that they cannot possibly devote sufficient attention to each client's case. Because each county that uses public defenders employs a set number of attorneys with a fixed annual budget, these attorneys must handle all of the criminal cases for poor defendants, no matter how many cases arise. In some cities, limited funding has meant that individual public defenders are handling more than 100 cases at any given moment. These attorneys may be interested in criminal law and dedicated to their clients' best interests, but budgetary constraints may make it impossible for them to provide thorough, zealous advocacy in each case.

The issue of adequate representation is especially important in adversary systems. By contrast, inquisitorial systems protect the defendant against the harm of inexperienced or uncommitted defense attorneys by making the judge responsible for ensuring that all evidence is adequately examined in court, including evidence favorable to the defendant.

Another Alternative

In Ontario, Canada, which employs the adversary system, criminal defendants receive advice and assistance earlier and more easily than U.S. defendants. In Ontario, police officers must inform arrestees of their right to counsel after arrest. By contrast, U.S. police can place suspects in an investigative lineup or administer a Breathalyzer test without informing the suspect of the right to counsel. U.S. police are not required to inform arrestees about the right to counsel until they wish to question a person being held in custody (*Miranda v. Arizona* [1966]). Even if the arrestee requests an attorney at that point, an attorney may not be actually appointed for days or weeks so that bail hearings and other processes may occur without any professional to advise the defendant and represent the defendant's interests. Ontario has a toll-free telephone number staffed by attorneys around the clock to provide initial legal advice and immediate assistance to people who have been arrested. These attorneys can help defendants avoid losing their rights or damaging the subsequent preparation of their court cases by providing early advice about how to respond to questions and requests from police officers (Roach and Friedland 1996).

What is the best way to provide representation to poor criminal defendants? This is an important question for any court system that relies on the adversary approach for processing cases and seeking the truth. This issue is especially difficult for the United States. Its relatively high rates of violent crimes draw many defendants into a justice system that does not always have sufficient funds to provide adequate representation. Moreover, the consequences of inadequate representation may be especially harsh because the United States imposes more severe sentences compared to other industrialized democracies. In the eyes of some observers, the manner in which countries such as the United States address this issue is one measure of the commitment to the adversary system and the concept of equal justice.

The Capacity of Citizen-Jurors to Make Judicial Decisions

Citizens who have no training or experience in law can make important court decisions in their roles as jurors for criminal and civil trials. When serving as jurors, laypeople must observe court proceedings, evaluate lawyers' presentations of evidence and arguments, and listen to judges' explanations about the relevant law before rendering decisions. Juries do not hear evidence and reach verdicts in all trials. About half of all U.S. trials each year are *bench trials* in which a judge is the lone decisionmaker. In the remaining trials, however, adult citizens are drawn randomly from the community to serve as jurors. Although some states prohibit people with criminal records from serving on juries, there are generally no other qualifications. Because trials are complicated events in which legal professionals use the language and concepts of law, there are serious questions about whether ordinary citizens are truly capable of understanding court proceedings and rendering fair, accurate, and unbiased decisions.

The History of Jury Trials

In English criminal proceedings prior to the thirteenth century, determinations of guilt were based on very different processes than those employed today. People charged with crimes were given a trial, but not the familiar legal proceeding. Trials in the eleventh and twelfth centuries were either trials by battle or trials by ordeal. These trials were usually initiated by private prosecutions (rather than prosecutions pursued on behalf of the king) in which one individual accused another. Over time, the government took responsibility for prosecuting an increasing number of offenses. This process also changed punishments from the payment of compensation to victims under the system of private prosecution to the widespread use of fines, physical mutilation, and capital punishment when crimes came to be treated as offenses against the king's law.

In these early trials, the guilt of criminal defendants was determined by their performance in or reaction to painful physical tasks. In a trial by battle, the defendant was forced to fight in a duel with the presumption that God would protect an innocent combatant from harm. If a combatant was killed or seriously injured, it was viewed as a statement from God about guilt. Trials by ordeal required defendants to undertake a painful task, such as placing their hands in boiling water or carrying a red-hot iron bar in their bare hands. Their skin was examined to determine the extent of injury caused by the ordeal, as there was a presumption that God would protect innocent people from serious harm. There were also more harsh ordeals, such as binding the defendant's feet and hands and then tossing the defendant into a lake or pond. If the defendant drowned, then God had taken an innocent person to heaven, but if the person managed to escape the bonds and float to the surface, then he or she faced execution as a guilty criminal (Heller 1969). Obviously, such severe ordeals condemned the accused individual to death whether or not a crime had actually been committed. Yet the religious belief in the power of God to control human events was apparently so powerful that the results of ordeals and battles were accepted as the basis for determining criminal guilt.

The use of trials by ordeal and battle ended after Pope Innocent III issued a decision in 1215 that barred priests from endorsing such procedures or performing any religious ceremonies in conjunction with such trials. By withdrawing its support for these methods of determining guilt, the church effectively eliminated the basis for believing that God's actions identified criminal offenders. In the absence of religion-based ordeals, the determination of guilt shifted into the hands of citizens called to court to serve on juries (Heller 1969).

Jury trials did not develop spontaneously to fill the vacuum left when the church withdrew its endorsement of ordeals and battles. Under King Henry II in the twelfth century, the government had begun to use a process in which twelve respected men from a community were chosen to take oaths that required them to report anyone suspected of committing a felony. Thus the concept of the jury, even while ordeals were used to determine guilt, had developed as the means of accusing individuals of committing serious crimes. When the use of ordeal and battle ended after 1215, the jury began to take a broader role by making determinations of guilt. These determinations in trials by jury were based on the jurors' personal knowledge as members of the community and by their observations of the defendant's reaction during the court proceedings when the accusations were described in public (Green 1985). These early trials did not include elaborate presentations of evidence. In small communities, the respected men called to serve on juries were presumed to have personal knowledge about people and events; this knowledge was considered to be sufficiently trustworthy to serve as the basis for determining the fate of the accused.

Jury Trials around the World

Trial by jury became a central feature of England's legal system. As the British Empire later spread colonies throughout the world, trial by jury was incorporated into many colonial legal systems, and the institution remained in effect even after the colonies became independent countries. Thus the use of trial by jury in the United States, Canada, Australia, and elsewhere has its roots in English legal history. In some former British colonies, such as New Zealand and Australia, juries are seldom used in the trial of civil cases but are still used in serious criminal cases. Some former British colonies, such as India, eliminated the use of juries and joined most other countries in employing trials before a single judge or a panel of judges for making determinations of guilt in criminal cases or determining liability in civil lawsuits.

Interestingly, two countries that previously relied on judges for determining outcomes in criminal cases, Russia and Spain, introduced the use of juries during the 1990s. In Russian and Spanish jury trials, jurors do not render general verdicts of guilty or not guilty as in the United States and countries that follow English traditions. Instead, jurors are asked by the judge to vote on a series of questions so that when their decisions are announced in court the judge understands the basis for their conclusions (Doran and Jackson 2000). By contrast, juries in the United States simply announce whether a criminal defendant is guilty or whether a civil defendant is liable without ever providing any explanation for the decision. The U.S. jury is presumed to have followed the law as described by the presiding judge, although there is no guarantee that the final decision is not based on erroneous assumptions, misunderstandings, or biased conclusions.

Other countries use mixed systems that combine judges and citizens as decisionmakers. In France, for example, nine citizens drawn from the community sit with three judges as the decisionmakers in serious criminal cases. At the end of the trial, the judges actively deliberate with the jurors before the decision is made through voting by secret ballot. Eight of the twelve participants must vote for guilt in order for a defendant to be convicted of a crime (Jacob et al. 1996). Thus the judges alone cannot determine the outcome of the case because they must persuade the jurors to adopt their views and conclusions.

U.S. Jury Trials

The Sixth Amendment to the U.S. Constitution guarantees many criminal defendants a right to trial by jury. The right has been applied to state criminal trials as well as federal court proceedings since the Supreme Court's 1968 decision in *Duncan v. Louisiana* that interpreted the right as applying in all U.S. courts. The right to a jury trial applies in all U.S. courts, but it does not apply to all cases. According to the U.S. Supreme Court's interpretation of the Sixth Amendment, the right to a jury trial applies only for defendants who are charged with serious offenses that can lead to a punishment of six months or more of incarceration. There is no right to a jury trial for petty offenses that are punishable by sentences of less than six months in jail (*Lewis v. United States* [1996]). In serious cases for which the right to trial by jury applies, defendants may waive their right to a jury and request that the case be argued in front of and decided by a judge. Defendants may make this choice because they fear that jurors will not understand complex issues in the case or because they fear that the nature of the charges, such as a sex offense, may upset the jurors and prevent them from making an objective decision. Defendants are often afraid that jurors will react emotionally to dramatic evidence rather than think carefully and critically about whether the evidence is accurate.

English juries were traditionally composed of twelve members. In most U.S. criminal courts, juries still have twelve members. However, the Supreme Court has ruled that the Sixth Amendment right to trial by jury does not require twelve-member juries (*Williams v. Florida* [1970]). It is permissible to have juries with as few as six members for criminal cases. In addition, U.S. juries are not required to reach unanimous verdicts. A few states permit individuals to be convicted of crimes by votes of 10-2 or 9-3. Jury trials in civil cases often have as few as six jurors. The size of civil juries is governed by the law of each state, and states can permit civil juries to reach verdicts by nonunanimous votes.

The size and unanimity rules for juries may affect their decisionmaking processes. When a jury has only six members, fewer perspectives will be represented during jury deliberations. In smaller juries, it is not likely that the full diversity of a community's demographic composition will be represented on the jury. When unanimous verdicts are not required, the majority of jurors can ignore the viewpoints of dissenting jurors and, as a result, potentially ignore useful insights that not all of the jurors immediately recognized during the course of the trial. In addition, the existence of nonunanimous verdicts in some states means that criminal defendants receive differential treatment depending on where they are placed on trial. Someone who is convicted by a nonunanimous verdict would not have been convicted if prosecuted for the same crime with the same evidence in a state that requires unanimity.

Complex Information and the Jury

In criminal cases, jurors may listen to detailed testimony that continues for days or even weeks. They must remain attentive to the details presented in the testimony of each witness, even if they are not especially interested in the case. In addition, they must attempt to set aside their emotions and biases to remain neutral and objective. It may be difficult for many jurors to maintain this emotional detachment, especially if they hear emotional testimony, see gruesome crime-scene photos, or learn about criminal acts that were previously committed by the defendant. They may also be required to listen to complex testimony from expert witnesses. There may be testimony about DNA evidence found at the crime scene, and the prosecution and defense may each present testimony from experts who disagree about whether the scientific testing was conducted properly or whether the test results actually indicate anything about the defendant's possible guilt. In other cases, each side may present testimony from psychiatrists who disagree with each other about the defendant's sanity and capacity to form the mental intentions necessary for conviction of certain crimes. Are citizen-jurors capable of making reliable decisions concerning scientific matters about which educated experts disagree?

Jurors must also attempt to make their consideration of evidence and decisionmaking conform to the requirements of the law. Textbook descriptions of jury trials often say that jurors determine the facts in a case (i.e., what happened?) after listening to all of the evidence, whereas the judge determines whether and how specific legal rules apply. In reality, however, jurors must incorporate explanations and understandings of law into their decisions about who did what to whom and whether legal liability should be imposed as a result of their conclusions about the chain of events. Thus jurors are continually confronted with legal issues and concepts that affect their consideration of a case. Throughout a trial, for example, lawyers and judges may regularly use legal terms such as *negligence* and *criminal intent*. Even before the judge attempts to provide a clear definition of these terms during the final jury instructions, jurors inevitably interpret, misunderstand, or ignore these terms as they attempt to absorb and process all the information being presented. A related issue concerns jurors' ability to follow legal rules in incorporating or excluding information into their decisionmaking. In open court, an attorney may refer to facts that cannot be legally submitted as evidence. Thus the judge often says to the jury, "Please disregard the statements you just heard from this attorney and do not consider them as part of the evidence in the case." Can a juror consciously erase statements and information presented by attorneys in court? Even if some jurors are capable of excluding such statements from their deliberations, there must be serious doubts about the ability of all jurors to do so.

Jurors must also attempt to understand the jury instructions at the conclusion of the case. In a criminal case, the judge informs the jury that it cannot find a defendant guilty unless it concludes that the evidence shows guilt beyond a reasonable doubt. This is a high standard of proof that can be difficult to establish. In civil cases, the decisions must be based on a preponderance of the evidence. This is a lesser standard of proof that requires civil litigants to prove only that it was more likely than not that the person or business being sued is legally liable. These are vague legal standards that cannot be defined with precision and that may be perceived differently by different jurors. The judge must also explain the elements of the crime and other relevant laws, which the jury must consider in making a decision. Sometimes it takes hours for the judge to explain all of the legal rules relevant to a specific case. Many experts believe that jurors lack the necessary attentiveness and comprehension to retain and apply complicated legal rules accurately in their decisions.

Supporters of juries argue that jurors can handle the complexities of decisionmaking because they work together in groups in which they share recollections and understandings to sort out the issues. If one juror misunderstands an element of the judge's instructions or forgets witness testimony, other jurors will contribute necessary explanations; the interactive processes of jury decisionmaking will lead to accuracy in the collective decision. More important, proponents of jury trials see jurors as serving important functions for a democratic governing system. Jurors prevent abusive prosecutions and dictatorial decisions by judges. When jurors reach a verdict, they demonstrate to the defendant or civil litigants that the decision comes from the community and is not merely being imposed by elite governmental decisionmakers.

Thus jurors sometimes override the law to advance the community's sense of justice, such as when a victim who seriously injures her attacker is acquitted of a crime even though the victim used excessive force or weapons that did not fit within the technical requirements of self-defense under the law. For example, an elderly woman who shoots a purse snatcher probably has used force that exceeds that permitted by law for self-defense, yet a jury may acquit the woman of felony assault charges because of its sense that it would be unjust to punish this crime victim under these circumstances. In other circumstances, the application of local values may be detrimental if, for example, they represent biases that equal-treatment laws are intended to prevent. Historically, for example, U.S. juries have sometimes failed to protect women victimized by their husbands' violent behavior and African Americans victimized by whites.

The jury represents an element of democratic decisionmaking in a branch of government dominated by educated elites who are trained in law. The institution of the jury permits ordinary citizens to participate in important judicial decisions that affect the lives of their fellow citizens. However, there are significant questions about whether juries are capable of addressing complex issues, especially those presented through complicated legal rules and processes. Even if it is desirable to keep lay citizens involved in judicial decisionmaking, there are questions about how jury processes can be organized to best enable the historic institution to serve its functions.

Accessibility of Civil Courts for Dispute Resolution

Courts are dispute-processing institutions. One of their primary functions is to provide a forum and a set of rules for resolving disputes peacefully and effectively. However, the costs associated with litigation often make it impossible for ordinary citizens to use courts. In the United States, it can cost as much as $200 just to file the papers to initiate a civil lawsuit. There are additional fees associated with *service of process* (the delivery of legal papers to the opponents to notify them of the lawsuit). It is possible for people to request that costs be waived if they can demonstrate that their income is so low as to make payment impossible. However, many people with modest incomes will not qualify for waiver even though they may not feel that they can afford to pay court costs. Moreover, the waiver applies only to fees charged by the court, not to attorneys' fees, litigation expenses, photocopying, and other matters that make it very expensive to pursue lawsuits.

In addition, there is no right to counsel for civil cases. The Sixth Amendment right to counsel provides free attorneys only to poor people who face serious criminal charges. Legal-services agencies that provide free legal advice to the poor on civil matters typically handle a limited number of specific issues such as divorces and landlord-tenant disputes. If the impediments of costs and legal representation keep ordinary citizens from using courts to process their disputes, then courts are, in effect, government-subsidized dispute-processing agencies that serve affluent individuals and corporations.

Small-Claims Courts

One mechanism for making courts accessible is to have special legal proceedings that do not require the participation of lawyers for disputes over small amounts of money. Many U.S. cities have *small-claims courts* that are designed to give lay citizens an opportunity to present cases in an informal manner when they are seeking no more than a few thousand dollars from the person or business that allegedly injured them or violated a contract. In small-claims courts, the usual rules of evidence and court procedure do not apply. Each side can present its own version of events to the presiding judicial officer, usually a lawyer serving as a part-time court referee, and the referee can ask questions to clarify the facts and issues in the case. As in any other legal case, there are risks that one person in the dispute will be more educated, articulate, and well-organized, and therefore the case will be determined by the mismatched capabilities of the disputants rather than a complete illumination and examination of the relevant facts.

Some critics of small-claims courts argue that such courts erroneously assume that disputes over modest sums of money present simple factual and legal issues. In fact, disputes over even small sums can be complicated. Indeed, many cases may be so complicated that the average layperson has little hope of effectively identifying, organizing, and presenting the appropriate issues. Moreover, small-claims courts are notorious for their ineffectiveness in enforcing judgments. Even when someone wins a

case in small-claims court, there is often little action by court officials to ensure that the losing party pays the required compensation to the prevailing party. Because such courts may process
dozens of cases with few staff resources, they are generally not
well equipped to monitor whether the losing party complied with
the decision. In many cases, the prevailing party may need to file
a new case to seek enforcement of the original judgment, and the
frustrating prospect of going through litigation again can lead
claimants to give up any hope of obtaining justice.

Contingency Fees

Even when small-claims courts work effectively, they do not
address the needs of nonaffluent claimants who seek large sums
of money for personal injuries, damage to property, or violations
of other interests protected by law. U.S. courts attempt to open
access for less affluent litigants by permitting the use of *contingency fees*. Contingency fees are a method of compensating attorneys in which the client pays no money but instead surrenders a
portion of any settlement or award produced by the case. For
example, in contingency-fee cases, people typically agree to pay
the attorney 30 percent of any recovery plus court fees and litigation expenses. In return, the attorney pays the court fees and prepares the case at his or her own expense and thereby assumes the
financial risk of losing a significant amount of money if the
client's claim is not successful. As a result, attorneys usually
accept contingency fees only in cases for which they anticipate a
substantial recovery. For example, many attorneys will accept
contingency fees for personal injury cases, medical malpractice
cases, and other claims against insurance companies, corporations, and wealthy individuals. If the lawsuit is filed against an
individual of modest means, such as an uninsured motorist who
is at fault in a serious injury-causing automobile accident, attorneys may not accept the case on a contingency basis because they
do not see any prospect of recovering money even if they win.

Contingency-fee cases can create gigantic windfalls for
lawyers. If someone hires a lawyer on a contingency basis after
being injured in the crash landing of a commercial airplane and the
lawyer negotiates a quick $1 million settlement in the case, the
lawyer may receive more than $300,000 for only a few hours' work.
The windfall profits received by the lawyer come from money that
otherwise would have gone to compensate the injured person.

Other countries prohibit the use of contingency fees because of a belief that such fees cause ethical problems for lawyers. When contingency fees are permissible, lawyers have a financial incentive to solicit clients and perhaps encourage unnecessary litigation. For example, many U.S. lawyers sponsor TV commercials that encourage people to consider suing doctors if their babies had any birth defects. Birth defects may have many causes that are not attributable to actions by doctors, yet these lawyers know that the doctors' insurance companies will often feel pressured to settle such claims by paying substantial sums of money rather than risk losing a larger amount if a jury decides that a doctor is to blame. When lawyers have such a personal financial stake in the outcomes of cases, they may not make objective professional judgments about whether a case actually provides an appropriate basis for legal liability.

In the United States, there is little to deter an attorney from initiating a plausible claim, especially if the lawsuit is against an affluent person or organization and the lawyer sees the possibility of a substantial recovery for a contingency-fee case. The person or organization being sued must pay its own attorneys' fees and court costs, even if it ultimately prevails in the case. As a result, these defendants or their insurance companies may be willing to settle cases by paying a sum of money that is less than the projected litigation expenses even if they strongly believe that they would prevail on the merits if the case went all the way to trial. By contrast, other countries deter lawsuits by requiring the losing party to pay the litigation expenses for the winning side. Thus, for example, lawyers in Great Britain and Germany must think long and hard before filing a lawsuit because their clients may end up paying substantial attorneys' fees and court costs for the opponents if the lawsuit is unsuccessful (Smith 1997). Such a system may be an especially powerful deterrent for less affluent people because they may not want to assume the risk of being liable for the other side's litigation expenses, even when they believe that they have a very strong case.

European Approaches

European countries take different approaches to solving the problem of providing access to the courts for less affluent people. In Italy and Portugal, attorneys may be required to represent poor people without compensation. Because such cases take time away from profitable cases involving paying clients, it is not surprising that studies show lawyers may put forth relatively little effort when assigned to handle uncompensated cases. Individual states' courts and lawyers' associations in the United States expect attorneys to provide a certain number of hours of free legal services, *pro bono work*, each year as part of their professional responsibilities. Many attorneys do not fulfill this expectation. Others fulfill their pro bono obligation by providing advice to churches or nonprofit organizations. By contrast, the Netherlands has such a liberal income test for an entitlement to legal assistance that most people in the country qualify for free advice from an attorney. In Sweden, legal fees are adjusted according to each person's wealth to make law and courts accessible to the populace (Smith 1997).

Sweden also has a variety of alternative dispute resolution (ADR) mechanisms, such as a consumer ombudsman and a public complaint board, that attempt to process citizens' grievances without requiring expensive and time-consuming court processes (Smith 1991). These processes are intended to resolve disputes without requiring people to undertake the time and expense of court processes. By diverting disputes away from courts, there is a hope that they can be resolved in a more informal manner that will create a compromise producing a higher level of satisfaction to both parties rather than making one the winner and the other the loser.

Some local U.S. governments have experimented with nonjudicial dispute resolution mechanisms to reduce litigation and associated costs. Local mediation agencies, including some that specialize in specific types of conflicts such as landlord-tenant disputes, have attempted to provide a means to solve disputes quickly, informally, and inexpensively. By reducing costs and the requirement of legal expertise, these approaches seek to diminish the difficulties experienced by people who lack the resources to use court processes. Critics question whether these mechanisms are effective. They also wonder whether such nonjudicial processes create a second-class justice system for poor people who find their disputes processed by individuals of unknown qualifications who fail to apply predictable formal rules designed to ensure consistent protection of legal interests and rights. For those who see courts as providing predictable professional decisions, the diversion of poor people's cases to nonjudicial processes has the undesirable effect of reserving courts for the affluent. From this perspective, access problems should be addressed by increasing opportunities for the poor to use courts rather than creating mechanisms that divert parties away from courts. At the heart of debates about the desirability of nonjudicial processes is a disagreement among observers about whether such processes are fair and effective.

Court Access and Governmental Priorities

Governments create and operate courts as institutions responsible for processing disputes between individuals and businesses. Although all citizens pay taxes that support these institutions, courts are not easily accessible to everyone in society. Litigants must pay court costs and attorneys' fees to initiate and pursue lawsuits. Thus people who lack the necessary funds are unlikely to make use of courts' dispute-processing capabilities. Countries use different mechanisms to increase accessibility. Some require attorneys to represent poor people without compensation. Others devote governmental resources to compensating attorneys for representing people who cannot easily afford to hire their own attorneys. Although some U.S. agencies provide limited representation for poor people, courts attempt to facilitate broader accessibility through small-claims courts that do not require attorneys, as well as contingency fees that encourage attorneys to accept and assume the risk for certain civil cases that might generate significant financial settlements or verdicts.

Several questions underlie the choices about whether and how to increase the accessibility of courts. First is the question of how much money a government is willing to devote to the goal of ensuring that less affluent people can make use of courts for processing disputes. The second question is whether governments believe that there is too much litigation, either because courts are overburdened, or because litigation costs from lawsuits are having a broad adverse impact on insurance companies and other businesses. In the United States, many members of Congress and state legislatures believe that there is too much litigation already, and thus little effort is made and few resources are devoted to making courts accessible for all citizens. Because governments have limited resources and must make decisions about how much money to devote to each public policy issue, officials inevitably strike a balance between priorities. Access to the courts has been a lower priority in the United States. But U.S. officials have created a few mechanisms, such as small-claims courts, the waiver of court costs, and limited representation for qualifying poor people, that provide greater court access than would otherwise be available.

Civil Justice Reform

Litigation is an expensive method for resolving disputes. The opposing parties must pay for lawyers to prepare and present their cases. Litigation involves lengthy formal processes for gathering information and presenting it to decisionmakers in accordance with rules of evidence. When legal disputes reach the trial stage, each case expends public resources. Court clerks, court reporters, bailiffs, and other public employees who work in courts must spend time focusing on one specific dispute. The judge is preoccupied with supervising the trial, enforcing the rules of evidence, and ensuring that jurors are not unfairly swayed by inflammatory arguments, improper evidence, and incorrect interpretations of law. For bench trials, in which there are no juries, judges must also focus on rendering decisions. In jury trials, a panel of citizens may be asked to disrupt their lives by coming into the courthouse, sometimes for many weeks, to listen to detailed and often confusing evidence and arguments about individuals' disputes. Litigation is valuable as a method to process disputes because it attempts to impose procedures and rules that are fair to each side, and it places dispute resolution under the government's authority so that the outcome of each case can be enforced peacefully through the application of governmental powers. Yet litigation is also very expensive and slow as well as a drain on government resources. When judges and other court officials are preoccupied with a civil lawsuit, they cannot spend their time on criminal cases, child welfare cases, and other matters that are also very important to society.

The time and expense involved in civil litigation has been a source of dissatisfaction for many litigants and court officials. Others in U.S. society are also unhappy about the operation of court processes in civil lawsuits. In particular, entities that are the targets of lawsuits may change their behavior or be unable to obtain insurance as a result of potential liability. For example, companies that make vaccines to prevent many diseases sometimes receive financial guarantees from the government. Otherwise they are at risk of massive lawsuits if even a small number of people suffer allergic reactions or side effects from vaccines that are beneficial for the majority. Some physicians change their specialties or retire early if their insurance rates rise as a result of medical malpractice lawsuits against doctors in their specialty. As a result, reform efforts in the United States frequently seek to reduce the time and expense of litigation. Many of these reform efforts are advocated by interest groups, such as the medical profession and product manufacturers, who will avoid significant financial losses if legislators make it more difficult for people to win substantial lawsuits against them.

Tort Reform

The most controversial cases typically involve tort law. Torts are civil wrongs. They are cases in which one party seeks compensation from someone for an injury to a person or property. Thus tort cases sometimes lead to huge financial awards in the aftermath of airplane crashes, automobile collisions, injuries from defective products, and botched surgeries. The central focus of tort reform in the United States has been to reduce the power of juries to hold defendants responsible for the injuries of others and to limit the amount of money that juries may award to injured plaintiffs. According to the American Tort Reform Association, forty-five states have enacted tort reform legislation since 1985 (www.atra. org). These statutes often focus on limiting the amount that may be recovered in lawsuits against medical doctors. Such laws create the awkward result of giving people injured by doctors less money than that given to people who suffer comparable injuries and disabilities from some other sources, such as automobile accidents or plane crashes. Tort-reform statutes also typically limit punitive damages. Punitive damages are extra sums of money, beyond that needed to compensate for injuries and medical expenses, that a jury awards for the specific purpose of punishing the party responsible for causing injuries. In some cases, punitive damage awards run into the millions of dollars and far exceed the compensation for the actual documented injuries suffered by the injured plaintiff.

Tort-reform statutes also impose fines and other sanctions against people who initiate frivolous lawsuits. Many large companies and government agencies believe that people file groundless lawsuits because they know that it is cheaper for large entities to settle the claim than it is to actually litigate. Thus even if a corporation or municipality knows that it will win the case at trial, it may still pay $10,000 to settle a phony or weak claim rather than spend the $50,000 or more necessary to defeat the claim in the expensive and time-consuming processes of litigation. Sanction statutes are intended to deter groundless lawsuits and provide a mechanism to sanction plaintiffs and attorneys who attempt to use the civil litigation process for quick undeserved profits.

Tort reform is generally opposed by consumer advocates, civil rights activists, and trial attorneys. Consumer advocates believe that civil lawsuits are an effective means to pressure manufacturers to develop safer products, including medicines, automobiles, toys, and other items that have caused serious injuries to people. They also believe that corporations should be held fully responsible for injuries caused by manufactured products. Civil rights activists see civil litigation as a means to push government agencies to develop policies and practices that respect peoples' rights. For example, police policies concerning the use of force and pursuit driving have primarily been shaped by a desire to avoid being sued. As a result of several multimillion dollar lawsuits against criminal justice officials, policies and training have been developed to teach officers to chase, apprehend, and restrain criminal suspects in ways that cause fewer injuries and deaths than in prior decades, when police officers were much more inclined to draw and fire their weapons.

Trial attorneys argue that tort reform improperly allows wrongdoers to avoid responsibility for injuries that they cause. The attorneys also claim that tort reform improperly deprives citizens of the opportunity to make important decisions because such reform proposals typically limit the power of juries to make decisions. Reform advocates counter that trial attorneys are seeking to advance only their own self-interest because many attorneys have become wealthy through contingency fee cases in which they take 30 percent. Tort reform is the source of political battles in legislatures as society seeks to find the balance between compensating injured plaintiffs and avoiding excessive costs that may drive some manufacturers, doctors, and others out of business.

Cyber Court

In 2001 the Michigan state legislature enacted a statute creating the nation's first cyber court. The purpose was to make use of available technology to handle court proceedings more conveniently and inexpensively than traditional litigation. The cyber court can meet in any location that has access to suitable communications technologies. The litigants in a civil lawsuit can participate from other locations. Witnesses can even be located at completely different locations. The cyber court is intended to make use of video conferencing, conference calls, and Internet conferencing to hold hearings without requiring litigants to travel to a courthouse. The initial legislation expressed the objective of having cyber court proceedings publicly available on the Internet. Participants in a civil lawsuit can communicate while sitting in conference rooms at their own offices. The cyber court is expected to save travel expenses and make court proceedings more accessible and easier to schedule. The court is expected to make business litigation, in particular, less expensive and more easily resolved. Businesses are presumed to have access to the necessary computer and telecommunications technology to make the cyber court workable. Moreover, businesses are expected to take advantage of any court reforms that will enable them to save money. In some kinds of cases, individual plaintiffs and witnesses will want to have face-to-face contact with judges and juries so that their expression of human emotion will persuade the decisionmakers about the validity of their statements and claims. By contrast, business litigation is often based almost entirely on financial calculations. Businesses settle lawsuits with each other based on the strategies that will produce the most favorable financial outcomes, which frequently means quick compromises and settlements. Because businesses may be less likely to be emotionally involved in their cases, the cyber court may facilitate communications between parties and between the judge and parties that will lead to quicker and more mutually satisfying resolutions.

Immediately after Michigan created its cyber court, other states expressed interest in adopting this innovation within their own jurisdictions.

Court-Annexed Alternative Dispute Resolution

As indicated in the preceding section, some jurisdictions seek to avoid putting disputants through the expensive, time-consuming litigation process by creating mechanisms outside of courts to process disputes. Sweden's ombudsman is an example of alternative dispute resolution mechanisms that divert disputes away from the courts and legal processes. However, ADR mechanisms are not always separate from courts. In the United States, many judicial systems have created court-annexed ADR processes. Court-annexed ADR processes are those that are administered by the court rather than those run by private entities, such as mediation services or arbitration consultants, to whom disputants may turn if they want to avoid court processes completely. After a civil lawsuit is filed, the litigants may be expected to take their dispute through a court-sponsored mediation or arbitration process prior to proceeding to a courtroom trial. Sometimes ADR processes are offered to the parties as an opportunity to facilitate settlement quickly and inexpensively. Increasingly, however, courts actually require litigants to take their cases through ADR processes before the judges permit the cases to be heard in court. In court-annexed procedures, litigants may have no choice. If a judge determines that the parties must pursue an ADR procedure or if court rules require all civil cases to use ADR mechanisms, then litigants must follow the mandated steps before their cases can be heard in a courtroom. In some courts, litigants may be required to use more than one ADR process if the first process does not produce a negotiated settlement.

One commonly used ADR mechanism is *mediation.* In court-annexed mediation, a disinterested third party meets with the two opposing sides and attempts to assist in the negotiation of a mutually agreeable solution. This third party, whether an individual or a panel of lawyers, serves as a facilitator rather than as a judge. The solution may not make either side happy. However, the mediator seeks to discover if a compromise solution may be preferable to the risk and expense of facing a win-or-lose decision in a trial. Sometimes the compromise solution may satisfy one party's preference for an outcome, such as the payment of money to an injured plaintiff, while simultaneously satisfying the other party's desire to avoid a lengthy trial. Typically, the mediator does not have any authority to require the parties to reach agreement. Instead, the mediator seeks to ensure that each party clearly recognizes the advantages and disadvantages of possible settlement agreements and compares those factors against the risks and uncertainty of proceeding to trial. Some courts imposed the risk of penalties upon parties who declined to accept a negotiated resolution in the litigation process. For example, a party that rejected a mediated settlement may be required to pay the opposing side's attorneys' fees if the ultimate trial verdict did not place them in a more favorable position than they would have enjoyed with the settlement. However, such experiments with the use of ADR sanctions tended to be eliminated after attorneys complained that they effectively served as coercive measures that impeded litigants' ability to enjoy their right to trial.

Another commonly used ADR mechanism is *arbitration*. In court-annexed arbitration, an attorney with experience in the area of law involved in the dispute acts as a quasijudge who examines both sides' arguments and evidence. The attorney issues a non-binding decision about how the case should be resolved. The decision is, in effect, a prediction about how a real judge or jury will decide the case if it proceeds to trial. Depending on the pre-cise arbitration processes employed in a particular jurisdiction, the arbitrator may also suggest compromise settlements. Because the arbitrator's decision is nonbinding, the parties to the case use it as information to consider the desirability of settlement in light of an expert's prediction about the probable trial outcome.

An ADR method pioneered in U.S. district courts is called *summary jury trials*. In these proceedings, citizens called for jury duty who are not actually selected to serve on juries are required to participate in the ADR process. These citizens are formed into a mock jury to hear arguments, but not evidence, from both sides in a civil lawsuit. During a morning session, lawyers for each side summarize the arguments and evidence that they plan to present at trial. After the completion of these presentations, the jury deliberates in the afternoon and announces its decision the same day. The jury issues a nonbinding verdict that indicates it assess-ment. When the jurors in a summary jury trial issue a nonbinding verdict in favor of one side, the decision sends a message to the other side that its case may not be as strong as it believes. Usually, the jurors' decision leads the losing party to think seriously about the possibility of a negotiated settlement. Even the party that pre-vails in a summary jury trial may be encouraged to consider set-tlement, especially if the jury says that it would award less money than the plaintiff expected.

ADR methods are intended to encourage negotiated reso-lutions for civil lawsuits without absorbing the time of judges and other court personnel. They are also intended to provide informa-tion to the opposing parties about their prospects for success at trial. Such information frequently facilitates a negotiated settlement.

Critics of ADR believe that it serves to drag out the civil litigation process and make it more difficult for litigants to obtain the trial to which they are entitled. This criticism seems especially powerful for those cases that are required to pass through multiple ADR processes before the judge agrees to set a trial date. In addition, critics believe that ADR methods are inherently coercive and effectively pressure people to settle, even when they would prefer to make full use of the trial process.

Binding Arbitration

The ever-present threat of expensive litigation has led many businesses to emphasize arbitration as a quicker, less costly method to solve disputes. Based on experiences with civil litigation, many businesses now include binding arbitration clauses in formal contracts that they enter with other businesses and with other agreements, such as those for credit cards, that they have with consumers. Under these contractual agreements, the parties to the contract agree to have disputes resolved through arbitration rather than through civil litigation. Some critics contend that consumers are often unknowingly surrendering their right to file lawsuits when they sign credit card agreements and other transactional contracts with corporations that are filled with confusing legal terms and paragraphs full of fine print. Few consumers read these contracts carefully and may never realize that they are bound to abide by arbitration until a dispute arises and they seek to obtain remedies for financial losses and other legal injuries for which the corporation may be responsible.

Public Access to Information about Court Cases

The Sixth Amendment to the U.S. Constitution provides a right to public trials in criminal cases. The underlying purpose of this right is to prevent secret trials in which the government might use unfair procedures or even punish people without evidence of guilt. Democratic systems seek to prevent abusive practices by government through the use of public accountability. When citizens are the decisionmakers who control the selection of officials through their roles as voters, they can keep officials from behaving improperly by monitoring the officials' decisions and actions. In theory, the effectiveness of accountability depends on the openness of decisionmaking processes, including those in courts. In reality, many important decisions in democratic governments occur behind closed doors. Legislators vote in legislative sessions that are open to the public, but many decisions are made prior to those votes in closed-door meetings among legislators, staff members, and lobbyists. Similarly, many decisions in the judicial system occur beyond the purview of the public. Plea bargaining is conducted in private. Judges deliberate and draft decisions in private. Jury deliberations are protected from any outside scrutiny. The constitutional provision requiring public access applies literally to "trials" and other formal proceedings rather than to all activities within the judicial branch. These formal proceedings are exceptionally important, however, because they represent the moments when procedural rights are activated and evidence is presented and challenged. Thus the public nature of trials and formal proceedings ensures that officials follow the rules of law and that the public can remain confident that courts are functioning properly and making reliable decisions about people's fates.

Conflicts between Public Access and Other Goals

Open judicial proceedings can cause a clash with competing policy goals, such as the public's desire to gain information and the defendant's opportunity for a fair trial. If, for example, there is widespread pretrial publicity about a defendant and the alleged facts of a case, it may be difficult to find enough unbiased jurors to empanel a jury. In Great Britain and Canada, the laws favor limiting access to information to ensure that the defendant will receive a fair trial before an impartial jury. Newspapers in these countries have been barred from providing detailed information about defendants prior to trial, and some media outlets have been fined for disseminating specific information about defendants (Abraham 1988).

By contrast, U.S. courts prefer to avoid placing any limitations on the First Amendment right of the press to report the news, even if there appears to be a risk that public information may affect potential jurors. U.S. courts presume that the trial can be moved to a new location if potential jurors in a particular community are biased by news reports and personal knowledge. For example, when Timothy McVeigh was charged with killing more than 168 people in Oklahoma City by blowing up the federal building in 1995, the trial was moved to Denver because of publicity in the case as well as concerns that too many potential jurors in Oklahoma City might have friends or relatives who were killed or injured in the bombing. In reality, however, the information about high-profile cases, especially McVeigh's, is trumpeted on the national news; in fact, there is nowhere in the country where people have not heard about the case. In rare cases, judges may impose limitations on what participants in a case can say to the press or what the press can report prior to the start of a trial. When such gag orders are imposed, news organizations often appeal to higher courts because they believe that judicial proceedings should be open to provide information to the public about the actions of their government. In some circumstances, news outlets cooperate voluntarily in certain cases by declining to identify or present pictures of jurors in trials of defendants from organized crime or terrorist organizations that might try to intimidate, bribe, or seek revenge against participants in a case. Many news organizations also have policies against revealing the identities of child victims or victims of sex crimes who may be humiliated or otherwise adversely affected by widespread public knowledge about their victimization.

Cameras in the Courtroom

One of the biggest controversies affecting public access to courts concerns televising judicial proceedings. In many states, news organizations are permitted to take TV cameras into courtrooms to film segments of hearings or even televise complete trials. A cable TV network called Court TV devotes all its programming to murder trials and cases involving high-profile defendants. Advocates of televised trials argue that broadcasting judicial proceedings serves to educate citizens about law and legal processes and provides the best insurance against secretive or improper actions by judges and prosecutors. According to this argument, judges, prosecutors, and defense attorneys will be on their best behavior and make careful decisions because they know that the entire world may be watching everything they do. Moreover, because all courtrooms have limited seating capacity, television provides the only means to ensure that all interested members of the public can have access to proceedings conducted by the judicial branch.

By contrast, critics of televised proceedings believe that cameras are a disruptive influence. These critics argue that cameras are distracting to jurors, who are supposed to be focused on listening intently to the evidence being presented. There are concerns that jurors will be more concerned about how they look on camera than about carefully listening to testimony from witnesses. Moreover, critics argue that prosecutors and defense attorneys become especially flamboyant and combative when they know they are on camera. Prosecutors in most states are elected officials who must gain voter support to be reelected. Televised trials provide an opportunity for them to show off in public, with the attendant risk that their arguments are tailored to please voters' ideological inclinations rather than appropriately focused on the details of the case. Similarly, defense attorneys in private practice must attract a steady stream of clients to build lucrative law practices. Thus they may use televised proceedings as an opportunity to make theatrical performances that detract from the solemn nature of judicial proceedings and distract jurors from the real issues in a case. The 1995 murder trial of football Hall-of-Famer O. J. Simpson is often cited as a case in which the attorneys' inflammatory statements and theatrical performances before millions of TV viewers allegedly diminished the quality of justice as well as the image and legitimacy of courts. Because of these concerns, federal courts do not televise judicial proceedings or even permit still cameras in courtrooms. Any members of the public who are not personally able to attend a federal trial or appellate hearing must gain their information about the proceedings from news reporters' descriptions and drawings by courtroom artists.

Twenty-first-century Americans are increasingly accustomed to having instant access to information through round-the-clock cable news networks and Internet news services. As a result, news media organizations are likely to clamor for greater access to judicial proceedings, especially in highly publicized cases of national interest. Despite increasing expectations about instant and complete access to information about current events, the collision between access to the courts and other policy goals may create additional limits on the ability of citizens to monitor judicial proceedings. This clash became especially apparent as a result of the terrorist attacks against the United States in September 2001.

Security Risks and Open Trials

In the aftermath of September 11, President George W. Bush issued an order declaring that suspected terrorists from abroad would be tried in military tribunals rather than through regular criminal trial processes. These proceedings would not provide defendants with the rights usually available under the U.S. Constitution, including the right to a public trial. Other countries have used secret military trials by claiming that national security required such proceedings or that civilian courts are incapable of protecting judges, jurors, and prosecutors who participate in regular proceedings. Alternatively, these countries attempt to add an element of secrecy by permitting decisionmaking officials to wear masks and hoods that disguise their identities to protect them from potential retribution. Great Britain used secret military trials to convict and imprison people accused of politically motivated bombings and other acts of terrorism in Northern Ireland. Colombia used secret trials for drug traffickers after many prosecutors and judges were murdered. Peru uses such proceedings for trials of accused rebels.

In the U.S. context, special military trials would be conducted in secret without opportunities for observation by the public and the news media. President Bush claimed that secret military proceedings would be needed so that participants would not be subjected to intimidation and retribution by terrorist organizations and the government would not be forced to reveal secret intelligence information in open court. In addition, defendants in such proceedings would not necessarily be guaranteed other rights under the Sixth Amendment. Such proceedings were used for the trials and death sentences of German saboteurs who were caught in the United States during World War II. Under President Bush's order, he would choose which suspected terrorists would be tried in military proceedings and which would be entitled to the processes and protections of normal criminal trials. In these secret proceedings, evidence could be kept secret from the defense attorney prior to the trial. The prosecution would not need to prove guilt beyond a reasonable doubt, and the defendant could be convicted by a two-thirds vote of the military officers presiding at the trial. In addition, there would be no right to appeal, so a convicted defendant could be sentenced to death and executed immediately after the trial (Cohen 2001). Bush's actions demonstrated that the Constitution does not provide absolute guarantees about how all cases will be handled.

Not surprisingly, critics were concerned that secret trials could lead to mistakes and abuses, especially because defendants would lack the usual protections of the Constitution and the opportunity to appeal. Critics were troubled by the fact that Bush's order seemed to demonstrate that the U.S. justice system was not genuinely committed to an adversarial process in which defendants possess rights intended to guard against abusive practices and erroneous convictions. In addition, the use of such proceedings may preclude the United States from ever again effectively criticizing other countries that have used secret proceedings as the means for imprisoning or executing political dissidents, including U.S. citizens accused of engaging in subversive activities abroad.

Is public access to judicial proceedings necessary to ensure that courts use fair processes and produce proper results? If so, how open should courts be? Should news media have unlimited opportunities to broadcast proceedings and discuss the details of cases? Because there are continuing debates about the impact of public access on defendants' rights to fair trials and unbiased jurors, the image and effectiveness of courts, and the need to protect national security, this issue will continue to be a source of controversy.

Sentencing Reform

In the 1980s critics began to argue that judges had too much discretion in sentencing convicted criminal offenders. Such concerns primarily focused on the perception that judges were not imposing tough sentences. Historically, most U.S. judges had broad authority to define an offender's sentence within a range of punishments specified by the state legislature. In many states, for example, judges could sentence offenders to terms of imprisonment ranging from one year to life for a specific felony. As a result, offenders who committed identical offenses could receive significantly different sentences, and the public perceived some of those offenders as receiving sentences that were insufficiently punitive.

Mandatory Sentences

Legislators responded to public perception and criticism by revising statutes defining criminal punishments. The underlying purposes of these changes were the reduction of judges' discretion in sentencing, as well as the enhancement of sentence severity. Some states initiated mandatory sentences. Under such laws an offender convicted of a specific crime would receive a sentence mandated by the legislature rather than be punished according to the judge's discretionary assessment of the individual's need for punishment and prospects for rehabilitation. These laws typically enhanced punishments for repeat offenders. The most extreme mandatory sentencing laws are habitual offender statutes. When offenders are convicted under habitual offender statutes, judges are required to sentence the offenders to long terms in prison or life sentences, even if the multiple offenses on the offenders' record were nonviolent theft or drug felonies. In California, Washington, and other states, laws created by state legislatures or through popular vote imposed a three-strikes rule, under which a third felony conviction could bring a mandatory life sentence.

The effectiveness of mandatory sentences was undercut by prosecutors' ability to make discretionary decisions about which charges to pursue against a defendant. In some states, prosecutors must formally charge repeat offenders under the habitual offender statute to make the offender subject to a long mandatory sentence. Frequently, the mere threat of imposing the habitual offender statute is sufficient to induce a defendant to plead guilty to a serious felony in exchange for avoiding a life sentence. Under a three-strikes law, the life sentence may be mandatory upon conviction for any third felony, but prosecutors still have the ability to charge defendants with misdemeanors rather than felonies for a third offense and thereby avoid the harsh third strike. Thus prosecutors may only prosecute for a felony on a third offense when they believe that the individual deserves to receive a life sentence. In light of the prosecutor's discretionary authority, the efforts to reform sentencing did not succeed in guaranteeing equal and more severe sentences for each convicted offender.

Sentencing Guidelines

Minnesota pioneered the use of sentencing guidelines as a means to equalize sentences for comparable offenders and reduce judges' discretion in sentencing. Various states followed Minnesota's example, and Congress established the U.S. Sentencing Commission to create sentencing guidelines for federal criminal cases. The creation of sentencing guidelines often coincided with increases in the severity of punishment, so judges found that they could no longer consider probation, fines, community service, and other options as alternatives to incarceration. Under sentencing guidelines, judges rely on a grid to determine the sentence for each offender. One axis of the grid reflects the seriousness of the offense, and the other axis reflects the offender's prior record. In order to find the mandated sentence, the judge looks across the grid to the sentencing box at the point where the offender's crime and prior record meet. In that box, there is a specified sentence range, such as 36–48 months of imprisonment. The judge sets the sentence within that range. In some jurisdictions, the judge can deviate from the range, but only if a formal opinion is issued to justify a greater or lesser sentence. Thus, for example, someone convicted of burglary with only one prior conviction may face a sentence within the range of 24–36 months, whereas a convicted burglar with two prior convictions may fall within the 48–60 month range.

Although research indicates that the use of sentencing guidelines reduces disparities in punishments, including disparities that previously might have been attributable to racial discrimination or other improper products of judges' discretionary decisions, many judges complain about the use of guidelines. They believe that the guidelines have reduced their role in sentencing to that of a clerk. Instead of permitting judges to use their wisdom and judgment in assessing each offender's culpability and rehabilitative potential, the guidelines tie the judges' hands and prevent consideration of special circumstances. In addition, prosecutors' discretion in defining criminal charges and negotiating plea agreements can defeat the fundamental purposes of the guidelines. For example, a drug dealer may negotiate a guilty plea in which he is convicted of a minor offense in exchange for providing information about other drug dealers. The sentencing guidelines would mandate a sentence based on the crime for which he was convicted, but there would be no sentence enhancement for the many other crimes for which the dealer may have admitted involvement. This drug dealer would receive a shorter sentence than someone he hired on one occasion to drive a car to a drug delivery location but who has no useful information about drug trafficking to exchange for a lesser charge. Thus first offenders who played modest roles in drug-trafficking organizations sometimes received more severe sentences than their bosses—the drug dealers who actively oversaw the sale of illegal narcotics. Many judges would like to use their discretion to include consideration of each offender's actual culpability in defining punishments, but the use of sentencing guidelines severely limits their ability to do so.

Conclusion

Countries face many issues in determining whether and how to reform their courts in order to best achieve the functions served by judicial processes. The decisions about which reforms to implement will depend largely on the dominant values of the governing system. If a country seeks greater efficiency in court proceedings, then reforms may focus on making judicial processes simpler and faster. Such reforms may not, however, advance other values, such as careful decisionmaking and equal outcomes for everyone in society. The United States faces special challenges in reforming its courts because its laws claim to place a greater emphasis on equal justice for all citizens, yet it is a society with greater inequalities among citizens then other industrialized democracies around the world. Thus the United States is challenged to consider how to make courts more accessible to people who lack the knowledge and resources needed to make use of judicial processes. This challenge is evident in debates about poor people's access to civil justice processes and representation for indigent defendants in criminal cases. Reform debates also focus on such issues as the public visibility of court proceedings and the power of judges to make discretionary decisions. As such debates continue and experiments with reform are initiated, new issues are likely to emerge, especially as technological advances, such as the cyber court, make it possible to reconceptualize the nature of courts and their processes.

References and Further Reading

Abraham, Henry J. 1988. *Freedom and the Court,* 5th ed. New York: Oxford University Press.

Adler, Stephen J. 1994. *Jury: Trial and Error in the U.S. Courtroom.* New York: Times Books.

Cappelletti, Mauro, and Bryant Garth, eds. 1978. *Access to Justice: A World Survey.* Milan, Italy: Giuffre.

Cohen, Adam. 2001. "Rough Justice." *Time.* December 10, pp. 31–38.

Doran, Sean, and John Jackson, eds. 2000. *Judicial Role in Criminal Proceedings.* Oxford, UK: Hart Publishing.

Frank, Jerome. 1973. *Courts on Trial.* Princeton, NJ: Princeton University Press.

Friedland, M. L., and Kent Roach. 1997. "Borderline Justice: Choosing Juries in the Two Niagaras." *Israel Law Review* 31: 120–157.

Gatto, Charles, ed. 1991. *Trial and Court Procedures Worldwide.* London: Graham and Trotman.

Giles, Robert, and Robert W. Snyder. 1999. *Covering the Courts: Free Press, Fair Trials, and Journalistic Performance.* New Brunswick, NJ: Transaction Books.

Green, Thomas Andrew. 1985. *Verdict According to Conscience: Perspectives on the English Criminal Jury, 1200–1800.* Chicago: University of Chicago Press.

Heller, Francis H. 1969. *Sixth Amendment to the Constitution of the United States.* New York: Greenwood Press.

Jacob, Herbert, et al. 1996. *Courts, Law, and Politics in Comparative Perspective.* New Haven, CT: Yale University Press.

Munsterman, G. Thomas, Paula L. Hannaford, and G. Marc Whitehead. 1997. *Jury Trial Innovations.* Williamsburg, VA: National Center for State Courts.

Roach, Kent, and M. L. Friedland. 1996. "Borderline Justice: Policing in the Two Niagaras." *American Journal of Criminal Law* 23: 241–352.

Smith, Christopher E. 1997. *Courts, Politics, and the Judicial Process,* 2nd ed. Chicago: Nelson-Hall.

———. 1991. *Courts and the Poor.* Chicago: Nelson-Hall.

Cases Cited

Argersinger v. Hamlin, 407 U.S. 25 (1972)

Duncan v. Louisiana, 391 U.S. 145 (1968)

Gideon v. Wainwright, 372 U.S. 335 (1963)

Lewis v. United States, 518 U.S. 322 (1996)

Miranda v. Arizona, 384 U.S. 436 (1966)

Scott v. Illinois, 440 U.S. 367 (1979)

Williams v. Florida, 399 U.S. 78 (1970)

3

Chronology

This chapter presents a chronological overview of major events in the development of courts, with primary attention on the history of courts in the United States, including famous trials.

1070s   An early form of judicial proceeding is used in England and eventually developed into the modern jury trial. Judicial proceedings on land tenure during the reign of William the Conqueror are held before the king's commissioners in the presence of tenants-in-chief with the involvement of Saxon-originated shire courts of the counties in which the disputed land is located. Disputes arise because this is a transitional era, as control of the land went from the Saxons to the Normans. The role of the members of the shire courts evolves so that they swore oaths and served as witnesses, making declarations about existing customs. The proceedings are also used in other matters, such as taxation, and are known as sworn inquests (Keeton 1966).

Early   During the reign of Henry I, a step is taken toward con-
1100s   solidating courts under national authority and creating consistency in court decisionmaking in England because the king sends his justices throughout the countryside to supervise the local administration of justice (Keeton 1966).

1215   Under pressure from barons and the public, John I signs the Magna Carta, the forerunner document of later con-

1215,
cont.

stitutional law. One of the rights in the document is the precursor to Anglo-American expectations about the use of courts and legal processes before a person is imprisoned or otherwise punished by government. According to clause 39, "No free man shall be arrested, or imprisoned, or deprived of his freehold, or outlawed, or banished, or in any way molested; and we will not set forth against him, nor send against him, unless by lawful judgment of his peers, by the law of the land" (Keeton 1966).

With respect to criminal cases, during prior decades the guilt of accused suspects was established when they were required to carry hot irons or thrust their limbs into boiling water. It was presumed that God would protect the innocent from harm during such "trials," known as trial by ordeal. As the practice is being used less frequently, Pope Innocent III effectively extinguishes its use by issuing an order in 1215 that forbids clergy from sanctioning trials by ordeal. Without the endorsement of the church to indicate that such procedures represented divine communications, the criminal process switches to the use of jurors to decide the fates of others in their community accused of crimes. Initially, jurors are local people who serve as witnesses by swearing oaths to tell what they know about local events. Over the years, however, the institution of the jury evolves into its present role of hearing evidence and making determinations of guilt (Heller 1951).

Mid-
1300s

From the reign of Edward III onward, the legal profession arises and forms the judiciary in England, which contrasts with earlier eras in which clerics and knights were appointed to serve as judges. The legal profession begins to develop prior to the reign of Edward III as the English common-law courts become exclusively focused on legal matters and follow existing law rather than being involved in the development of public policy. As the courts become more narrowly focused on law, the need for legal specialists intensifies, and gradually the judges are exclusively legal specialists too (Keeton 1966).

1648

Laws and Liberties of Massachusetts, one of the earliest law books about colonial America, is published. The book contains references to juries, judges, various English legal documents, and a system of private property, thereby demonstrating how transplanted English legal traditions serve as the basis for courts and law in America. Because few of the earliest colonists are lawyers, the colonists have to adapt legal institutions and processes as they understand them to their own situation. Thus the court proceedings and rules as applied in the U.S. colonies are not controlled by the courts in England. Indeed, many U.S. colonies behave independently in setting up laws and judicial institutions. Although the court system in England is very complicated, with separate courts of law and equity and a variety of specialized courts, the U.S. colonies generally organize their courts according to a simple structure (Friedman 1998).

1692   The infamous witch trials take place in Salem, Massachusetts. As a result of public hysteria about witches, people are accused, convicted, and executed for witchcraft based on the flimsiest rumors and fears. Nineteen people go to the gallows, and five others die in prison. The case demonstrates the potential power of religion and public fear in determining the outcomes of cases. The existence of courts does not guarantee that those courts are guided in their decisions by neutral principles of law.

1735   One of the most famous early U.S. trials is that of John Peter Zenger, a printer charged with "seditious libels" for publishing a newspaper with articles praising critics of the British-appointed governor. When the twelve jurors in the case rebelled against the stated law and instructions of the governor's hand-picked judge to acquit Zenger, their decision helps lay the foundation for the traditions of free speech and press in the United States. The outcome of the case is considered to be a tribute to Andrew Hamilton, Zenger's defense attorney, who is considered to be one of the most effective and eloquent attorneys of the colonial era (Linder 2002).

The British parliament passes the Stamp Act, which specifies that people in the American colonies accused of re-

1735, fusing to pay the stamp tax would be tried before a sin-
cont. gle judge in the vice-admiralty court rather than before a
jury in regular courts. The colonies are unified in their
protests against this withdrawal of a judicial process
right that is highly valued, so parliament later repeals the
law in the face of protests (Bodenhamer 1992).

1770 In March 1770, amid growing unhappiness in the American colonies about the imposition of British taxes and
customs duties, a crowd of people in Boston throws ice,
lumps of coal, and other objects at British soldiers near
the Customs House. The soldiers fire on the crowd,
killing five. The incident becomes known as the Boston
massacre. A British captain and eight soldiers are in-
dicted for murder. At their trial, the soldiers are defended
by Josiah Quincy and John Adams. The captain and six
soldiers are acquitted, but two soldiers are convicted of
manslaughter. As punishment, they are branded on their
thumbs. John Adams believes that proper verdicts were
rendered. He defends the soldiers, in part, because he
fears that public passions might improperly lead to murder convictions and executions when manslaughter
charges are most appropriate (Linder 2002).

1777 Vermont begins to select judges through elections. Other
states later adopt elections for judicial selection (Friedman 1998).

1787 The U.S. Constitution is drafted at the Constitutional
Convention in Philadelphia. The document is intended
to replace the Articles of Confederation, an earlier constitution that did not give the federal government sufficient power to ensure economic growth, national defense, and other essential aspects of creating a new
country. The Constitution specifies that federal judges
would be appointed by the president and confirmed by
the Senate. Moreover, it protects their tenure in office as
a means to ensure that they would be independent decisionmakers. The Constitution also creates the U.S.
Supreme Court and specifies that other federal courts
can be created by Congress.

1789   The first Congress to meet under the Constitution enacts the Judiciary Act of 1789. The act specifies that the U.S. Supreme Court would have a chief justice and five associate justices. In the nineteenth century, new laws set the size of the Court at nine justices. The Judiciary Act also creates federal trial courts in each state in the union and specifies how appeals would move from those courts to the Supreme Court (Rehnquist 1987). The act also divides the country into three circuits and requires two Supreme Court justices to travel twice annually in each circuit to hear cases in a three-judge panel with the district's judge. The Supreme Court's justices find their travel responsibilities to be a source of irritation, especially when justices are required to travel through the larger Southern states far from Philadelphia where the Supreme Court originally meets (Carp and Stidham 1991).

1791   Enough states ratify the Bill of Rights, the first ten amendments to the U.S. Constitution that provide legal protections for individuals. These include important rights affecting courts and trials, such as the Fifth Amendment right against double jeopardy and the Sixth Amendment rights to speedy trial, trial by jury, and defense counsel in criminal cases.

1801   The outgoing administration of President John Adams passes the Judiciary Act of 1801, which ends the circuit-riding responsibilities of Supreme Court justices and creates sixteen new circuit judgeships. The incoming administration of President Thomas Jefferson views the legislation as an attempt to fill the judiciary with numerous life-tenured Adams appointees (Carp and Stidham 1991).

1803   President Thomas Jefferson's administration succeeds in repealing the Judiciary Act of 1801. Congress enacts the Circuit Court Act of 1802, which restores circuit-riding by Supreme Court justices, expands the number of circuits, and expands the power of district judges to handle circuit court matters on their own (Carp and Stidham 1991).

        The U.S. Supreme Court issues its famous decision in *Marbury v. Madison*. The case arises when newly elected

1803,   President Thomas Jefferson refuses to deliver an official
cont.   commission to Marbury, a last-minute appointee of out-
        going President John Adams, thereby preventing Mar-
        bury from assuming office as a justice of the peace in
        Washington, D.C. The U.S. Supreme Court considers
        whether it could and should order President Jefferson to
        deliver the commission. Chief Justice John Marshall's fa-
        mous opinion asserts the Court's authority to make such
        an order but declines to do so on the grounds that Mar-
        bury brought his claim to the Court under an invalid pro-
        vision of the Judiciary Act. Thus the Supreme Court ex-
        ercises its power of judicial review by declaring a portion
        of an act of Congress to be unconstitutional. This case so-
        lidifies judicial power in the United States by exercising
        a power that had been discussed by the Framers of the
        Constitution but not placed directly into the words of the
        nation's fundamental legal document.

1807   Vice President Aaron Burr is placed on trial for treason.
        He is accused of plotting a rebellion against the United
        States. The trial judge is U.S. Supreme Court Chief Jus-
        tice John Marshall. President Thomas Jefferson advo-
        cates the prosecution. The prosecutors are Charles Lee,
        former U.S. Attorney General, and William Wirt, a future
        presidential candidate. The defense attorneys are Ed-
        mund Randolph and Luther Martin, two men who had
        participated in the drafting of the Constitution. Burr is
        ultimately acquitted because Chief Justice Marshall
        finds that the prosecution had failed to prove Burr's ac-
        tive participation in warlike actions against the United
        States (Linder 2002).

1833   The U.S. Supreme Court's decision in *Barron v. Baltimore*
        declares that the Bill of Rights provides protections for in-
        dividuals only against actions by the federal government.
        As a result, it takes more than a century for new interpre-
        tations to lead to the application of the trial rights in the
        Fifth and Sixth Amendments to state court proceedings.

1839–   Famous trials and appeals occur in relation to a slave
1840   revolt in which Africans recently captured and placed in
        slavery are being transported by ship around Cuba. They

revolted, killed the captain, and steered the ship to the United States. The Africans are first placed on trial in Connecticut for murder, mutiny, and piracy. The judge dismisses the charges after several days of arguments on the grounds that the alleged crimes took place at sea beyond the jurisdiction of U.S. courts. In a second civil trial concerning the surviving Spanish crew members' claim to ownership of the Africans as slaves, the judge rules that the Africans should be freed because they had been captured and placed into slavery illegally. The case proceeds to the U.S. Supreme Court, where former President John Quincy Adams along with Roger Baldwin argues for the release of the Africans. The Supreme Court upholds the lower-court decisions, and the Africans are taken by missionaries to Sierra Leone. This represents an early example of a judicial decision against aspects of slavery. The famous case is immortalized in the 1997 Hollywood film *Amistad* (Linder 2002).

1868   The Fourteenth Amendment is ratified and added to the U.S. Constitution. This amendment explicitly provides individuals with constitutional rights to protect them against actions by state and local governments. The amendment provides the rights of "privileges and immunities of citizenship," "due process of law," and "equal protection of the laws." Because of their vague phrasing, the meanings of these rights are developed through decisions by the U.S. Supreme Court.

1869   Arabella Mansfield becomes the first woman to receive a license to practice law in the United States when she passes the Iowa bar exam and state judges permit her to be sworn in as an attorney.

Congress enacts legislation authorizing the creation of nine new circuit judgeships to cope with burdensome caseloads in the federal courts. The statute also reduces Supreme Court justices' circuit-riding duties to one term every two years (Carp and Stidham 1991).

1873   Susan B. Anthony, a leading activist on behalf of gaining women the right to vote, registers to vote and votes in an

1873,   election. She is charged and placed on trial for illegal vot-
cont.   ing. After the presentation of evidence and arguments, the
        judge instructs the jury to issue a verdict of guilty. An-
        thony is fined $100 for her crime, but she refuses to pay it.
        This trial, like some others in U.S. history, demonstrates
        how courts and trials can become vehicles for debates
        about contemporary issues in policy and politics. Women
        did not gain the right to vote nationally until the ratifica-
        tion of the Nineteenth Amendment in 1920 (Linder 2002).

1875   Chief Justice Horace Grey of the Massachusetts Supreme
        Court is credited with being the first U.S. judge to em-
        ploy a law clerk, a recent law school graduate to assist
        with the judge's research and writing. Eventually the use
        of law clerks spreads, especially in federal courts and
        state appellate courts, and law clerks become important
        and sometimes influential actors in the judicial decision-
        making processes. The influence of law clerks stems
        largely from their recommendations to judges about
        which cases to accept for hearing and which issues
        within a case deserve the greatest attention (Carp and
        Stidham 1991).

1880   The U.S. Supreme Court decides in *Strauder v. West Vir-
        ginia* that state statutes cannot categorically exclude men
        from jury service because of their race. West Virginia's
        statute excludes African Americans from jury service, but
        the Supreme Court declares the statute to be unconstitu-
        tional as a violation of the Fourteenth Amendment's Equal
        Protection Clause. Despite this early judicial decision
        against racial discrimination, many states simply develop
        new exclusionary mechanisms that do not rely on explicit
        discriminatory language in statutes. For example, many
        states exclude African-American voters by using rigged
        literacy and citizenship tests. Congress and the U.S.
        Supreme Court eventually wipe away these other dis-
        criminatory mechanisms in the 1960s.

1891   Congress enacts legislation creating new courts called the
        circuit courts of appeals. The new circuit courts of ap-
        peals each consisted of one circuit judge from the old cir-
        cuit courts, one circuit court of appeals judge from the

new courts, one Supreme Court justice, and one district judge. Any two of these judicial officers could constitute a quorum to hear and decide cases. The country is divided into nine circuits.

1893   Congress creates an additional circuit court of appeals for the District of Columbia.

1899   Illinois creates the first juvenile court. Later, other states emulate Illinois by creating special juvenile court systems to handle delinquency, neglect, and other issues concerning children and teenagers.

1907   Clarence Darrow, one of the most famous U.S. defense attorneys of the twentieth century, successfully defends "Big Bill" Haywood, a labor leader, against criminal charges connected to the assassination of a former Idaho governor. The trial arises amid violent conflicts between mine workers attempting to unionize and mine owners, supported by government officials, who oppose unionization. The man who confesses to planting the assassination bomb seeks leniency by claiming that the killing had been ordered by the leaders of the Western Federation of Miners, including Haywood. Darrow defends the mine leaders and, in one of his famous courtroom performances, gains acquittals. The trial establishes Darrow's reputation as a famous trial attorney and also demonstrates the ways in which courts and trials can become involved in national policy conflicts, such as the labor movement (Linder 2002).

1911   Congress enacts legislation to abolish the circuit courts that had been created by the original Judiciary Act of 1789. Their work overlapped with that of district courts, and their name caused confusion with the younger circuit courts of appeals (Carp and Stidham 1991).

1921   The famous Sacco and Vanzetti trial took place in Dedham, Massachusetts. The two men are Italian immigrants involved in anarchist organizations. Some anarchists had carried out bombings and robberies during the World War I era and its aftermath. After the Bolshevik revolution in

1921,   Russia, a Red scare among the U.S. public led to the arrests
cont.   and persecution of political dissidents feared to be intent
on overthrowing the U.S. government. Sacco and Vanzetti
are prosecuted for the murders of two shoe-company employees during a robbery. They are acquainted with other
Italian-American anarchists who may have been involved
in the robbery, but there are serious debates about the
strength of the evidence against them. During their trial,
they became symbolic victims of excessive government
persecution of dissidents in the eyes of people who are
concerned about discrimination against immigrants as
well as threats to civil liberties. They are convicted and executed for the murders. Debates about their guilt continue
long after their deaths (Linder 2002).

1922   Congress enacts legislation to create the Judicial Conference of the United States, the official policymaking body
of the federal judiciary. The conference is chaired by the
chief justice and includes judges who represent the circuits around the country. The legislation requires the conference to submit an annual report to Congress, including
proposed legislation that the judges recommend. The conference becomes the official entity for communicating
with Congress on behalf of the federal judiciary.

1924   At the murder trials of Nathan Leopold and Richard
Loeb, attorney Clarence Darrow makes memorable arguments against the death penalty that are quoted for
decades afterward by opponents of capital punishment.
Leopold and Loeb are brilliant, wealthy students at the
University of Chicago who decided to commit the perfect
crime. They abducted and murdered a teenage boy but
were identified and captured when Leopold's special
prescription eyeglasses were found with the body. At
trial, Darrow does not contest his clients' guilt, but he
uses an eloquent twelve-hour argument against the death
penalty to avoid execution (they do receive prison sentences). The case stands as one of the nation's most famous murder trials and is immortalized in the 1959 Hollywood film *Compulsion* (Linder 2002).

1925   The Scopes monkey trial in Dayton, Tennessee, is one of the most famous trials in U.S. history. It concerns the prosecution of a local high school science teacher for teaching of evolution in a state where the law mandates that creationism be taught. The trial is set up when Scopes volunteers to be prosecuted to challenge the state law, which is regarded as an attack on the development of modern science. The trial is broadcast on radio and covered intensively by national newspapers. It features a courtroom confrontation between Clarence Darrow, the famous defense attorney, and William Jennings Bryan, the orator and presidential candidate who presents himself as an expert witness on the infallibility of the Bible. Darrow's cross-examination of Bryan is renowned. Scopes is convicted and sentenced to pay a fine of $100, but the state court of appeals overturns the conviction on technical grounds. As in several other famous trials, the courts provide a setting for illuminating and debating prominent issues of public policy (Linder 2002).

Congress enacts the Judges' Bill that gives the U.S. Supreme Court complete discretion to select which cases it will hear from among thousands of petitions submitted.

1925   The U.S. Supreme Court's decision in *Gitlow v. New York* is the first application of a constitutional protection for individuals from the Bill of Rights to a state government action. The Court declares that the First Amendment right to free speech is incorporated into the Fourteenth Amendment's Due Process Clause to protect individuals against state actions in the same manner as it protects against federal government actions. Although this decision has little impact on court proceedings, it sets the stage for later decisions that will apply Fifth and Sixth Amendment trial rights to state court proceedings.

1925–   During an era in which thousands of white Detroiters are
1926   members of the Ku Klux Klan and African Americans who purchased homes in all-white neighborhoods find themselves violently evicted by angry mobs of white neighbors, Dr. Sweet, an African-American physician, moves into a home in a white neighborhood. A crowd of whites gathers outside the home, howling threats and

1925–   throwing objects at the house. The Sweets and their rela-
1926,   tives and friends are barricaded inside the house. They
cont.   believe that they are being fired upon with guns, and
          someone in the house fires a gun from a window, killing
          one person and wounding another among the mob out-
          side. All ten adults inside the house are charged with
          murder. They are represented by Clarence Darrow, in a
          case that is famous for his eloquent verbal attack against
          racism in the United States. After a hung jury in the first
          trial, the prosecution proceeds against Dr. Sweet's
          younger brother, Henry, a college student, in the second
          trial. With the help of Darrow's eloquent defense, Henry
          Sweet is acquitted by an all-white jury. The trial judge in
          the case is Frank Murphy, a future justice of the U.S.
          Supreme Court. The case illuminates issues of racial dis-
          crimination and demonstrates the potential for legal
          processes to be used to make important statements
          against racism (Linder 2002).

1929   Congress creates an additional circuit court of appeals
          (the Tenth Circuit).

1931–   The Scottsboro trials concern rape charges filed against
1937   nine young African-American men in Alabama as a result
          of an altercation with some whites as they all hitched a
          ride aboard a freight train and traveled from town to town
          in search of work during the Depression. The defendants
          are initially convicted and sentenced to death in a quick
          trial in which they are not represented by counsel. The
          trial occurs in an atmosphere of racial hostility because
          the alleged victims are white women. Military personnel
          had to guard the defendants at the local jail to prevent
          them from being lynched by an angry mob of whites. In
          Powell v. Alabama (1932), the U.S. Supreme Court over-
          turns the convictions and declares that indigent defen-
          dants facing the death penalty must receive legal repre-
          sentation. The prosecutions become national symbols for
          racial discrimination in Southern courts, and thousands of
          protestors march in Washington, D.C., seeking dismissal
          of the charges. Northern attorneys provide assistance in
          subsequent trials, but the young men are convicted again
          in the Alabama courts, despite the fact that one of the al-

leged victims recants her claim that a rape occurred. Eventually, five of the young men serve prison sentences. The case is regarded by historians as a demonstration of unjust court proceedings when local political offices and jury-selection procedures are in the hands of officials with powerful racial biases (Goodman 1994).

1934   President Franklin D. Roosevelt appoints Ohio Supreme Court Justice Florence Allen to the U.S. Court of Appeals for the Sixth Circuit. Judge Allen becomes the first woman to serve as a federal judge.

1935   The Lindbergh kidnapping trial occurs after the abduction and murder of the baby son of national aviation hero Charles Lindbergh, the first man to make a solo flight across the Atlantic Ocean. Bruno Hauptmann, an immigrant from Germany, is charged, convicted, and executed for the crime. He continues to proclaim his innocence throughout the trial and until his execution. The case is controversial because many believe that Hauptmann is innocent and that he is convicted on questionable evidence. The prosecution presents evidence that the wood and unusual nails in the ladder left at the kidnapping scene matched wood and nails from Hauptmann's apartment. A witness also testified that he had seen Hauptmann prowling around the Lindbergh estate in the days prior to the crime. The case is noted for attracting strong national interest and receiving tremendous attention from the news media because it involves a national hero (Linder 2002).

1939   Congress enacts legislation to create the Administrative Office of the United States Courts. It provides a centralized administrative entity for monitoring the federal courts' needs and allocating resources efficiently to district and circuit courts throughout the country.

1949   Missouri implements a merit-selection process for judges. Gradually, many other states follow Missouri's lead, creating their own merit-selection plans.

1950   Congress creates the U.S. Court of Military Appeals to handle cases produced by the military's separate court

1950,   system; it processes cases concerning violations of mili-
cont.   tary law by military personnel (Carp and Stidham 1991).

1951   Julius and Ethel Rosenberg are tried, convicted, and exe-
        cuted for passing U.S. atomic secrets to the Soviet Union,
        secrets that allegedly enabled the Soviets to build nu-
        clear weapons. Julius had been involved with the Com-
        munist Party and subsequently revealed evidence shows
        that he met with Soviet officials. There are serious
        doubts, however, about whether Ethel is involved in
        spying or stealing atomic secrets. The case generates sig-
        nificant controversy because it arises at a time when
        Americans are fearful of the Soviet Union after it demon-
        strates nuclear weapon capabilities. In addition, strong
        anticommunist feelings are generated during this era by
        the takeover of China by communists and U.S. involve-
        ment in the Korean conflict. Although others are in-
        volved in passing secrets to the Soviets, several cooper-
        ate with authorities by testifying against the Rosenbergs
        in exchange for lighter sentences. Justice William O.
        Douglas of the U.S. Supreme Court originally issues a
        stay of execution, but he is overruled by other justices.
        The executions take place despite pleas for clemency.
        The Rosenbergs are the only defendants executed; in
        light of questions about their culpability in the minds of
        many observers, this leads to continuing debates about
        whether there was a just and fair result to the trial pro-
        ceedings (Linder 2002).

1953   President Dwight Eisenhower appoints California Gov-
        ernor Earl Warren to be the new chief justice. During
        Warren's tenure at the Supreme Court from 1953 to 1969,
        the high court decides a variety of cases expanding the
        definitions of constitutional rights, including the applica-
        tion of trial rights from the Bill of Rights to state court
        proceedings.

1962   The U.S. Supreme Court's decision in *Robinson v. Califor-
        nia* applies the Eighth Amendment prohibition on cruel
        and unusual punishments to state courts. This decision
        means that the U.S. Constitution applies to sentences pro-
        duced by state criminal trials.

1963   The U.S. Supreme Court's decision in *Gideon v. Wainwright* applies the Sixth Amendment right to counsel to state criminal proceedings in which indigent defendants face serious criminal charges.

1964   The U.S. Supreme Court's decision in *Malloy v. Hogan* applies the Fifth Amendment privilege against compelled self-incrimination to state court proceedings.

1965   The U.S. Supreme Court's decision in *Pointer v. Texas* applies the Sixth Amendment right to compulsory process to state court proceedings.

1967   The U.S. Supreme Court's decision in *Klopfer v. North Carolina* applies the Sixth Amendment right to a speedy trial to state court proceedings.

President Lyndon B. Johnson appoints U.S. Solicitor General Thurgood Marshall to the U.S. Supreme Court. Justice Marshall becomes the first African American to serve as a justice on this nation's highest court. He had previously been a famous civil rights attorney who argued many racial discrimination cases before the Supreme Court, as well as a federal judge on the U.S. Court of Appeals for the Second Circuit in New York.

Congress creates the Federal Judicial Center as the research and training agency of the federal courts (Carp and Stidham 1991).

1968   Congress enacts the Federal Magistrates Act. The legislation creates a new judicial office designed to assist U.S. district judges. The new office is created, in part, to provide new resources for the federal judiciary without the partisan political conflicts attendant to the creation of new district judgeships.

The U.S. Supreme Court's decision in *Duncan v. Louisiana* applies the Sixth Amendment right to trial by jury to state court criminal trials involving serious charges.

1969   President Richard Nixon appoints Warren Burger to re-

1969,
cont.
place retiring Chief Justice Earl Warren. Burger's appointment leads to an era in which the Supreme Court begins to reduce and limit constitutional rights applicable to trial processes.

1969–
1970
The famous trial of the Chicago Seven occurs in the aftermath of civil disturbances at the 1968 Democratic National Convention in Chicago. The city of Chicago had refused to grant permits for people to camp out in public parks as part of planned antiwar and civil rights protests at the Democratic convention. The city imposed an 11 P.M. curfew in the parks, and when demonstrators violated the curfew, they were attacked by club-wielding police officers. Some demonstrators responded with attacks on police officers and property. Eventually, the leaders of the organizations that had coordinated the protests, including Abbie Hoffman, founder of the Youth International Party (Yippies), and Bobby Seale of the Black Panther Party, are put on trial. Eight leaders are prosecuted for violating the recently created federal Anti-Riot Act. Bobby Seale's outbursts and complaints in the courtroom about wanting a different attorney lead the judge to order him bound and gagged in his chair. Later, his case is severed for a separate trial. Although some of the defendants want to defend themselves in a traditional way, other defendants want to use the trial as a moment of theater in which they can gain continuous national publicity by cracking jokes, swearing, challenging the judge's authority, and generally indicating in explicit ways that they did not accept the legitimacy of the proceedings. The defense attorneys, William Kunstler and Leonard Weinglass, are in constant conflict with the judge, Julius Hoffman, who often overreacts to the defense and finds the attorneys and defendants in contempt of court. As the jury is deliberating the riot charges, the judge begins to sentence the attorneys and defendants to long prison terms for 159 contempt-of-court citations. Attorney Kunstler, for example, is summarily given a sentence of more than four years in prison. The court of appeals later overturns the contempt convictions and punishments. Although five of the defendants are convicted on riot charges, the court of appeals also overturns those convictions. The trial em-

bodies the national turmoil and intergenerational political conflict over changing social values. Because of the national publicity given to the daily events in the trial, it may have helped to politicize less-involved observers who believed that the government was undertaking excessive actions in seeking to prosecute and punish political dissidents (Linder 2002).

1970   The U.S. Supreme Court's decision in *Williams v. Florida* determines that juries in criminal cases do not need to have twelve members. It is permissible for states to create laws permitting juries to have as few as six members. This decision creates the possibility for criminal juries to be comparable to civil juries. Many states use juries of fewer than twelve members for civil cases. Although federal criminal juries have twelve members, federal civil juries have only six members.

1971   Each federal circuit court of appeals is authorized to hire a full-time court administrator, called the circuit executive, to oversee budget, personnel, and other management issues within the courts (Carp and Stidham 1991).

1972   The U.S. Supreme Court's decision in *Apodaca v. Oregon* determines that juries do not need to make a unanimous decision in order to render a guilty verdict in a criminal case. It is permissible for states to enact statutes permitting criminal convictions to be determined by supermajority votes of 11-1, 10-2, or 9-3. Even after the Supreme Court's decision, most states continue to require unanimous verdicts to convict criminal defendants.

1974   Congress enacts the Speedy Trial Act, which provides statutory guidelines for time limits on federal criminal trial processes.

1975   The U.S. Supreme Court's decision in *Taylor v. Louisiana* determines that states cannot have statutes that exclude women from jury service, even if those statutes purport to help women by avoiding judicial interference with women's child-care responsibilities. Under the invalidated Louisiana scheme, women needed to specifically

1975,   request that their names be placed on the jury lists. As a
cont.   result, women were significantly underrepresented on juries. The Court's decision effectively requires states to
treat men and women equally in creating jury lists.

1977   President Jimmy Carter fulfills a campaign promise by issuing an executive order to create the U.S. Circuit Judge
Nominating Commission. Carter wants to reduce the use
of partisan politics and political patronage as the basis for
selecting federal judges. Instead, he hopes to initiate a
merit-selection system for federal judges. The commission created by Carter is supposed to consider potential
appointees for federal appellate judgeships and recommend nominees to the president based on the individual's experience and qualifications. Carter also strongly
encourages U.S. senators to create merit-based nominating commissions within their home states to produce recommendations for nominees for district court judgeships. Carter also wants U.S. magistrates to be selected
through merit processes, and he succeeds in having a
merit-selection process eventually included in the Federal Magistrates Act of 1979. Carter also makes a con-
scious effort to increase diversity in the federal judiciary,
and his nominations increase the number of women and
minorities appointed to federal judgeships. With the ex-
ception of the selection process for U.S. magistrate
judges, which is enshrined in the 1979 statute, the other
aspects of Carter's judicial selection reforms end when
Ronald Reagan wins the presidency in 1980 and returns
the judicial selection process to its traditional emphasis
on partisan politics and ideology.

1978   The Minnesota legislature creates the Minnesota Sentencing Guidelines Commission to develop standard
sentences that will increase fairness and equity in imposing consistent criminal punishments. Minnesota's
development and use of sentencing guidelines is later
emulated by other states as well as Congress and the
federal system.

Congress enacts the Omnibus Judgeship Act, which creates 177 new federal district judgeships and 35 new court

of appeals judgeships. This is the largest number of federal judgeships ever created by a single piece of legislation. The judgeships are needed to lessen caseload burdens in the federal courts (Carp and Stidham 1991).

1979   The Federal Magistrates Act of 1979 changes the title of U.S. magistrates to U.S. magistrate judges, long sought by these judicial officers because of a belief that they would receive more respect if their title included the word *judge*. The legislation also seeks to enhance flexible case processing in the federal courts by granting magistrate judges the authority to handle any task performed by U.S. district court judges, except for presiding over trials in felony cases.

1981   Congress creates a new circuit court of appeals by dividing the Fifth Circuit and making a new Eleventh Circuit (with jurisdiction over federal cases from Florida, Georgia, and Alabama). The Fifth Circuit retains its jurisdiction over Texas, Louisiana, and Mississippi (Carp and Stidham 1991).

President Ronald Reagan fulfills a campaign promise by appointing Arizona Court of Appeals Judge Sandra Day O'Connor to the U.S. Supreme Court. Justice O'Connor becomes the first woman to serve on the nation's highest court.

1982   Congress enacts the Federal Courts Improvement Act of 1982. The act creates an additional specialized circuit court of appeals, the U.S. Court of Appeals for the Federal Circuit. The new court consolidates the old Court of Claims and the Court of Customs and Patent Appeals (Carp and Stidham 1991).

John Hinckley Jr. is tried in Washington, D.C., for the attempted assassination of President Ronald Reagan. In firing six shots at Reagan outside a hotel, Hinckley hit Reagan, Reagan's press secretary, Jim Brady, a Secret Service agent, and a Washington, D.C., police officer. Hinckley apparently shoots Reagan in an effort to impress film actress Jodie Foster, the focus of his romantic obsession.

1982,   Hinckley's responsibility for the shooting is not in doubt.
cont.   There are dozens of witnesses, and the shooting is filmed
        by news cameras trailing the president. Hinckley's
        lawyers put forward an insanity defense. Thus the jurors
        in the case hear competing testimony from government
        psychiatrists, who judge Hinckley to be sane, and de-
        fense psychiatrists, who conclude that Hinckley is insane.
        In an enormously controversial decision, the jury decides
        that Hinckley is not guilty by reason of insanity. Hinckley
        is sent into secure custody at a mental hospital. As a re-
        sult of the Hinckley case, many jurisdictions reexamine
        and revise their laws concerning the insanity defense to
        make it more difficult for offenders to gain acquittals on
        that basis (Linder 2002).

1983   After several years of experimentation in various federal
        courts with mediation and nonbinding arbitration, the
        first formal recognition of alternative dispute resolution
        (ADR) in the federal courts is stated in amendments to
        Rule 16 of the Federal Rules of Civil Procedure, providing
        for the use of extrajudicial procedures to resolve disputes.
        In the years that follow, the use of ADR procedures ex-
        pand as a means to settle civil lawsuits without trials, and
        many courts formalize the use of such procedures for
        most or all civil cases (Stienstra and Willging 1995).

1984   Congress enacts the Bail Reform Act, which explicitly
        permits federal judges to deny pretrial release for certain
        suspects after presentation of evidence at a pretrial hear-
        ing that shows there are no conditions of release that will
        ensure the suspect will appear in court or that the suspect
        will pose a danger to the community if released prior to
        trial.

        Congress enacts the Sentencing Reform Act, which cre-
        ates the U.S. Sentencing Commission and initiates the de-
        velopment and implementation of sentencing guidelines.
        These guidelines diminished judges' discretion in de-
        signing convicted offenders' punishments and seeks to
        add equity and consistency to sentencing. Critics charge
        that the guidelines are excessively harsh for some of-
        fenses and offenders and that the guidelines prevent con-

sideration of individual circumstances when deciding punishments.

Congress makes bankruptcy courts subunits of district courts after the Supreme Court rules that it is unconstitutional to make these specialized courts independent entities with delegated judicial powers from Article III of the Constitution. Bankruptcy judges are appointed for fourteen-year terms. They can handle most bankruptcy matters, but some issues must be decided by district judges, usually based on a report and recommendation from the bankruptcy judge (Carp and Stidham 1991).

1986   The U.S. Supreme Court's decision in *Batson v. Kentucky* determines that defendants can challenge a prosecutor's actions in excluding potential jurors from a specific racial group by asking the judge to request a nonrace-based explanation for the prosecutor's exclusions. This case focuses on the use of peremptory challenges, which traditionally permit discretionary exclusions of potential jurors without providing any reason. Prosecutors are not permitted to use race as the reason for excluding potential jurors. The Supreme Court later expands the prohibition on race-based exclusions to criminal defense attorneys and attorneys in civil cases.

1988   Congress enacts legislation to create the Court of Veterans Appeals to hear appeals from claims concerning veterans benefits. The court's judges serve fifteen-year terms, and thus their authority, position, and tenure differ from district, circuit, and Supreme Court judicial officers, whose courts are created under Article III of the Constitution. Article III judges serve during good behavior, which effectively means lifetime tenure (Carp and Stidham 1991).

1990   Congress enacts the Civil Justice Reform Act to encourage innovations in the federal courts that would increase case-processing efficiency while reducing costs and delays. The act encourages district courts to develop case-management plans and to utilize ADR mechanisms.

1992–   Los Angeles police officers involved in a car chase with
1993   African-American motorist Rodney King kicked King
         and beat him with metal batons when they finally catch
         him. A man in an apartment overlooking the scene films
         their actions with his new video camera. The man gives
         the video to a TV station, and it is played on local and na-
         tional newscasts. Later, suspicions are raised that the of-
         ficers may have had inappropriate racial motivations.
         This suspicion stems from frequent complaints by minor-
         ity citizens about the actions of Los Angeles police offi-
         cers as well as a computer message sent by one of the of-
         ficers involved in the King incident that seemed to refer
         to African Americans as gorillas. Four officers face state
         criminal charges for their actions. Their attorney per-
         suades the court to move the trial out of central Los An-
         geles, and it is held instead in Simi Valley, California, a
         predominantly white and politically conservative com-
         munity. The defense attorneys and their witnesses per-
         suade the jurors that the force applied to King as por-
         trayed in the videotape, including more than fifty blows
         with batons, is reasonable and necessary. The jury, which
         had no African-American members, find the defendants
         not guilty. About an hour after the announcement of the
         verdict, riots break out in Los Angeles. Youths loot stores,
         attack motorists, and take over sections of neighborhoods
         as the police retreat in the face of large, violent crowds.
         After five days of civil disturbances, fifty-four people are
         dead, and there is more than $1 billion in property dam-
         age. As the riot occurs, federal authorities work to pre-
         pare a second trial on federal civil rights charges. The
         U.S. Supreme Court has limited the definition of double
         jeopardy only to those cases in which a defendant faces
         identical charges in the same court after acquittal in the
         first trial. The defendants cannot be charged with state
         assault crimes but a trial on separate federal charges of
         violating King's civil rights would not violate the Fifth
         Amendment right against double jeopardy. The second
         trial occurs in Los Angeles with a jury of mixed racial
         composition. The prosecutors improve the presentation
         of their case and identify additional evidence. As a result,
         two of the officers are convicted. Many people wonder
         whether the jurors may have felt pressured to convict the

officers because of the risk that acquittals would trigger more riots. The case demonstrates the connection between courts, trial processes, and contemporary conflicts within society, including debates about racism and police brutality (Linder 2002).

1994   The U.S. Supreme Court determines in *J.E.B. v. Alabama ex rel. T.B.* that trial attorneys cannot use gender to exclude potential jurors through peremptory challenges.

1995   Football Hall-of-Famer O. J. Simpson is tried for the murders of his former wife and a waiter who, at the moment that the killer arrived at the woman's house, is apparently returning sunglasses that she had left at a restaurant. Simpson is a suspect because he had apparently physically abused his wife during their marriage and behaved suspiciously after the murder, ultimately leading police on a nationally televised car chase through the highways of Los Angeles. The trial is covered intensively by the national news media. Over the course of the nine-month trial, attorneys, witnesses, and the judge become national figures. Ultimately, the jury, composed predominantly of African Americans, finds Simpson, an African-American defendant, not guilty because the evidence did not prove his guilt beyond a reasonable doubt. Debates about the trial illuminate a racial divide in the United States, with public opinion polls showing that most whites believe Simpson is guilty while many African Americans believe he is merely a target of the police. The racial elements within the case are exacerbated when evidence reveals that a Los Angeles detective who investigated the case and claimed to find a key piece of evidence—a bloody glove—at Simpson's house had expressed overtly racist attitudes in the past. In the aftermath of the trial, there are also debates about whether juries make appropriate decisions and whether trial processes should be reformed to give juries less power. In a subsequent civil lawsuit against Simpson by the families of the murder victims, a predominantly white jury finds that by a preponderance of the evidence (a lesser standard of proof than that applicable in criminal cases) that Simpson is responsible for the deaths. The jury

1995, awards the family $8.5 million in compensatory dam-
cont. ages. As in other highly publicized and controversial trials, the courtroom proceedings illuminate divisions and
debates in society in the human drama of a legal conflict.
In addition to issues of racism and jury competence
raised in the Simpson case, it also demonstrates how civil
legal proceedings can be used against suspected criminal
offenders, even when criminal trials do not produce
enough evidence to secure a conviction and criminal
punishment (Linder 2002).

1996 In response to lobbying from state attorneys general,
Congress enacts the Prison Litigation Reform Act, which
creates limitations on prisoners' ability to file civil rights
lawsuits in the federal courts. Although the act also limits federal judges' authority to order remedies in prisoner
civil rights lawsuits, many federal judges welcome the
legislation as a mechanism to reduce the significant caseload of prisoner lawsuits in federal courts.

1997 Timothy McVeigh and Terry Nichols stand trial for the
1995 bombing of the federal building in Oklahoma City
that killed 168 people. The trial is moved from Oklahoma
to Denver, Colorado, in an effort to ensure that the defendants receive a fair trial. There are fears that potential
jurors in Oklahoma would have difficulty being objective
in hearing the evidence because so many people had
friends and acquaintances affected by the blast and because of the intense media attention. McVeigh and
Nichols are convicted after lengthy trials. McVeigh, who
is regarded as the mastermind and who is convicted of
actually planting and detonating the bomb, is sentenced
to death; eventually he is executed by lethal injection. The
jury cannot reach agreement on whether Nichols should
also receive the death penalty; the judge sentences him to
life in prison.

2000 In the presidential contest between Republican George
W. Bush and Democratic Vice President Al Gore, the U.S.
Supreme Court responds to a petition from the Bush campaign, terminating the ongoing recount of votes previously ordered by Florida state courts in the contested

Florida counties that controlled the outcome to the national election. Despite the Court's controversial decision, which effectively gave the presidency to the candidate who lost the national popular vote through an
unprecedented application of the Equal Protection
Clause to protect Bush voters in Florida, the country accepted the decision. The case seems to demonstrate that
the legitimacy of the Supreme Court is so well established that its reputation and stature can survive even the
most controversial interventions into partisan political
processes.

2001   In the aftermath of the terrorist attacks on New York City
and on the Pentagon in Washington, D.C., that killed
more than 2,000 people, the United States launches a military action in Afghanistan to capture and kill the people
and organizations that allegedly planned and supported
the attacks. As the United States begins to capture people
suspected of involvement, detainees are sent to a U.S.
naval base in Cuba as the federal government begins to
figure out if and how to place them on trial and punish
them for their actions. President George W. Bush issues
an executive order declaring that the detainees will face
trial in military tribunals in which they would not enjoy
the protections of the constitutional rights applicable to
civilian courts within the borders of the United States.
Bush's executive order generates significant debates in
the United States about the fairness of the planned proceedings and about the country's commitment to the use
of courts, trials, and constitutional rights to punish
people who violate laws and cause harm to U.S. society.
The episode raises questions about the role of courts and
trials in cases of mass killings, as well as continuing fears
about the threat of terrorism.

The Michigan state legislature creates the nation's first
cyber court. The cyber court is intended to permit hearings and other court proceedings to take place without
the time and expense of gathering all parties in the same
location. By using video conferencing, conference calls,
and Internet conferencing, the cyber court's objective is to
make judicial processes accessible and efficient for people

2001,   in remote locations. One of the primary objectives of the
cont.   cyber court is to enable businesses located outside of
         Michigan to process their disputes with Michigan busi-
         nesses and individuals quickly and efficiently. Businesses
         are presumed to have the technological resources and
         know-how to make use of the cyber court format. After
         Michigan created the cyber court, politicians in other
         states began to urge their own jurisdictions to follow
         Michigan's lead by taking judicial proceedings into the
         technological age.

2002   For the first time, the U.S. Foreign Intelligence Court re-
         jects a request by the Federal Bureau of Investigation (FBI)
         to conduct electronic surveillance on terrorism suspects.
         The special court had been created to provide judicial
         oversight over U.S. national security agencies to ensure
         that they did not violate people's constitutional rights
         when using wiretaps and other forms of electronic surveil-
         lance. Throughout its history, the court had been consid-
         ered to be a rubber stamp for the FBI and other agencies
         because it was never known to reject a request to conduct
         electronic surveillance. Moreover, because the court, com-
         posed of three federal judges appointed for temporary
         special service by the chief justice of the U.S. Supreme
         Court, meets in secret to protect classified information, the
         public has little knowledge about its actions. The informa-
         tion about the court's action becomes public only because
         it is released in documents provided to the news media by
         Congress. By rejecting the FBI's request, the court demon-
         strates that judges may be capable of providing oversight
         and accountability for national security agencies, even
         during a period of great public fears about terrorism.

References and Further Reading

Bodenhamer, David J. 1992. *Fair Trial: Rights of Accused in U.S. History.*
New York: Oxford University Press.

Carp, Robert, and Ronald Stidham. 1991. *The Federal Courts,* 2nd ed.
Washington, DC: Congressional Quarterly Press.

Friedman, Lawrence M. 1998. *U.S. Law: An Introduction.* New York: W. W.
Norton.

Goodman, James. 1994. *Stories of Scottsboro.* New York: Random House.

Heller, Francis. 1951. *The Sixth Amendment to the Constitution of the United States.* New York: Greenwood Press.

Keeton, George W. 1966. *The Norman Conquest and the Common Law.* London: Ernest Benn.

Linder, Douglas. 2002. *U.S. Trials Website.* http://www.umkc.edu/ famoustrials.

Rehnquist, William H. 1987. *The Supreme Court: How It Was, How It Is.* New York: William Morrow.

Stienstra, Donna, and Thomas E. Willging. 1995. *Alternatives to Litigation: Do They Have a Place in the Federal District Courts?* Washington, DC: Federal Judicial Center.

Cases Cited

Apodaca v. Oregon, 406 U.S. 404 (1972)

Barron v. Baltimore, 32 U.S. 243 (1833)

Batson v. Kentucky, 476 U.S. 79 (1986)

Duncan v. Louisiana, 391 U.S. 145 (1968)

Gideon v. Wainwright, 372 U.S. 335 (1963)

Gitlow v. New York, 268 U.S. 652 (1925)

J.E.B. v. Alabama ex rel. T.B., 511 U.S. 127 (1994)

Klopfer v. North Carolina, 386 U.S. 213 (1967)

Malloy v. Hogan, 378 U.S. 1 (1964)

Marbury v. Madison, 5 U.S. 137 (1803)

Pointer v. Texas, 380 U.S. 400 (1965)

Powell v. Alabama, 287 U.S. 45 (1932)

Robinson v. California, 370 U.S. 660 (1962)

Strauder v. West Virginia, 100 U.S. 303 (1880)

Taylor v. Louisiana, 419 U.S. 522 (1975)

Williams v. Florida, 399 U.S. 78 (1970)

4

Biographical Sketches

This chapter presents biographical sketches of people who have played important roles as developers of judicial institutions, legal principles, and court procedures or as prominent participants in important trials. The performance of prominent judges and attorneys during trials is especially influential because other judges and attorneys look to these role models in shaping their own behavior. In addition, the experiences of individual judges and lawyers often serve as the basis for court reform proposals as these actors identify ways in which courts and trials can be structured to better serve society. Although these individuals have been selected for attention, they do not represent a complete list of influential people. In light of the number of court systems in each U.S. state and in countries around the world, it is important to remember that every court system has its own history and its own set of influential actors.

Shirley S. Abrahamson (1931–)

Shirley S. Abrahamson was the first female justice on the Wisconsin Supreme Court and later became the first woman to serve as that court's chief justice. Among chief justices of state supreme courts, she gained exceptional national visibility as a leader in court reform and other efforts to improve law and the legal system.

She was born in New York City and earned her college degree at New York University in 1953. She earned her law degree at Indiana University and an advanced doctorate in law at the University of Wisconsin. She practiced law in Madison, Wis-

consin, and taught at the University of Wisconsin School of Law
before she was appointed to the state supreme court in 1976. She
subsequently won elections to remain on the court in 1979, 1989,
and 1999. She became chief justice of the Wisconsin Supreme
Court in 1996. Unlike most state judges who are visible, if at all,
only within their own states, Abrahamson gained national visibility and influence through active participation in organizations
concerned with reforming and improving courts and law. She
held leadership positions in the Institute for Court Management,
the American Law Institute, and the American Bar Association.
She has also published articles on various subjects concerning
court operations and equal justice.

Florence Allen (1884–1966)

Florence Allen was a legal pioneer and was the first woman to serve
as a judge on several courts. She is best remembered as the first
woman to serve as a judge in the federal courts. By breaking barriers established by gender discrimination, Judge Allen set an example for men and women that helped to prove how capable women
could be in the field of law. She served as a role model for many
women who followed in her footsteps as lawyers and judges.

She graduated from Western Reserve University in Ohio and
then worked as a journalist and teacher before enrolling in the University of Chicago School of Law. She transferred to New York University and passed the Ohio bar exam after graduation. Because
law firms would not hire women as attorneys, she opened her own
firm in Cleveland. She became active in Democratic politics and
worked for women's suffrage. She was elected to a state judgeship
in 1920, and she presided over many trials, including one of an
organized crime figure whose associates sent death threats to
Judge Allen. After two years as a trial judge, she successfully cam-
paigned for election to the Ohio Supreme Court in 1922. In 1934
President Franklin D. Roosevelt appointed Allen to the U.S. Court
of Appeals for the Sixth Circuit. In each of her judicial positions she
had been the first woman to serve, and she encountered hostility
from many male colleagues. She remained in active service as an
appellate judge until 1959. No other woman was appointed to
serve on a federal appellate court until more than thirty years after
Judge Allen began her service on the Sixth Circuit.

Although few women had the opportunity to serve as judges
until the 1970s, Judge Allen's performance as a respected judicial

officer helped prove that gender discrimination barriers were artificial and unfair. By serving as an early pioneer and role model, Judge Allen helped pave the way for the hundreds of women who would serve as judges throughout the United States afterward.

Gloria Allred (1941–)

Gloria Allred gained a national reputation as an outspoken, effective attorney who specialized in cases concerning discrimination, women's issues, and family law. She was regularly selected by lawyers' associations and media outlets as one of the most prominent attorneys in the United States. She has served as president of the Women's Equal Rights Legal Defense and Education Fund. Her fame as an attorney was enhanced by her role as a TV commentator and radio talk-show host in Los Angeles.

After earning degrees from the University of Pennsylvania and New York University, Allred worked for several years as a public school teacher. She later earned her law degree from Loyola University School of Law in Los Angeles. Eventually, she became the principal partner in her own Los Angeles law firm, Allred, Maroko & Goldberg. As an attorney, she won lawsuits affecting women in various spheres of life, such as hairstylists who charge women more than men for haircuts, and clothing retailers who charge women but not men for alterations. She also successfully represented divorced women who wanted to move with their children away from their former husbands to seek better employment and educational opportunities. Previously, many divorced parents were forbidden from moving their children away from the location of their former spouses. Allred also won a large financial judgment against a TV production company for firing an actress because she was pregnant. She gained national media attention when she represented the family of murder victim Nicole Brown Simpson in dealing with the news media and the court during the murder trial of football Hall-of-Famer O. J. Simpson. She also submitted written arguments on behalf of Paula Jones in the sexual harassment case filed by Jones against President Bill Clinton for actions he allegedly undertook while serving as governor of Arkansas.

Gloria Allred's career demonstrates that attorneys can impact the policies and practices of many businesses and government agencies when they specialize in specific areas of law and successfully represent individuals in lawsuits. Although civil lawsuits are ostensibly focused on the interests of an individual plaintiff, they often lead to broader policy changes because a successful lawsuit educates corporate and governmental defendants about the likelihood of future litigation if they do not change their harmful behavior. In Allred's career, she had a particularly important impact on issues affecting women in discrimination and divorce cases. Like many other attorneys who gain prominence, Allred successfully used her access to the news media to advance her clients' interests and to increase her own name recognition and influence.

F. Lee Bailey (1933–)

F. Lee Bailey became one of most famous criminal defense attorneys in the United States by representing clients in highly publicized and controversial cases. Bailey sought publicity and was frequently accused of focusing on enhancing his own fame. Despite these criticisms, Bailey developed a legendary record and reputation for success in many of his controversial cases. Bailey gained fame in the 1960s by representing Dr. Sam Sheppard, the Cleveland physician accused of murdering his wife who claimed that the killing was actually committed by a mysterious intruder. A TV series as well as a Hollywood film (*The Fugitive*, 1993) were based on the Sheppard case. Bailey also represented the accused Boston Strangler in 1966. Later, he successfully represented Captain Ernest Medina, an army officer accused of involvement in an infamous massacre of civilians at My Lai during the Vietnam War. Bailey also handled the defense for Patty Hearst, the heiress who was kidnapped by radicals and who was later convicted of helping them to commit armed robberies. Later, during the 1990s, Bailey assisted in the successful defense of O. J. Simpson, the football star who was accused of killing his wife and another person.

Bailey has a reputation for careful pretrial preparation and careful cross-examination of witnesses. He is also regarded as an attorney who uses the news media and public attention effectively. Because he was involved in so many of the most famous U.S. criminal trials in the second half of the twentieth century, any discussion of influential criminal defense attorneys must include attention to F. Lee Bailey.

Myra Bradwell (1831–1894)

Myra Bradwell was one of relatively few American women in the nineteenth century to become a lawyer. She is notable for her effort to use the litigation process as the means to make the legal profession open its doors to women. Although overt gender discrimination initially prevented her from obtaining her law license, her struggle to change the legal profession eventually succeeded after she spent more than two decades fighting for equal rights.

Bradwell, the wife of a judge/state legislator, founded and ran the *Chicago Legal News,* a respected publication that kept lawyers up to date about developments in law. Although she passed the Illinois bar exam in 1869, the Illinois Supreme Court refused to grant her a license because she was a woman. She challenged the state court's decision and pursued her cause all the way to the U.S. Supreme Court. In an infamous decision that proved to be a major setback for efforts to obtain legal equality for women, the U.S. Supreme Court rejected her claim (*Bradwell v. State* [1873]). Instead of relying on constitutional principles, the Supreme Court justices reflected the biases of their historical era by declaring, in effect, that God and nature required women to focus their time on home and family rather than on professional careers. One justice wrote,

> The natural and proper timidity and delicacy which belongs to the female sex evidently unfits it for many of the occupations of civil life. The constitution of the family organization, which is founded in the divine ordinance, as well as in the nature of things, indicates the domestic sphere as that which properly belongs to the domain and functions of womanhood.

Despite the setback, Bradwell maintained her activity in legal publishing and eventually obtained her law license in 1890 after the state of Illinois eliminated its legal barrier to women's access into the profession. Bradwell was an important pioneer in the effort to make legal careers open to women.

Warren Burger (1907–1995)

During his service as chief justice of the U.S. Supreme Court from 1969 through 1986, Warren Burger advocated reforms to improve the administration of justice. He was instrumental in developing the Federal Judicial Center, a government agency that studies courts and their processes. These studies frequently serve as the basis for court reform proposals and for the evaluation and refinement of reforms already implemented. He played an important role in developing other institutions, such as the Institute for Court Management at the National Center for State Courts. He strongly believed in the need for improving the administration of courts to make them more efficient and effective. The institutions that he helped develop used research, technology, training, and the dissemination of knowledge to improve court administration throughout the United States.

Burger was born in St. Paul, Minnesota, in 1907, the son of a railway cargo inspector. Burger worked as an insurance salesman to pay for undergraduate studies at the University of Minnesota. He continued to work as he earned his law degree in the evening program at St. Paul College of Law. He practiced law in Minneapolis and became active in Republican politics. He became an assistant U.S. attorney general in 1953. In 1956 President Dwight D. Eisenhower appointed Burger to be a judge on the U.S. Court of Appeals for the District of Columbia Circuit. While serving on that court, Burger gained a reputation as a law-and-order judge who believed that rights for criminal suspects had been interpreted too expansively. President Richard Nixon appointed Burger to become chief justice of the U.S. Supreme Court in 1969, in part because of Burger's reputation as a judge who would diminish the scope of criminal suspects' rights and expand the flexibility of law enforcement officials' authority.

During Burger's years as chief justice, the Supreme Court faced its initial encounters with many of society's controversial issues, including abortion, affirmative action, busing to achieve school desegregation, and prisoners' rights. In addition, the Court also addressed a potential constitutional crisis when Nixon refused a special prosecutor's request for audiotapes of White House conversations related to the president's potential involvement in the Watergate scandal. Although the Supreme Court justices were frequently divided about controversial issues and Burger was not always able to persuade his colleagues to follow his views, he led the Court to a unanimous decision in *United States v. Nixon* that ultimately played an important role in Nixon's decision to resign in 1974.

Warren Burger played a role in many of the Supreme Court's most important and controversial decisions about social issues. Unlike some of his colleagues who wrote revered judicial opinions that continued to influence judges' decisions decades later,

Burger's judicial opinions are not regarded as especially influential. However, Burger is considered a monumental figure in pushing the modernization of court administration and in developing institutions that could improve the administration of justice.

Jose Cabranes (1940–)

Jose Cabranes gained national prominence as an experienced federal trial judge whose outstanding record and reputation led him to be considered as a prime candidate for appointment to the U.S. Supreme Court. He eventually was appointed to be an appellate judge and continues to be a candidate for the highest court. He also gained national prominence as a critic of sentencing reform laws affecting federal courts.

Jose Cabranes was born in Mayaguez, Puerto Rico, in 1940. He earned degrees at Columbia University, Yale Law School, and Cambridge University in England. After practicing law in New York City, he taught on the law school faculty at Rutgers University. He subsequently became special counsel to the governor of Puerto Rico before assuming a post as general counsel and director of governmental relations for Yale University. President Jimmy Carter appointed Cabranes to a judgeship on the U.S. District Court for the District of Connecticut in 1979. Subsequently, President Bill Clinton appointed him to a judgeship on the U.S. Court of Appeals for the Second Circuit in 1994.

Judge Cabranes developed such an impressive reputation as a thoughtful, moderate judge that he was considered by both Republican President George H. W. Bush and Democratic President Bill Clinton as an attractive candidate for possible appointment to the U.S. Supreme Court. Cabranes also enhanced his national reputation as a thoughtful analyst of issues affecting courts and trials by coauthoring a book (*Fear of Judging: Sentencing Guidelines in the Federal Courts* [1998]) that criticized the design and implementation of sentencing guidelines because of the detrimental impact on the role of trial judges in making deliberative decisions about criminal case outcomes.

Clarence Darrow (1857–1938)

Clarence Darrow was one of the most famous trial attorneys in U.S. history. He gained fame for his effective representation of unpopular clients in controversial cases. Darrow's involvement in controversial cases helped shape public opinion on important issues in the development of U.S. political history. His courtroom arguments had influence outside the courtroom for their effect on people's views about such subjects as the labor movement, evolutionary biology, and the death penalty.

Darrow was the son of an undertaker in a small Ohio town. Like other lawyers of his era, he had relatively little formal training. He attended Allegheny College and then studied briefly at the University of Michigan before becoming a lawyer in Ohio and later a railroad lawyer in Chicago. Darrow came to instant prominence when he abandoned his career as an attorney for the Chicago and Northwestern Railway to defend the leader of U.S. socialists Eugene Debs, who faced criminal charges in connection with a railway strike. Darrow's prominence as a trial attorney and as a defender of the labor-union movement increased when he successfully defended labor leader William Haywood in 1907 against murder charges for alleged involvement in the assassination of the former governor of Idaho. The trial occurred in an era of violent clashes involving mine owners, federal soldiers, and union miners.

Another one of Darrow's famous cases took place in 1924. Two wealthy and brilliant teenage students at the University of Chicago, Nathan Leopold and Richard Loeb, were accused of abducting and murdering a younger teenager, apparently for the mere purpose of experiencing the thrill of carrying out what they thought would be the perfect crime. They were caught when Leopold's unique eyeglasses were found with the victim's body and traced back to him. The nationally publicized case led to loud public calls for the death penalty for the two young men. In order to avoid the passions of a jury, Darrow had the two men plead guilty. He focused his attention on the sentencing hearing in which he made a renowned attack on capital punishment to save the lives of his clients. Darrow succeeded in persuading the judge to sentence the young killers to imprisonment despite widespread public support for their executions.

Darrow's most famous courtroom performance occurred in the so-called Scopes monkey trial in 1925. A high school science teacher in Tennessee faced criminal charges for teaching the theory of evolution in violation of state laws mandating support for religious theories of creationism. Renowned orator and former presidential candidate William Jennings Bryan came to the trial to assist the prosecution as part of his effort to ensure that Darwin's theory of evolution would never be taught as an alternative to the Bible's book of Genesis. The trial was broadcast live on radio and covered extensively by national newspapers. During the trial, Darrow called Bryan to the stand as an expert witness to testify about the Bible and proceeded to dismantle Bryan's claims about the Bible's consistency and infallibility. The courtroom battle between Darrow and Bryan—two giants in U.S. history—became legend in the struggle for acceptance of scientific methods and evolutionary biology. Their encounter was immortalized in the popular play *Inherit the Wind.*

Clarence Darrow's renown as a courtroom attorney made him a role model for succeeding generations of U.S. lawyers. Moreover, his career demonstrated how courts and trials can serve as important forums for debates about social problems and policies. As a result, many people who aspire for careers as attorneys see themselves as helping to shape larger social developments and public policies.

Morris Dees (1936–)

Morris Dees was a successful white businessman who put aside his career to become a crusading civil rights lawyer. He founded the Southern Poverty Law Center (SPLC) and actively litigated cases concerning racial discrimination and other issues. He specialized in the use of civil lawsuits against racist organizations such as the Ku Klux Klan. He sued on behalf of people victimized by violence from hate groups and gained financial awards that helped to force some of these organizations to surrender their property and other financial resources to the victims.

Dees was born in 1936, the son of an Alabama farmer. As an undergraduate at the University of Alabama, he started a successful mail-order business and expanded it into a successful publishing business after graduating from the University of Alabama School of Law. After gaining financial success in his private law practice and business ventures, he went through a period of soul-searching in which he decided to completely change his focus. He sold his business ventures and began to litigate actively on behalf of civil rights causes. He filed cases in the 1960s intended to combat the extensive application of racial segregation in Alabama. In 1971 he became cofounder of the Southern Poverty Law Center. Supported by contributions from donors around the country, the SPLC files lawsuits against hate groups that commit acts of violence, maintains the Klan Watch project to monitor the activities of racial hate groups throughout the United States, and publishes *Teaching Tolerance,* a magazine and curriculum to assist schoolteachers in teaching their students about racial tolerance and the value of diversity in U.S. society.

Because of his success in suing hate groups, Dees received death threats, and an attempt on his life was made when the SPLC offices were bombed. As a successful national fund-raiser on behalf of civil rights causes, Dees was able to raise money to build a new SPLC facility with increased security and to commission the construction of a famous monument at the SPLC offices in Montgomery, Alabama, that contains the names of people who lost their lives in the struggle for racial equality and civil rights in the South during the mid–twentieth century.

Richard A. Enslen (1931–)

The career of Richard A. Enslen reflects the development and implementation of court reforms, which require consistent efforts by advocates who must counter the resistance to change that exists in most institutional settings. In his role as a U.S. district judge in the western district of Michigan, Enslen was a national leader in the implementation of alternative dispute resolution (ADR) mechanisms in federal trial courts. In the federal courthouse in Kalamazoo, Enslen insisted that litigants make use of various pretrial procedures designed to encourage the development of negotiated settlements. In some cases, such settlements may be able to achieve appropriate compromises between litigants and simultaneously spare the court the time and expense of prolonged civil trials.

Prior to being appointed as a federal judge by President Jimmy Carter in 1979, Enslen practiced law in Kalamazoo, directed the Peace Corps in Costa Rica, and served as a state trial court judge. In his service as a judge, Enslen gained a keen insight into the burdens faced by clients when their lawyers focus on prolonged courtroom battles rather than attempt to resolve disputes through negotiations. As a result of his sensitivity to clients' interests, Enslen began to use various ADR processes within his courthouse, including summary jury trials, mediation, and arbitration. He experimented with other innovations. For example, he appointed a special master to assist him in resolving a difficult case about Native American fishing rights (*Grand Traverse Band of*

Chippewa and Ottawa Indians v. Director, Michigan Department of Natural Resources [1995]). When handling major litigation about unconstitutional prison conditions, he required corrections officials to come up with their own suggestions for how the problems could be remedied.

Although some lawyers initially resented what they perceived to be judicial pressure to settle cases, ADR mechanisms became increasingly accepted as part of the civil litigation process. Enslen wrote about ADR and gave talks about the subject to lawyers and judges. Other judges drew from his example in using ADR mechanisms for their own cases. Because of his pioneering efforts and advocacy for ADR methods, Enslen was the only federal judge invited to testify before the Senate Judiciary Committee in support of the Civil Justice Reform Act of 1990. After the statute was enacted, Enslen's district court was selected by Congress as one of the demonstration districts that would develop innovations in case management that would later be evaluated and emulated by other federal courts. The efforts of Judge Enslen and other innovators led to the development and refinement of ADR methods as well as their implementation and acceptance in courts throughout the country.

Ruth Bader Ginsburg (1933–)

As an attorney, Ruth Bader Ginsburg was a renowned advocate of gender equality. Her arguments to the Supreme Court led to the high court's most important initial decisions against gender discrimination in the 1970s. Later, she became a justice on the U.S. Supreme Court, where she participated in many important decisions.

Ruth Bader was born in Brooklyn, New York, the daughter of a furrier. She excelled as a student and earned degrees at Cornell University and Columbia University School of Law. Despite graduating at the top of her class, no New York law firms would hire her. She was a victim of discrimination against both women and Jews. Eventually, a federal judge hired her as his law clerk. She later became a professor of law at Rutgers University and Columbia University. Professor Ginsburg worked with the American Civil Liberties Union (ACLU) to represent claimants in gender discrimination cases. She became the director of the national ACLU's Women's Rights Project. Her representation was not limited to women victimized by discrimination. She also argued

cases on behalf of men to challenge government policies that provided preferences for women. During the 1970s she argued six
cases in front of the U.S. Supreme Court, winning five. In *Craig v.
Boren* (1976), a case in which she submitted written arguments to
the Supreme Court, a majority of justices finally accepted her
argument that the Constitution's Equal Protection Clause should
protect against gender discrimination by government.

In 1980 President Jimmy Carter appointed Ginsburg to be a
judge on the U.S. Court of Appeals for the District of Columbia
Circuit. She served on that prestigious appellate court for thirteen
years and established a reputation as a thoughtful, moderate
judge. President Bill Clinton appointed her to the U.S. Supreme
Court in 1993. At her confirmation hearings, she described herself
as a moderate judge because she distinguished her role as a
lawyer from her role as a judge. As a lawyer, she saw herself as
bearing an obligation to zealously advocate on behalf of clients
and legal interpretations that composed her cases. By contrast, as
a judge she saw herself as carefully limiting her decisions and
actions within the boundaries of appropriate activity for judicial
officers. Thus she said her judicial role would keep her from
deciding in favor of causes she supported if she did not believe
that the law also supported that cause. Her performance as a
Supreme Court justice subsequently confirmed her moderate
approach and demonstrated, within the career of a single individual, that lawyers and judges play very different roles within
court processes.

William H. Hastie (1904–1976)

William H. Hastie was an important litigator for the National
Association for the Advancement of Colored People (NAACP).
The NAACP during the 1930s used civil lawsuits as a means to
illuminate and combat racial discrimination. He subsequently
became the first African American to serve as a federal appeals
court judge.

Hastie was born in Knoxville, Tennessee, and grew up in
Washington, D.C., where his father worked as a clerk in the federal government. He was the valedictorian of the class of 1925 at
Amherst College and subsequently graduated near the top his
class at Harvard Law School at a time when very few African
Americans had the opportunity to attend elite colleges and universities. During the 1930s he was a pioneering litigator for the

NAACP and faced great hostility from the public, attorneys, and judges as he prepared arguments concerning the illegality of racial discrimination. After serving as an attorney in the federal government, he was appointed by President Franklin D. Roosevelt as a district judge for the U.S. Virgin Islands. He later became dean of Howard University School of Law in Washington, D.C. President Harry Truman appointed Hastie to be governor of the U.S. Virgin Islands in 1946. In 1949 Truman appointed Hastie to be a judge on the U.S. Court of Appeals for the Third Circuit in Philadelphia. Hastie became chief judge of the appellate court in 1968. He served as a distinguished federal judge until his retirement in 1972.

William H. Hastie was a pioneering civil rights litigator, educator, and jurist. Through his work and the example he set during his performance in various public and judicial offices, he helped to break down discriminatory barriers that had long existed to exclude African Americans from professional opportunities in the legal profession and the judiciary.

Charles Hamilton Houston (1895–1950)

Charles Hamilton Houston was a prominent attorney and educator who led the strategic litigation campaign of the National Association for the Advancement of Colored People (NAACP) that eventually produced the U.S. Supreme Court's condemnation of school segregation in *Brown v. Board of Education* (1954). In addition, in his role as a professor and dean at Howard University's School of Law, he helped to mentor and train a generation of successful African-American attorneys, including future U.S. Supreme Court Justice Thurgood Marshall, who litigated and won many civil rights cases.

Houston was an honors graduate of Amherst College and Harvard Law School. He was the first African-American editor of the *Harvard Law Review*. After earning additional advanced law degrees at Harvard and the University of Madrid, he practiced law in Washington, D.C., and taught at Howard University School of Law. He eventually became the legal director of the NAACP, where he led the planning of a litigation strategy to attack racial discrimination in education through a series of cases that addressed higher education first and then public schools nationwide. In the Supreme Court, he argued important cases concerning racial discrimination in education, labor law, and the death penalty.

Charles Hamilton Houston was one of the most important attorneys in the early-twentieth-century legal battles against racial discrimination. As the architect of the NAACP's successful litigation strategy, he provided a model for using court cases to shape public policy that was emulated by many other groups in the decades following his death. In addition, he was an important teacher and mentor for many of the most important and effective African-American lawyers who waged many court battles to advance the principle of racial equality.

William Kunstler (1919–1995)

William Kunstler was a self-described radical lawyer who became famous for representing political dissidents accused of crimes during the 1960s and subsequent decades. He grew up in New York City and graduated from Columbia Law School. While stationed in the South during his military service in World War II, he became politically motivated because of his outrage over seeing the existence of oppressive racial segregation aimed at African Americans. He represented the defendants in the famous trial of the Chicago Seven, when the leaders of various hippie and radical groups were arrested on conspiracy charges in the aftermath of massive protests at the 1968 Democratic National Convention in Chicago. Kunstler advised Reverend Martin Luther King Jr., and he was the attorney for leaders of the Black Panthers. He also represented leaders of the American Indian Movement. When prisoners took over New York's Attica prison in an uprising that ultimately led to three dozen deaths when officials stormed the prison while firing weapons, the prisoners requested that Kunstler serve as their lawyer. He met with the uprising leaders within the prison prior to the retaking of the institution at the order of Governor Nelson Rockefeller.

Kunstler's representation of liberal political dissidents earned him the admiration of supporters and the contempt of opponents. However, Kunstler also represented other people whom he described as "pariahs," including a drug dealer who shot several police officers, and a Muslim man charged with shooting a politically active rabbi. He was also often accused of seeking excessive publicity so that he appeared to overemphasize his desire to gain news media attention for his political viewpoints. His actions in such cases made him a controversial figure to many politically sympathetic people who shared his skepticism about the fairness of the U.S. system of justice. Throughout his career, Kunstler used the litigation process to make statements about the flaws that he perceived in the U.S. governing system as well as to represent the interests of his controversial clients.

Thomas D. Lambros (1930–)

In his role as U.S. district judge for the northern district of Ohio, Thomas D. Lambros is credited with the invention of the summary jury trial, an alternative dispute resolution (ADR) mechanism that involves real jurors in one-day mock trials. The jurors issue a nonbinding verdict after hearing summarized arguments from both sides in a civil lawsuit. The jurors' reactions to and decisions about the brief presentation of the case are intended to educate the attorneys about how an actual jury may react to their arguments in a full-blown trial on the issues. In most cases, the nonbinding verdict encourages one or both sides to achieve a negotiated settlement that will avoid the expense, delay, and risk of an actual trial.

Lambros became a state judge in 1961 at the age of 31 and was appointed to serve as a federal district judge by President Lyndon Johnson in 1967, when he was only 37 years old. He served on the federal bench for an additional 28 years before retiring in 1995. During his years as a federal judge, Lambros was a strong advocate of ADR. He educated other judges and lawyers about summary jury trials and various ADR methods. When Congress enacted the Civil Justice Reform Act of 1990, the U.S. District Court for the Northern District of Ohio became a demonstration district for the development of case-management and dispute-resolution techniques because of Lambros's reputation as a national leader in the ADR movement. Lambros received many national awards for his work on developing ADR. After he retired from the bench, he founded the Lambros Dispute Management Center and today works privately to help settle disputes and thereby avoid the delay and expense of litigation.

Arabella Mansfield (1846–1911)

Arabella Mansfield was the first woman in the United States to be licensed to practice law as an attorney. During the nineteenth century, most lawyers gained knowledge by studying with a practicing attorney. Very few attorneys studied law at universities. After graduating from Iowa Wesleyan College, Mansfield studied law with an attorney and passed the Iowa bar exam in 1869. Iowa judges permitted her to be licensed as an attorney despite the fact that state law specifically referred to attorneys as males. Mansfield did not use her license to actually work as an attorney. Instead, she pursued a career as a college professor. Her historical importance stems from her initially breaking through a barrier that prevented women from becoming lawyers and judges, a barrier that continued to exist in many states for decades after Mansfield was admitted to practice law in Iowa.

Thurgood Marshall (1908–1993)

Thurgood Marshall was a noted attorney who used a litigation strategy of pursuing selected cases to shape public policy in favor of racial equality. Subsequently, he served as a judge on the U.S. Court of Appeals for the Second Circuit and as a justice on the U.S. Supreme Court. In addition, he spent three years as the U.S. Solicitor General, the attorney responsible for representing the government in arguments before the Supreme Court. Justice Marshall's distinguished career demonstrated how attorneys and judges working within courts can have a significant impact on the development of public policy.

Thurgood Marshall was born in Baltimore in 1908, the son of a waiter and a schoolteacher. As an African American, he experienced firsthand the humiliations of racial discrimination in an era when the best jobs, education, housing, and other benefits were reserved for whites. He ended up devoting much of his legal career to using courts and law to combat racial discrimination.

After graduating from Lincoln University and the Howard University School of Law, two institutions created for African Americans because they were denied access to most other universities, he became an attorney for the National Association for the Advancement of Colored People (NAACP). Eventually he became the director of litigation for the NAACP and traveled throughout the country advising attorneys and representing people who were victimized by racial discrimination. The NAACP developed a strategy of filing litigation against the racial segregation practices of universities. After winning several cases, the NAACP later pursued a case addressing racial segregation in public schools, a form of discrimination that affected hundreds of thousands of students. Marshall successfully argued the case of

Brown v. Board of Education (1954) before the U.S. Supreme Court. As a result, the high court declared that school segregation violated the Equal Protection Clause.

In 1961 President John F. Kennedy appointed Marshall to be a federal appeals court judge in New York. His nomination generated significant opposition from Southern senators who disliked Marshall's efforts to end racial segregation. President Lyndon Johnson appointed Marshall to be Solicitor General in 1965. Marshall had handled many cases for the NAACP, and now he argued thirty-two more cases before the U.S. Supreme Court on behalf of the U.S. government. In 1967 President Johnson appointed Marshall to the U.S. Supreme Court. Marshall was the first African American to serve on the country's highest court. During a twenty-four-year career as a Supreme Court justice, Marshall was notable for his many judicial opinions concerning racial discrimination, constitutional rights, and capital punishment. He retired from the Supreme Court in 1991.

Thurgood Marshall was a legendary courtroom advocate who eventually became a justice on this country's highest court. Throughout his legal career, Marshall demonstrated how courts and law can shape public policy and move a country toward fulfillment of its constitutional ideals.

Sandra Day O'Connor (1930–)

Sandra Day O'Connor's distinguished career gave her broad experience in all aspects of judicial affairs and culminated in her appointment and service as the first female justice on the U.S. Supreme Court. O'Connor grew up on a ranch in Arizona and earned her undergraduate and law degrees with honors at Stanford University. When she graduated near the top of her class from Stanford Law School, she was unable to obtain employment with a law firm because they generally only hired women to be legal secretaries in the 1950s. Eventually she found jobs in government service. Her legal career brought her experiences as an assistant county prosecutor, a private practice attorney, and an assistant state attorney general. She served for six years in the Arizona state legislature, where she helped to develop statutes that would affect courts' procedures, structure, and budgets. She was elected as a state trial judge in Arizona and served for four years before the governor appointed her to the Arizona Court of Appeals in 1979. In 1981 President Ronald Reagan fulfilled a campaign pledge to appoint the first woman to the U.S. Supreme Court by nominating O'Connor for a seat on the country's highest court.

During her years on the Supreme Court, O'Connor gained a reputation for supporting the authority of law enforcement officers and prosecutors and declining to expand rights for criminal suspects and defendants. Justice O'Connor repeatedly expressed the desire to permit states to handle their own affairs without excessive interference by Congress and the Supreme Court. In some cases, especially issues affecting women and children, O'Connor sometimes parted company with her usual conservative allies to provide the decisive fifth vote to give the Court's liberal majority control over the outcomes of such cases. Overall, her varied career and outstanding record make her a pioneering figure and role model for women lawyers and judges.

Roscoe Pound (1870–1964)

Roscoe Pound taught law at the University of Nebraska, Northwestern University, and the University of Chicago before becoming a professor and dean at Harvard Law School from 1910 to 1937. Pound is most famous for his many writings about the nature of law and the need to connect law to social conditions and problems in society. Because of his prominent position at Harvard and his influential writings, he is considered to be one of the most important figures in the development of U.S. law. Although Pound is best known for shaping the underlying philosophy of law in this country, he was also an active and influential early advocate of court reforms to improve the administration of justice. His speeches and writings included criticisms of inefficient courts that were unduly influenced by local politics. He used his position of prominence to highlight the problems of inefficient court administration, and other reformers looked to him for guidance and legitimacy.

William H. Rehnquist Jr. (1924–)

In his role as chief justice of the U.S. Supreme Court (where he continued to serve at the time of this writing), William Rehnquist has sought to educate Congress about the caseload pressures and resource needs of the federal courts. During Rehnquist's tenure, political battles between various presidents and the U.S. Senate have left many federal judgeships unfilled for months at a time whenever a judge died, retired, or resigned and needed to be replaced. He warned Congress that the creation of too many federal crimes and the emphasis on the federal prosecution of drug offenders would overburden the federal courts and prevent them from fulfilling their responsibilities to the full range of cases. He sought to reduce the caseload burdens of the federal courts by supporting efforts to limit the filing of petitions and lawsuits by convicted offenders. He also sought to permit state governments to handle their own affairs as much as possible, and therefore he was reluctant to make decisions that would expand constitutional rights or impose nationwide rules for trial processes.

William Rehnquist earned degrees at Stanford University, Harvard University, and Harvard Law School. After serving as a law clerk to Supreme Court Justice Robert Jackson, he practiced law in Phoenix for most of the 1950s and 1960s. He became an assistant attorney general in the administration of President Richard Nixon in 1969. After two years of government service, Nixon appointed Rehnquist to be an associate justice of the U.S. Supreme Court in 1971. Rehnquist began his service as a judicial officer on his country's highest court without any prior experience as a judge in any other state or federal court. In 1986, upon the retirement of Chief Justice Warren Burger, President Ronald Reagan elevated Rehnquist to the post of chief justice.

Justice Rehnquist earned a reputation as one of the Supreme Court's most conservative justices. He was among the justices least likely to support claims of civil rights violations by individuals. Instead, he usually endorsed governmental authority when there was an alleged collision between government practices and individual rights. Rehnquist's best-known activities affecting court administration concerned his efforts to reduce what he saw as ever-increasing caseload pressures on the federal courts due to the transfer of many issues from state courts to federal courts through the enactment of new statutes by Congress.

Gerry Spence (1929–)

Gerry Spence became a nationally renowned trial attorney by winning multimillion dollar verdicts in civil lawsuits and successfully defending criminal defendants in highly publicized cases. In addition, he became well known as the author of a dozen books and the founder of the Trial Lawyers College, which provides training in courtroom tactics and trial preparation for lawyers who litigate civil and criminal cases.

Gerry Spence was born in 1929 in Wyoming. He received his bachelor's degree and law degree from the University of Wyoming. After serving as a county attorney, he entered private practice and developed his reputation by winning high-profile cases. He won a $10 million verdict against Kerr-McGee Corporation on behalf of Karen Silkwood, a company employee who raised questions about worker safety issues and subsequently died in a mysterious automobile accident. Her story became the basis of the 1983 Hollywood film *Silkwood*. He later won multiple million-dollar verdicts against corporate entities such as Penthouse and McDonald's by representing individuals whose reputations or livelihoods were harmed through torts or contract violations committed by those companies. In highly publicized criminal cases, he gained acquittals for the former first lady of the Philippines, Imelda Marcos, who was charged with various financial improprieties, and Randy Weaver, a critic of the U.S. government whose wife and child were killed in a shootout at his isolated Idaho home that also took the life of a federal law enforcement officer.

Gerry Spence became a best-selling author by writing a dozen books about individual legal cases, strategies for argumentation, and the flaws in the U.S. system of justice. He became a familiar figure to the public through his books and through his TV talk show, which tackled many contemporary justice issues. His best-selling books include *Gunning for Justice, Justice for None*, and *How to Argue and Win Every Time*. Like other successful trial attorneys, Spence saw the litigation process as a means to achieve justice for individuals who find themselves in mismatched battles with larger, richer entities such as corporations and government.

Arthur T. Vanderbilt (1888–1957)

In his positions as president of the American Bar Association, dean of New York University Law School, and chief justice of the New Jersey Supreme Court, Arthur T. Vanderbilt remained involved in efforts to make courts professional, efficient institutions that could serve the needs of society. He was involved in the creation of the Administrative Office of the United States Courts and the development of the Federal Rules of Criminal Procedure as well as the reform of New Jersey's court system. The Institute for Judicial Administration at New York University Law School continues to have national prominence by providing training and information for judges and court administrators.

Vanderbilt earned degrees at Wesleyan University and Columbia University Law School before beginning work as an attorney in Newark, New Jersey, in 1913. He used his involvement and eventual prominence in Republican politics in New Jersey to help revise the state's constitution. His role in politics also led to his appointment as chief justice of the New Jersey Supreme Court in 1948. The appointment came after he had already gained prominence as an advocate of efficient judicial administration during his prior service as leader of the American Bar Association and as a law school dean. Under Vanderbilt's leadership. New Jersey's courts became more centralized and administratively efficient. Instead of operating independently in each county, courts became more effective as centralized management permitted a more efficient distribution of resources. Thanks to Vanderbilt's efforts, the centralization of judicial administration became recognized as an important element in making state court systems more efficient and effective.

Earl Warren (1891–1974)

Earl Warren had a distinguished career as a prosecuting attorney, state attorney general, governor, and chief justice of the U.S. Supreme Court (1953–1969). He is best remembered for his role in leading the Supreme Court during an era in which its decisions expanded individuals' rights and advanced racial equality. Warren played an influential role in many of the Court's decisions that shaped courts and trials by defining and expanding rights for individuals in the judicial process.

Earl Warren was born into modest circumstances as the son of a railroad-car repairman. After graduating from college and law school at the University of California, he became a prosecutor in Alameda County, California. For eighteen years he prosecuted criminal cases. Although he gained renown as a tough, effective prosecutor, he was also known to show concern about protecting the rights of the accused. After he became well known as a county prosecutor, he was elected to statewide office, first as California attorney general, and later as governor. He was considered a prime contender for the Republican nomination for president in the 1952 election, but he threw his support to Dwight

Eisenhower. After Eisenhower was elected president, he appointed Warren to be chief justice of the Supreme Court. At the time of his appointment, although Warren was a highly experienced and respected public official, he had no prior experience as a judge before becoming the leader of his country's highest court. Soon after arriving in Washington, D.C., Warren set the tone for his tenure on the Supreme Court by leading the justices to a unanimous, controversial decision declaring that racial segregation in public schools violates the Equal Protection Clause of the Constitution. As a result of this decision and later Supreme Court cases expanding rights for individuals, many political opponents harshly criticized Warren for forcing improper changes upon U.S. society. Despite strident criticism from some quarters, Warren continued to make decisions according to his honest interpretation of the Constitution without regard to whether those decisions would be popular with the public.

During Warren's service as chief justice, the Supreme Court reshaped trial processes and court procedures in criminal cases by expanding constitutional rights for suspects and defendants. Under Warren's leadership, the Supreme Court incorporated most of the Constitution's provisions concerning criminal justice into the Fourteenth Amendment's Due Process Clause for application to state and local officials, including prosecutors and judges. Previously, many constitutional rights for suspects and defendants provided protection only against actions by federal law enforcement and court officials. State and local officials were limited by state law only in their handling of criminal cases. In 1961, for example, the U.S. Supreme Court decided *Mapp v. Ohio,* which required all state courts to exclude from use at trial any evidence that was obtained through improper searches. This expansion of the so-called exclusionary rule had a significant impact on police officers' discretionary actions in criminal investigations and prosecutors' opportunities to use evidence obtained in violation of suspects' rights. The Supreme Court also required all states to provide defense attorneys for every defendant facing serious criminal charges (*Gideon v. Wainwright* [1963]). The introduction of defense attorneys into criminal cases changed the dynamics of prosecutions and trials in states that previously had made defendants defend themselves in court despite their lack of education and training about law and trial procedures. In addition, the Court declared that the right to trial by jury applied to serious cases in state courts just as it applied to similar cases in federal court (*Duncan v. Louisiana* [1968]). Prior to the Warren Court's decision, some states denied defendants' requests for a jury trial and forced them to be tried before a judge sitting alone. These three cases are some examples of the Supreme Court's impact on courts and trials under Earl Warren's leadership. There were dozens of other cases in which Warren led the Supreme Court to shape trial procedures by expanding the definition of constitutional rights for criminal defendants.

5

Documents and Statistics

Court procedures and trial processes are defined by many types of laws. Laws may come from national and state constitutions, statutes enacted by legislatures, and judicial decisions. Often the structure and authority of a court system are defined by a constitution. Statutes provide additional details about the design of the courts as well as the rules for court procedures. Judicial decisions interpreting constitutional provisions define rights for individuals in trial processes, and these decisions shape court procedures by telling judicial officials what they must do to comply with requirements of the law.

The nature of a court system's caseload and the number of cases processed in a court will be determined both by the laws applicable to that court and by the social conditions affecting that jurisdiction. If there is a low crime rate, then courts may not be burdened with a significant criminal caseload. If, however, a court's jurisdiction includes a national border where people are frequently caught trying to smuggle drugs or other contraband, then the court's substantial criminal caseload may cause long waiting periods for people within that jurisdiction who file civil lawsuits and want to have a trial.

The materials presented in this chapter provide perspective on the laws affecting courts and trials as well as the structure of courts and their caseload burdens.

Selected Provisions
of the U.S. Constitution

Article III

Article III of the U.S. Constitution describes the federal courts. Only the Supreme Court is created by the Constitution. All other federal courts are created by Congress and, therefore, can be altered or abolished by Congress. Article III also discusses the tenure of federal judges, which shall continue indefinitely during good behavior, which implies service for life if the judge does not misbehave. This gives federal judges significant protection against political pressures because it is so difficult to remove them from office. Presumably, their independence and insulation from political pressure will permit them to make courageous decisions, even those that are politically unpopular. This judicial structure differs considerably from that of judges in many state systems who must periodically stand for reelection and risk being thrown out of office if they displease the public. Article III also states that all trials shall be by jury, but the Supreme Court's decisions have actually limited the right to jury trial to cases involving serious charges (see Lewis v. United States).

Section 1: The judicial Power of the United States, shall be vested in one supreme court, and in such inferior Courts as Congress may from time to time ordain and establish. The Judges, both of the supreme and inferior Courts, shall hold their Offices during good Behaviour, and shall, at stated Times, receive for their Services a Compensation, which shall not be diminished during their Continuance in Office.

Section 2: [1] The judicial Power shall extend to all Cases, in Law and Equity, arising under this Constitution, the Laws of the United States, and Treaties made, or which shall be made, under their Authority; —to all Cases affecting Ambassadors, other public Ministers and Consuls; —to all Cases of admiralty and maritime Jurisdiction; —to Controversies to which the United States shall be a Party; —to Controversies between two or more States; between a State and Citizens of another State; —between Citizens of different States; —between Citizens of the same State claiming Lands under Grants of different States, and between a State, or the Citizens thereof, and foreign States, Citizens or Subjects.

[2] In all Cases affecting Ambassadors, other public Ministers and Consuls, and those in which a State shall be a Party, the

supreme Court shall have original Jurisdiction. In all the other Cases before mentioned, the supreme Court shall have appellate Jurisdiction, both as to Law and Fact, with such Exceptions, and under such Regulations as the Congress shall make.

[3] The Trial of all Crimes, except Cases of Impeachment, shall be by Jury; and such Trial shall be held in the State where said Crimes shall have been committed; but when not committed within any State, the Trial shall be at such Place or Places as the Congress may by Law have directed.

Section 3. [1] Treason against the United States, shall consist only in levying War against them, or in adhering to their Enemies, giving them Aid and Comfort. No Person shall be convicted of Treason unless on the Testimony of two Witnesses to the same overt Act, or on Confession in open Court.

[2] The Congress shall have the Power to declare the Punishment of Treason, but no Attainder of Treason shall work Corruption of Blood, or Forfeiture except during the Life of the Person attained.

Amendment V (1791)

The Fifth Amendment contains important rights related to courts and trial processes. Of particular importance are the privilege against compelled self-incrimination, the protection against double jeopardy, and the right to due process of law. These rights are not self-explanatory, so the U.S. Supreme Court's decisions give meaning to the Fifth Amendment's provisions.

No person shall be held to answer for a capital, or otherwise infamous crime, unless on a presentment or indictment of a Grand Jury, except in cases arising in the land or naval forces, or in the Militia, when in actual service in time of War or public danger; nor shall any person be subject for the same offence to be twice put in jeopardy of life or limb; nor shall be compelled in any criminal case to be a witness against himself, nor be deprived of life, liberty, or property, without due process of law; nor shall private property be taken for public use, without just compensation.

Amendment VI (1791)

The Sixth Amendment is known as the trial-rights amendment. It contains several important rights, including the right to trial by jury and the right to counsel, that are well known to the public. It contains other rights, including the right to confront adverse witnesses and the right to compulsory process to bring evidence and witnesses to court. The Sixth Amendment applies only to criminal cases, and its provisions do not affect the rules for civil lawsuits and civil litigation.

In all criminal prosecutions, the accused shall enjoy the right to a speedy and public trial, by an impartial jury of the State and district wherein the crime shall have been committed, which district shall have been previously ascertained by law, and to be informed of the nature and cause of the accusation; to be confronted with the witnesses against him; to have compulsory process for obtaining witnesses in his favor; and to have the Assistance of Counsel for his defence.

Amendment VII (1791)

The Seventh Amendment is one of the few parts of the Bill of Rights that the U.S. Supreme Court has never applied to state courts. Its provisions apply only to federal courts. The limited applicability reflects, in part, one woefully outdated specific statement in the amendment. At the time that the amendment was written, $20 was a significant sum of money, so people believed that they were entitled to a jury trial when that much money was in dispute. In the twentieth and twenty-first centuries, the accumulated effect of inflation and the nation's affluence have made $20 merely a modest sum of money. Thus the Supreme Court has not wanted to impose on state courts the requirements of mounting expensive jury trials whenever this sum is at issue in a civil lawsuit.

In Suits at common law, where the value in controversy shall exceed twenty dollars, the right of trial by jury shall be preserved, and no fact tried by jury, shall be otherwise re-examined in any Court of the United States, than according to the rules of the common law.

Amendment VIII (1791)

The Eighth Amendment concerns criminal punishments as well as bail and fines. The provisions on bail and fines have never been interpreted by the Supreme Court in a definitive manner to give guidance about what precise amounts of money would be "excessive." With respect to

*fines, the Court has decided that a seizure of $357,000 in cash is an im-
permissible "excessive fine" for an offense that is usually punishable by
a fine of only a few thousand dollars (United States v. Bajakajian
[1998]). However, other than that one example of an excessive fine, the
Court's decisions give little guidance about how this provision of the
Eighth Amendment limits the power of legislatures and judges to impose fines as criminal and civil punishments. The amendment's prohibition on cruel and unusual punishments applies only to protect people
convicted of crimes. It does not protect people being held in jail awaiting
trial, and it does not protect others under government control, such as
public school students and committed mental hospital patients. The
Cruel and Unusual Punishments Clause protects against torturous
punishments and those that are disproportionate to the offense being
punished.*

Excessive bail shall not be required, nor excessive fines imposed, nor cruel and unusual punishments inflicted.

Amendment XIV (1868)

*The Fourteenth Amendment was written and ratified after the Civil
War. One of its purposes was to protect newly freed former slaves from
unfair treatment at the hands of state governments. Unlike the Bill of
Rights, which was originally aimed to give individuals protections
against actions by the federal government, the Fourteenth Amendment
explicitly protects people against actions by state governments. By extension, it also protects against actions by local governments, which are
considered political subunits of states. The rights to due process and
equal protection are the primary provisions that affect the operations of
courts and trials.*

Section 1: All persons born or naturalized in the United
States, and subject to the jurisdiction thereof, are citizens of the
United States and of the State wherein they reside. No State shall
make or enforce any law which shall abridge the privileges or immunities of citizens of the United States; nor shall any State de-
prive any person of life, liberty, or property, without due process
of law; nor deny to any person within its jurisdiction the equal
protection of the laws.
[Sections 2–5 omitted]

Selected Examples of Additional Statutory and Other Materials

Merit Selection of Judges in Missouri

Missouri was the first state to develop a merit-selection plan for appointing judges. The plan served as a model for the states that later developed their own merit selection plans.

Missouri Constitution, Article V:

Section 25(a). Nonpartisan selection of judges–courts subject to plan–appointments to fill vacancies. Whenever a vacancy shall occur in the office of judge of any of the following courts of this state, to wit: The supreme court, the court of appeals, or in the office of circuit or associate circuit judge within the city of St. Louis and Jackson County, the governor shall fill such vacancy by appointing one of the three persons possessing the qualifications for such office, who shall be nominated and whose names shall be submitted to the governor by a nonpartisan judicial commission established and organized as hereafter provided. If the governor fails to appoint any of the nominees within sixty days after the list of nominees is submitted, the nonpartisan judicial commission making the nomination shall appoint one of the nominees to fill the vacancy.

Section 25(c)(1). Tenure of judges–declaration of candidacy—form of judicial ballot–rejection and retention. Each judge appointed pursuant to the provisions of sections 25(a)–(g) shall hold office for a term ending December thirty-first following the next general election after the expiration of twelve months in the office. Any judge holding office, or elected thereto, at the time of the election by which the provisions of sections 25(a)–(g) become applicable to his office, shall, unless removed for cause, remain in office for the term to which he would have been entitled had the provisions of sections 25(a)–(g) not become applicable to his office. Not less than sixty days prior to the holding of the general election next preceding the expiration of his term of office, any judge whose office is subject to the provisions of sections 25(a)–(g) may file in the office of the secretary of state a declaration of candidacy for election to succeed himself. If a declaration is not so filed by any judge, the vacancy resulting from the expiration of his term of office shall be filled by appointment as herein provided. If such declaration is filed, his name shall be submitted at said next general election to the voters eligible to vote within the state if his office is that of judge of the supreme court, or within the geographic jurisdiction limit of the district where he serves if his office is that of a judge of the court of appeals, or within the circuit if his office is that of a circuit judge, or within the county if his office is that of associate circuit judge on a separate judicial ballot, without party designation, reading:

"Shall Judge [name] of the [court title] be retained in office?"
        ☐ Yes   ☐ No

. . . If a majority of those voting on the question vote against retaining him in office, upon the expiration of his term of office, a vacancy shall exist which shall be filled by appointment as provided in section 25(a); otherwise, said judge shall, unless removed for cause, remain in office for the number of years after December thirty-first following such election as is provided for the full term of such office, and at the expiration of each such term shall be eligible for retention in office by election in the manner here prescribed.

Section 25(d). Nonpartisan judicial commissions—number, qualifications, selection and terms of members—majority rule—reimbursement of expenses–rules of supreme court. Nonpartisan judicial commissions whose duty it shall be to nominate and submit to the governor names of persons for appointment as provided by sections 25(a)–(g) are hereby established and shall be organized on the following basis: For vacancies in the office of judge of the supreme court or of the court of appeals, there shall be one such commission, to be known as "The Appellate Judicial Commission"; for vacancies in the office of circuit judge or associate circuit judge of any circuit subject to the provisions of sections 25(a)–(g) there shall be one such commission, to be known as "The. . . . Circuit Judicial Commission," for each judicial circuit which shall be subject to the provisions of sections 25(a)–(g); the appellate judicial commission shall consist of a judge of the supreme court selected by the members of the supreme court, and the remaining members shall be chosen in the following manner: The members of the bar of this state residing in each court of appeals district shall elect one of their number to serve as a member of said commission, and the governor shall appoint one citizen, not a member of the bar, from among the residents of each court of appeals district, to serve as a member of said commission, and the members of the commission shall select one of their number to serve as chairman. Each circuit judicial commission shall consist of five members, one of whom shall be the chief judge of the district of the court of appeals within which the judicial circuit of such commission, or the major portion of the population of said circuit is situated and the remaining four members shall be chosen in the following manner: The members of the bar of this state residing in the judicial circuit of such commission shall elect two of their number to serve as members of said commission, and the governor shall appoint two citizens, not members of the bar, from among the residents of said judicial circuit to serve as members of said commission, the members of said commission shall select one of their number to serve as chairman; and the terms of office of the members of such commission shall be fixed by law, but no law shall increase or diminish the term of any member then in office. No member of any such commission other than a judge shall hold any public office, and no member shall hold any official position in a political party. Every such commission may act only by the concurrence of a majority of its members. The members of such commission shall receive no salary or other compensation for their services but they shall receive their necessary traveling and other expenses incurred while actually engaged in the discharge of their official duties. All such commissions shall be administered, and all elections provided for under this section shall be held and regulated, under such rules as the supreme court shall promulgate.

Judicial Selection in New Mexico

New Mexico has taken an innovative approach in selecting judges. Its system attempts to use the accountability value of partisan elections as well as the merit-based value of retention elections for incumbent judges.

Constitution of the State of New Mexico, Article VI, Section 33:

A. Each justice of the supreme court, judge of the court of appeals, district judge or metropolitan court judge shall have been elected to that position in a partisan election prior to being eligible for a nonpartisan retention election. Thereafter, each such justice or judge shall be subject to a retention or rejection on a nonpartisan ballot. Retention of the judicial office shall require at least fifty-seven percent of the vote cast on the question of retention or rejection.

Alternative Dispute Resolution in Florida

Florida's statutes provide for the possibility of court-ordered mediation, court-ordered nonbinding arbitration, voluntary binding arbitration, or voluntary trial resolution as alternatives to the formal litigation process in civil lawsuits.

Florida Statutes, Title V, Chapter 44, Section 104:

(1) Two or more opposing parties who are involved in a civil dispute may agree in writing to submit the controversy to voluntary binding arbitration, or voluntary trial resolution, in lieu of litigation of the issues involved, prior to or after a lawsuit has been filed, provided no constitutional issue is involved.

(2) If the parties have entered into an agreement which provides in voluntary binding arbitration for a method of appointing one or more arbitrators, or which provides in voluntary trial resolution a method of appointing a member of The Florida Bar in good standing for more than 5 years to act as trial resolution judge, the court shall proceed with the appointment as prescribed. However, in voluntary binding arbitration at least one of the arbitrators, who shall serve as the chief arbitrator, shall meet the qualifications and training requirements adopted [under Florida law].

Sentencing Guidelines Commission in Minnesota

Minnesota led the nation in developing sentencing guidelines as a means to equalize and standardize sentences for criminal offenders. The Minnesota statute includes a description of the occupational groups that will be represented in developing the guidelines and who controls the composition of the commission.

Minnesota Statutes, Chapter Title: Criminal Sentences, Conditions, Duration, Appeals, Section 244.09:

Subdivision 2. The sentencing guidelines commission shall consist of the following:

(1) the chief justice of the supreme court or a designee;

(2) one judge of the court of appeals, appointed by the chief justice of the supreme court;

(3) one district court judge appointed by the chief justice of the supreme court;

(4) one public defender appointed by the governor upon recommendation of the state public defender;

(5) one county attorney appointed by the governor upon recommendation of the board of directors of the Minnesota county attorneys association;

(6) the commissioner of corrections or a designee;

(7) one peace officer as defined [by law] appointed by the governor;

(8) one probation officer or parole officer appointed by the governor; and

(9) three public members appointed by the governor, one of whom shall be a victim of a crime defined as a felony; . . .

North Dakota Rules on Cameras in the Courtroom

Rules regarding the use of cameras during courtroom proceedings in North Dakota are governed by an administrative regulation produced by the state supreme court:

North Dakota Supreme Court Administrative Rule 21—Electronic and Photographic Media Coverage of Court Proceedings:

. . .

Section 3. Media representative. Broadcasters and photographers shall designate a person with whom the court may consult as a representative of them.

Section 4. General. The court may permit expanded media coverage of a judicial proceeding in the courtroom while the judge is present, and in adjacent areas as the court may direct. Expanded media coverage provided for under this rule may be exercised only by media personnel. This rule does not apply to electronic recording of the official record of a judicial proceeding.

a. Coverage allowed. Media personnel may request the court before which a judicial proceeding is pending to authorize coverage of the proceeding or of all proceedings relating to a case. Expanded media coverage may be permitted of all judicial proceedings, except proceedings specifically excluded by statute, this rule, or in the exercise of the judge's discretion.

b. Judge's authority to deny expanded media coverage. The judge may deny expanded media coverage for any proceeding or portion of a proceeding in which the judge determines on the record, or by written findings:

1. Expanded media coverage would materially interfere with a party's right to a fair trial;

2. A witness or party has objected and shown good cause why expanded media coverage should not be permitted; . . .

3. Expanded media coverage would include testimony of a juvenile victim or witness in a proceeding in which illegal sexual activity is an element of the evidence; or

4. Expanded media coverage would include undercover agents or relocated witnesses.

c. Judge's authority to limit or end media coverage. The judge may limit or end expanded media coverage at any time during a proceeding, if the judge determines on the record, or by written findings:

1. The requirements of this rule or additional guidelines imposed by the judge have been violated; or

2. The substantial rights of an individual participant, or rights to a fair trial will be prejudiced by the expanded media coverage if it is allowed to continue.

d. Coverage prohibited. Proceedings held in chambers, proceedings closed to the public, and jury selection may not be photographed, recorded, or broadcast. Conferences between an attorney and client, witness or aide, between attorneys, or between counsel and the court at the bench may not be recorded or received by sound equipment. Close-up photography of jurors is prohibited.

e. No appeal of expanded media coverage decision. A judge's ruling on expanded media coverage is not appealable.

. . .

Section 7. Equipment and media personnel. Unless the court directs otherwise, equipment used in a judicial proceeding is limited to a single television camera operated by one person and one audio system for radio broadcasts. Only one still photographer is allowed in a judicial proceeding. Any media pooling needed because of these limitations on equipment and personnel is the sole responsibility of the media and must be arranged before coverage without calling the court to mediate. Every effort must be made for the joint use of broadcasting equipment within the courtroom. Wires, microphones, and similar equipment must be placed as unobtrusively as possible within the courtroom at least fifteen minutes before the proceeding and must be secured or taped down when appropriate. Artificial lighting and flashbulbs are not permitted. Only equipment that does not produce distracting noises is allowed in the courtroom. Media coverage outside the courtroom must be handled with care and discretion, but need not be pooled or held to the restrictions of this rule. The quantity and types of equipment permitted in the courtroom is in the discretion of the judge.

Michigan's Cyber Court

In 2001, Michigan initiated a cyber court to enable court hearings to take place through video, audio, or Internet conferencing. The court was created to reduce the expense and time involved in gathering witnesses and attorneys in a single courthouse. Other states expressed interest in copying Michigan's innovation.

Chapter 80. The Cyber Court.

Sec. 8001. (1) The Cyber Court is created. The purpose of the cyber court is to allow disputes between business and commercial entities to be resolved with the speed and efficiency required by the information age economy.

(2) The Cyber Court shall be located in 1 or more counties as determined by the Supreme Court. The Cyber Court shall sit in facilities designed to allow all hearings and proceedings to be conducted by means of electronic communications, including but not limited to, video conferencing and internet conferencing.

(3) The Cyber Court shall hold session and shall schedule hearings or other proceedings to accommodate parties or witnesses who are located outside of this state. A Cyber Court facility is open to the public to the same extent as a Circuit Court facility. When technologically feasible, all proceedings of the Cyber Court shall be broadcast on the internet.

Juror Note-Taking in Missouri

Traditionally, jurors were not permitted to take notes during trials. There were fears that jurors would be distracted and lose track of testi-

*mony as they wrote notes. Moreover, it was feared that erroneous un-
derstandings and interpretations of evidence would become more difficult to correct during jury deliberations if those understandings were
written on paper. In recent years, however, many courts have decided
that jurors may benefit from taking notes because they will have more
information available during deliberations.*

Supreme Court of Missouri, Rule 69.03, Juror Note-Taking:
Upon the court's own motion or upon the request of any party,
the court shall permit jurors to take notes. If jurors are permitted
to take notes, the court shall supply each juror with suitable materials. Jurors shall not take their notes out of the courtroom except to use their notes during deliberations. The court shall collect
all juror notes immediately before discharge of the jury. After the
jury is discharged, the court shall destroy the notes promptly
without permitting their review by the court or any other person.
Juror notes shall not be used to impeach a verdict.

Eligibility for Legal Assistance: Legal Services Corporation

*The Legal Services Corporation provides representation in certain cate-
gories of legal cases for poor people who meet eligibility criteria. The criteria, based on family income, are established and adjusted by the agency
as it updates relevant government regulations.*

45 Code of Federal Regulations 1611 Eligibility: Income Level
for Individual Eligible for Assistance
Summary: The Legal Services Corporation ("Corporation")
is required by law to establish maximum income levels for individuals eligible for legal assistance. This document updates the
specified income levels to reflect the annual amendments to the
Federal Poverty Guidelines as issued by the Department of
Health and Human Services (see Table 5.1).
Effective Date: This rule is effective as of February 25,
2002. . . .
Supplementary Information: Section 1007(a)(2) of the Legal
Services Corporation Act ("Act"), 42 U.S.C. 2996f(a)(2), requires
the Corporation to establish maximum income levels for individuals eligible for legal assistance, and the Act provides that other
specific factors shall be taken into account along with income.
Section 1611.3(b) of the Corporation's regulations establishes
a maximum income level equivalent to one hundred and twenty-

Table 5.1 Legal Services Corporation: 2002 Poverty Guideline

Size of family unit	48 contiguous states and Washington, D.C.	Alaska	Hawaii
1	$11,075	$13,850	$12,750
2	$14,925	$18,663	$17,175
3	$18,775	$23,475	$21,600
4	$22,625	$28,288	$26,025
5	$26,475	$33,100	$30,450
6	$30,325	$37,913	$34,875
7	$34,175	$42,725	$39,300
8	$38,025	$47,538	$43,725

Source: "Eligibility: Income Level for Individuals Eligible for Assistance," Title 45, *Code of Federal Regulations*, Section 1611, http://www.lsc.gov.

five percent (125%) of the Federal Poverty Guidelines. Since 1982, the Department of Health and Human Services has been responsible for updating and issuing the Poverty Guidelines. The revised figures for 2001 in table 5.1 are equivalent to 125% of the current Poverty Guidelines as published on February 14, 2002 (67 FR 6931).

Excerpts from the Testimony: President of the Legal Services Corporation

Legal Services Corporation, the agency that provides civil legal assistance for poor people in the United States, has frequently faced political attacks and budget cuts. As a result, the president of the nonprofit governmental corporation must keep Congress informed about the agency's activities and continually argue for financial support in the effort to provide poor people with access to the courts.

Statement of the Legal Services Corporation [LSC], John Erlenborn, President, February 28, 2002:

Although we live in the world's wealthiest nation, there are more than 43 million Americans that are potentially eligible for LSC-funded services. To continue to ensure these vulnerable Americans are not completely shut out of the justice system, a strong federal role in supporting legal services continues to be vital.

. . .

During this fiscal year, LSC will distribute $310 million dollars in federal grants to local, independent legal aid programs.

Through its annual appropriation from Congress, LSC remains the single largest funding source of civil legal assistance in the country.

Programs receiving LSC funding help handle more than one million legal cases annually. LSC-funded programs are focused on serving the basic, critical legal needs of low-income clients. Ten percent of LSC clients are elderly; over 50 percent of all clients are women with young children. The most common types of cases are family, housing, income maintenance, and consumer law issues. Almost one-sixth of all cases involve efforts to obtain protection from domestic violence. Other case types frequently handled by LSC grantees include evictions, foreclosures, child custody and support, child abuse and neglect, wage claims, access to health care, and unemployment and disability claims.

. . .

In 1996, Congress enacted fundamental changes to the national legal services program, reaffirming the federal government's commitment to providing free civil legal assistance to poor Americans. In order to refocus the LSC-funded system on individual clients with particular legal needs, Congress placed a series of new restrictions on LSC grantee programs. These new rules apply to all private and public funding received by an LSC grantee. LSC-funded programs are not allowed to file or litigate class action lawsuits, engage in many types of lobbying, seek or receive attorneys' fees, litigate on behalf of prisoners, or represent most undocumented aliens.

. . .

Since the passage of congressional reforms in 1996, LSC has been faithful to the will of Congress and steadfast in its commitment to uphold all new restrictions on our grantees' activities. Our strong focus on compliance has been matched by our diligent efforts to maximize the federal legal aid investment in every state and to help effect major reform where necessary. We have embraced our new vision with resolve and purpose, determined to help more Americans access the civil justice system to address their critical, basic legal problems.

Key Decisions of the U.S. Supreme Court Affecting Courts and Trials (chronological order)

Strauder v. West Virginia, 100 U.S. 303 (1880)

The U.S. Supreme Court declared that West Virginia had violated the Equal Protection Clause of the Fourteenth Amendment by having a law that prohibited African Americans from serving on juries. The Court's decision was an important statement in favor of equal treatment in court processes, but it had little practical effect. Many states developed other methods for excluding minority jurors, such as drawing jurors from lists of registered voters while making it nearly impossible for African Americans to register to vote. Most of these barriers to participation in voting and jury service by African Americans were defeated in the 1960s and 1970s.

Powell v. Alabama, 287 U.S. 45 (1932)

Several African-American men were convicted of rape and sentenced to death without representation by counsel in a very brief trial in the highly charged atmosphere of racial hatred in Depression-era Alabama. The Supreme Court ruled that indigent defendants facing capital charges must be provided with defense attorneys, especially when they are not sufficiently educated and experienced to represent themselves in court. In the words of the Court's opinion:

> In light of the facts outlined in the forepart of this opinion—the ignorance and illiteracy of the defendants, their youth, the circumstances of public hostility, the imprisonment and the close surveillance of the defendants by military forces, the fact that their close friends and family were all in other states and communication with them [was] necessarily difficult, and above all that they stood in deadly peril of their lives—we think the failure of the trial court to give them reasonable

time and opportunity to secure counsel was a clear denial of due process. . . . All that is necessary to decide now, as we do decide, is that in a capital case, where the defendant is unable to employ counsel, and is incapable adequately of making his own defense because of ignorance, feeble mindedness, illiteracy, or the like, it is the duty of the court, whether requested or not, to assign counsel for him as a necessary requisite of due process of law.

Johnson v. Zerbst, **304 U.S. 458 (1938)**

The U.S. Supreme Court declared that indigent criminal defendants facing serious charges in federal courts are entitled to have an attorney provided for them by government. Prior to such early decisions that began to give meaning to the Sixth Amendment's right to counsel, most criminal trials were brief, mismatched proceedings in which an uneducated, hapless defendant futilely attempted to defend himself against the evidence presented by trained prosecutors who could utilize police officers to conduct investigations. According to the Court's opinion:

> Since the Sixth Amendment constitutionally entitles one charged with crime to the assistance of counsel, compliance with this constitutional mandate is an essential jurisdictional prerequisite to a federal court's authority to deprive an accused of his life or liberty. When this right is properly waived, the assistance of counsel is no longer a necessary element of the court's jurisdiction to proceed to conviction and sentence. If the accused, however, is not represented by counsel and has not competently and intelligently waived his constitutional right, the Sixth Amendment stands as a jurisdictional bar to a valid conviction and sentence depriving him of his life or his liberty.

Griffin v. Illinois, **351 U.S. 12 (1956)**

Many states had rules that required people who wanted to appeal their cases to provide the court of appeals with a transcript of the trial proceedings that are to be challenged and reviewed on appeal. It is often very expensive to have trial proceedings transcribed. It is a time-consuming process for which court reporters must be paid when they translate their notes from the trial into a full transcript of the proceedings. The U.S. Supreme Court ruled that Illinois violated the Fourteenth Amendment's Equal Protection Clause because it did not provide free trial transcripts to indigent offenders to enable them to appeal their cases. Without transcripts provided by the state, many offenders would be unable to raise claims about errors that allegedly occurred in their trial proceedings. In the Court's words:

> There is no meaningful distinction between a rule which would deny the poor the right to defend themselves in a trial court and one which effectively denies the poor an adequate appellate review accorded to all who have money enough to pay the costs in advance. It is true that a State is not required by the Federal Constitution to provide appellate courts or a right to appellate review at all. . . . but that is not to say that a State that does grant appellate review can do so in a way that discriminates against some convicted defendants on account of their poverty.

The ruling applied only to criminal cases. It did not apply to civil cases.

Gideon v. Wainwright, 372 U.S. 335 (1963)

An indigent man was tried and convicted of breaking and entering in Florida. He asked that an attorney be appointed to represent him during his trial, but the trial judge informed him that he had no right to have an attorney. Because the defendant was literate and of average intelligence, the judge correctly informed the defendant that the law presumed that he could represent himself. As he began serving his five-year prison sentence, the man sent a handwritten petition to the U.S. Supreme Court asking the justices to decide whether his Sixth Amendment right to counsel had been violated when his request for an attorney had been denied. In one of its most famous and popular decisions, the Court decided that the Sixth Amendment right to counsel applies in state courts just as it applies in federal courts. Thus any indigent defendant facing serious changes that could lead to a sentence of six months or more of incarceration must be given an attorney at trial. When Gideon received his second trial, he was acquitted of all charges when he had the representation of an attorney. The attorney was able to show the jury that much of the evidence actually pointed to the lone witness for the prosecution whose testimony provided the basis for the conviction rather than to Gideon. The case was the focus of a best-selling book entitled *Gideon's Trumpet,* as well as a one-man theatrical show and film starring Henry Fonda as the uneducated prisoner, Clarence Earl Gideon.

The Court described its reasoning and conclusions about the need for appointed defense attorneys to ensure fairness for poor defendants:

> That government hires lawyers to prosecute and defendants who have the money hire lawyers to defend are the strongest indications of the widespread belief that lawyers in criminal courts are necessities, not luxuries. The right of one charged with crime to counsel may not be deemed fundamental and essential to fair trials in some countries, but it is in ours. From the very beginning, our state and national constitutions and laws have laid great emphasis on procedural and substantive safeguards designed to assure fair trials before impartial tribunals in which every defendant stands equal before the law. This noble ideal cannot be realized if the poor man charged with a crime has to face his accusers without a lawyer to assist him.

Douglas v. California, 372 U.S. 353 (1963)

In an opinion that emphasized the need to ensure that poor people receive equal treatment in court processes, the Court declared that indigent offenders are entitled to free representation after conviction when they pursue their first appeal of right. Typically, this means their constitutional right to counsel continues at the state court of appeals level. The Court's opinion described the underlying concern with equal justice:

> The present case, where counsel was denied petitioners on appeal, shows that the discrimination is not between "possibly good and obviously bad cases," but between cases where the rich man can require the court to listen to argument of counsel before deciding on the merits, but a poor man cannot. There is lacking that equality demanded by the Fourteenth Amend-

ment where the rich man, who appeals as of right, enjoys the benefits of counsel's examination into the record, research of the law, and marshalling of arguments on his behalf, while the indigent, already burdened by a preliminary determination that his case is without merit, is forced to shift for himself. The indigent, where the record is unclear or the errors are hidden, has only the right to a meaningless ritual, while the rich man has a meaningful appeal.

Pointer v. Texas, 380 U.S. 400 (1965)

The U.S. Supreme Court declared that the Sixth Amendment right to confrontation applies in state criminal cases just as it applies in federal cases. The right creates an entitlement for criminal defendants to hear and see witnesses against them in court. In this case, the Court reversed the conviction of a man after the prosecution used at trial a transcript of preliminary hearing testimony given by an absent codefendant. Thus, at the trial, the defendant had no opportunity to cross-examine the absent witness whose damaging testimony was being presented in the form of a written record of pretrial statements. In the words of the Court's opinion:

> It cannot seriously be doubted at this late date that the right of cross-examination is included in the right of an accused in a criminal case to confront the witnesses against him. And probably no one, certainly no one experienced in the trial of lawsuits, would deny the value of cross-examination in exposing falsehood and bringing out the truth in the trial of a criminal case. . . . The fact that this right appears in the Sixth Amendment of our Bill of Rights reflects the belief of the Framers of those liberties and safeguards that confrontation was a fundamental right essential to a fair trial in a criminal prosecution. . . . There are few subjects, perhaps, upon which this Court and other courts have been more nearly unanimous than in their expressions of belief that the right of confrontation and cross-examination is an essential and fundamental requirement for the kind of fair trial which is this country's constitutional goal.

Escobedo v. Illinois, 378 U.S. 478 (1965)

A murder suspect asked to see his attorney, but the police told the suspect that the attorney did not want to see him. At the police station, the suspect could see his attorney down the hall trying to speak with him, but the police kept the attorney away and refused to permit any contact with the client. The U.S. Supreme Court declared that criminal suspects in custody have a right to see their attorneys when they make a request to speak with them. The police cannot legally stop such meetings from occurring. The Court's opinion expressed its concern about the undesirable impact of interfering with suspects' communications with attorneys to try to gain a confession outside of the presence of counsel:

> We have learned the lesson of history, ancient and modern, that a system of criminal law enforcement which comes to depend on the "confession" will, in the long run, be less reliable and more subject to abuses than a system which depends on extrinsic evidence independently secured through skillful investigation. . . . We have also learned the companion lesson of history that no system of criminal justice can, or should, survive if it comes to depend for its continued effectiveness on the citizens' abdication through unawareness of their constitutional rights. No system worth preserving should have to *fear* that if an accused is permitted to consult with a lawyer, he will become aware of, and exercise, these rights. If the exercise of constitutional rights will thwart the effectiveness of a system of law enforcement, then there is something very wrong with that system.

Miranda v. Arizona, 384 U.S. 436 (1966)

A rape suspect was questioned alone in a private interrogation room by two detectives. The detectives emerged from the room with his confession. The Supreme Court faced the issue of whether suspects are entitled to have lawyers appointed to represent them during questioning and whether officers must inform suspects of this right. In one of its most controversial decisions, the Court decided that police officers have an affirmative obligation to inform suspects that they have a right to remain silent and a right to have an attorney present during custodial questioning. Many police officials and politicians complained that the Court's decision would cause guilty people to go free by preventing anyone from confessing. In reality, many suspects continue to make incriminating statements.

Chief Justice Earl Warren's famous majority opinion demonstrated skepticism about police methods and great concern about the possible abuse of suspects' rights:

> In each of these cases, the defendant was thrust into an unfamiliar atmosphere and run through menacing police interrogation procedures. The potentiality for compulsion is forcefully apparent, for example, in *Miranda*, where the indigent Mexican defendant was a seriously disturbed individual with pronounced sexual fantasies, and in *Stewart*, in which the defendant was an indigent Los Angeles [African American] who had dropped out of school in the sixth grade. To be sure, the records do not evince overt physical coercion or patent psychological ploys. The fact remains that in none of these cases did the officers undertake to afford appropriate safeguards at the outset of the interrogation to insure that the statements were truly the product of free choice. It is obvious that such an interrogation environment is created for no purpose other than to subjugate the individual to the will of his examiner. This atmosphere carries its own badge of intimidation. To be sure, this is not physical intimidation, but it is equally destructive of human dignity. The current practice of incommunicado interrogation is at odds with one of our Nation's most cherished principles— that the individual may not be compelled to incriminate himself. Unless adequate protective devices are employed to dispel the compulsion inherent in custodial surroundings, no statement obtained from the defendant can truly be the product of his free choice.

Klopfer v. North Carolina, 386 U.S. 213 (1967)

In one of a continuing series of cases concerning the applicability of individual provisions of the Bill of Rights to state courts and trial proceedings, the U.S. Supreme Court declared that the Sixth Amendment right to a speedy trial applies to state courts just as it applies to federal courts. According to the Supreme Court:

> We hold here that the right to a speedy trial is as fundamental as any of the rights secured by the Sixth Amendment. That right has its roots at the very foundation of our English law heritage. Its first articulation in modern jurisprudence appears to have been made in Magna Carta (1215). . . . The history of the right to a speedy trial and its reception in this country clearly establish that it is one of the most basic rights preserved by our Constitution.

Duncan v. Louisiana, 391 U.S. 145 (1968)

A young African-American man intervened in an altercation to pull his cousins away from some white youths with whom they were arguing. One of the white youths claimed that the man "slapped his elbow." Because the event occurred in a parish (county) in Louisiana that was notorious for racial discrimination, this minor event led to serious criminal charges against the man. He was convicted of assault and sentenced to a term of incarceration. Prior to the trial, he had requested to be tried before a jury rather than in a bench trial before a judge. His request was denied. He later appealed by claiming that the proceeding violated his Sixth Amendment right to trial by jury in criminal cases. The U.S. Supreme Court agreed with his claim and declared that the right to trial by jury applies to state courts in the same manner that it applies to federal courts. As stated in the Court's opinion:

> Our conclusion is that in the American States, as in the federal judicial system, a general grant of jury trial for serious offenses is a fundamental right, essential for preventing miscarriages of justice and for assuring that fair trials are provided for all defendants. We would not assert, however, that every criminal trial—or any particular trial—held before a judge alone is unfair or that a defendant may never be as fairly treated by a judge as he would be by a jury. Thus we hold no constitutional doubts about the practices, common in both federal and state courts, of accepting

waivers of jury trial and prosecuting petty crimes without extending a right to jury trial. However, the fact is that in most places more trials for serious crimes are to juries than to a court alone; a great many defendants prefer the judgment of a jury to that of a court. Even where defendants are satisfied with bench trials, the right to a jury trial very likely serves its intended purpose of making judicial or prosecutorial unfairness less likely.

Benton v. Maryland, 395 U.S. 784 (1969)

A man tried in state court on larceny and burglary charges was acquitted on the larceny charge but convicted on the burglary charge. Because of an error in the jury process, he was granted a new trial. At the second trial, he was convicted of both charges. The Supreme Court ruled that the Fifth Amendment protection against double jeopardy applies to state courts as well as federal courts, and therefore he could only be reconvicted on the burglary charge in the second trial. Because he had been acquitted on the larceny charge in the first trial, he could not face trial on that charge again. In the Court's words:

> The fundamental nature of the guarantee against double jeopardy can hardly be doubted. Its origins can be traced to Greek and Roman times, and it became established in the common law of England long before this Nation's independence.... "[T]he underlying idea, one that is deeply ingrained in at least the Anglo-American system of jurisprudence, is that the State with all its resources and power should not be allowed to make repeated attempts to convict an individual for an alleged offense, thereby subjecting him to embarrassment, expense and ordeal and compelling him to live in a continuing state of anxiety and insecurity, as well as enhancing the possibility that even though innocent he may be found guilty." This underlying notion has from the very beginning been part of our constitutional tradition. Like the right to trial by jury, it is clearly "fundamental to the American scheme of justice."

Williams v. Florida, 399 U.S. 78 (1970)

Trial juries in criminal cases were traditionally composed of twelve members. Some jurisdictions began to use smaller juries to decrease costs and administrative problems. In this case, the U.S. Supreme Court declared that the Sixth Amendment right to trial by jury did not require that criminal juries have twelve members. Instead, states were permitted to use juries of smaller than twelve in criminal cases just as such smaller juries are frequently used in civil trials. The Constitution does not require that juries have a fixed number of members that is defined by Anglo-American traditions. According to the majority opinion:

> [T]he essential feature of a jury obviously lies in the interposition between the accused and his accuser of the commonsense judgment of a group of laymen, and in the community participation and shared responsibility that results from that group's determination of guilt or innocence. The performance of this role is not a function of the particular number of the body that makes up the jury. To be sure, the number should probably be large enough to promote group deliberation, free from outside attempts at intimidation, and to provide a fair possibility for obtaining a representative cross-section of the community. But we find little reason to think that these goals are in any meaningful sense less likely to be achieved when the jury numbers six, than when it numbers 12—particularly if the requirement of unanimity is retained. And, certainly the reliability of the jury as a factfinder hardly seems likely to be a function of its size.

Barker v. Wingo, 407 U.S. 514 (1972)

Two men were arrested for murder. The prosecution first sought to place on trial and convict the man against whom they had the most evidence with the hope that he could then be persuaded to serve as a witness for the prosecution in the second trial. However, it took the prosecution a long time to obtain the first conviction. The first man went through six trials because of hung juries and successful appeals. There were further delays in the second trial due to the health of certain witnesses. Ultimately, more than five years passed between the crime and the completion of the second defendant's trial. Throughout the process, the prosecution kept returning to the court to request delays. After the second man was convicted, he filed an appeal claiming that his conviction should be overturned because the lengthy delays violated his Sixth Amendment right to a speedy trial. When the Supreme Court considered the case, it developed a flexible test for identifying violations of the right to a speedy trial. Rather than set a definite time limit for the completion of trials, the Court created a four-part balancing test. In the Court's words:

> A balancing test necessarily compels courts to approach speedy trial cases on an *ad hoc* basis. We can do little more than identify some of the factors which courts should assess in determining whether a particular defendant has been deprived of his right. Though some might express them in different ways, we identify four such factors: Length of delay, the reason for the delay, the defendant's assertion of his right, and prejudice to the defendant.

Thus for each case in which a claim arises concerning the right to a speedy trial, the trial judge must balance the following factors: (1) the length of the delay—was it a delay of months or years?; (2) the reason for the delay—was it caused by the prosecution, the defense, or the court?; (3) whether the defendant demanded a trial during the period of the delay; and (4) whether the delay harmed the defendant's case. When the test was applied to this case, the Court found that no violation had occurred. Despite the very lengthy delay caused by the prosecution, two factors weighed against a finding of violation, the defendant never demanded a trial during the five-year delay, and the delay did not harm the defendant's case because his witnesses were still available. Thus the right to a speedy trial does not have a precise definition. The assessment of the right will vary depending on the circumstances of each case.

Apodaca v. Oregon, 406 U.S. 404 (1972)

Oregon and Louisiana permitted criminal defendants to be convicted in jury trials by less-than-unanimous votes of the jurors. Traditionally, jurors needed to reach a unanimous decision in order to convict someone accused of a crime. The U.S. Supreme

Court considered the question of whether the Sixth Amendment's right to a fair trial or right to a jury trial required unanimous jury verdicts in order to convict the accused. The Court decided that the Constitution does not impose a unanimity requirement on juries. In the words of the Court's opinion:

> Our inquiry must focus upon the function served by the jury in contemporary society. . . . "[T]he essential feature of a jury obviously lies in the interposition between the accused and his accuser of the common-sense judgment of a group of laymen. . . ." [quoting *Williams v. Florida* 1970]. . . . A requirement of unanimity, however, does not materially contribute to the exercise of commonsense judgment. . . . Requiring unanimity would obviously produce hung juries in some situations where non-unanimous juries will convict or acquit. But in either case, the interest of the defendant in having the judgment of his peers interposed between himself and the officers of the State who prosecute and judge him is equally well served.

Thus states can permit convictions to occur through nonunanimous verdicts. The use of nonunanimous verdicts creates risks. Jurors have less incentive to listen to arguments from members with minority viewpoints if dissenters can merely be ignored in voting on a verdict. Most states continue to require unanimous verdicts in criminal cases.

Argersinger v. Hamlin, 407 U.S. 25 (1972)

The U.S. Supreme Court expanded the right to counsel for indigent defendants by requiring the government to provide attorneys in any case in which incarceration may be the punishment rather than just for serious charges drawing sentences of six months or more. The Court's opinion presented reasons for requiring counsel even when defendants face only short jail sentences:

> The requirement of counsel may well be necessary for a fair trial even in a petty-offense prosecution. We are by no means convinced that legal and constitutional questions involved in a case that actually leads to imprisonment even for a brief period are any less com-

plex than when a person can be sent off for six months or more. . . . Beyond the problem of trials and appeals is that of the guilty plea, a problem which looms large in misdemeanor as well as in felony cases. Counsel is needed so that the accused may know precisely what he is doing, so that he is fully aware of the prospect of going to jail or prison, and so that he is treated fairly by the prosecution. In addition, the volume of misdemeanor cases, far greater in number than felony prosecutions, may create an obsession for speedy dispositions, regardless of the fairness of the result. . . . There is evidence of the prejudice which results to misdemeanor defendants from this "assembly-line justice." One study concluded that "[m]isdemeanants represented by attorneys are five times as likely to emerge from police court with all charges dismissed as are defendants who face similar charges without counsel." . . . We must conclude, therefore, that the problems associated with misdemeanor and petty offenses often require the presence of counsel to insure the accused a fair trial.

Ross v. Moffitt, 417 U.S. 600 (1974)

According to the U.S. Supreme Court's decision, there is no right to counsel for discretionary appeals to a state supreme court or the U.S. Supreme Court. Other cases made it clear that there is no right to counsel for habeas corpus petitions and civil rights lawsuits filed by prisoners or for civil lawsuits by poor people. Thus indigent people must represent themselves except when on trial for criminal charges that can bring incarceration as a punishment and the first appeal of right following such a trial.

The Court's opinion justified its conclusion that counsel is required for appeals of right in state intermediate appellate courts but not for discretionary appeals in courts of last resort:

This is not to say, of course, that a skilled lawyer, particularly one trained in the somewhat arcane art of preparing petitions for discretionary review, would not prove helpful to any litigants able to employ him. An indigent defendant seeking review in the Supreme Court of North Carolina is therefore somewhat handicapped in comparison with a wealthy defendant who has counsel assisting him in every conceivable manner at every stage in the proceeding. But both the opportunity to have counsel prepare an initial brief in the Court of Appeals and the nature of discretionary review in the Supreme Court of North Carolina make this relative handicap far less than the handicap borne by the indigent defendant denied counsel on his initial appeal as of right in *Douglas v. California* (1963). And the fact that a particular service might be of benefit to an indigent defendant does not mean that the service is constitutionally required. The duty of the State under our cases is not to duplicate the legal arsenal that may be privately retained by a criminal defendant in a continuing effort to reverse his conviction, but only to assure the indigent defendant an adequate opportunity to present his claims fairly in the context of the State's appellate process.

Gregg v. Georgia, 428 U.S. 153 (1976)

In 1972 a slim majority of justices on the U.S. Supreme Court declared that the death penalty was being imposed in an impermissibly arbitrary manner (*Furman v. Georgia* [1972]). As a response to the Court's decision, states that were committed to capital punishment revised their procedures for death penalty cases to satisfy the justices' concerns about arbitrary decisionmaking. The primary reforms enacted by states concerned two aspects of death penalty cases. First, death penalty trials were split into two phases, a guilt-determination phase and a punishment-determination phase. This scheme reflected the underlying idea that juries and judges would make more carefully considered judgments about which convicted murderers should live or die if they focused their attention solely on the question after the offender's guilt had already been established. Second, the punishment phase was to include careful consideration of aggravating and mitigating factors. *Aggravating factors* are those that make the specific crime or offender more deserving than other offenders of receiving the ultimate punishment. Factors such as a prior criminal record, excessive cruelty in the commission of the offense, or the simultaneous commission of other felonies, such as kidnapping or robbery, in conjunction with a murder could make an offender more deserving of the death penalty. By contrast, *mitigating factors* are those that make the offender less deserving of the death sentence. Such factors might include low intelligence, youthfulness, child-abuse victimization early in life, or other circumstances that might weigh against the most severe punishment. After examining the development of these reformed procedures, a majority of Supreme Court justices approved the resumption of the death penalty as a constitutionally permissible criminal punishment.

The opinion of the Court describes the aspects of the new procedures that made the death penalty permissible as a punishment:

> These [new] procedures require the jury to consider the circumstances of the crime and the criminal before it recommends sentence. No longer can a Georgia jury do as Furman's jury did: reach a finding of the defendant's guilt and then, without guidance or direction, decide whether he should live or die. Instead, the jury's attention is directed to the specific circumstances of the crime: Was it committed in the course of another capital felony? Was it committed for money? Was it committed upon a peace officer or in a manner that endangered the lives of many persons? In addition, the jury's attention is focused on the characteristics of the person who committed the crime: Does he have a record of prior convictions for capital offenses? Are there any special facts about the defendant that mitigate against imposing capital punishment (e.g., his youth, the extent of his cooperation with the police, his emotional state at the time of the crime)? As a result, while some jury discretion still exists, "the discretion to be exercised is controlled by clear and objective standards so as to produce nondiscriminatory application." . . . As an important additional safeguard against arbitrariness and caprice, the Georgia statutory scheme provides for automatic appeal of all death sentences to the State's Supreme Court.

Bordenkircher v. Hayes, 434 U.S. 357 (1978)

During the course of plea-bargaining negotiations, a prosecutor threatened to charge a repeat offender with an additional count under a habitual offender statute, which would, upon conviction, produce a very long sentence. The prosecutor said he would forego the additional charge if the defendant would plead guilty to the crime and accept a sentence of several years in prison. The defendant refused, and he was subsequently convicted as a habitual offender and given a long sentence. He appealed by claiming that the prosecutor's threat of an additional charge was a form of improper pressure that should not be permitted in plea-bargaining processes. The U.S. Supreme Court disagreed. The Court declared that prosecutors can threaten to impose additional charges as long as they are legitimate charges. Thus it is permissible to apply pressure during plea negotiations as long as that pressure stems from criminal charges and punishments that are permitted under the law. A prosecutor could not threaten phony charges for which there is no substantiation. Charges supported with evidence, by contrast, are permissible. As the Court stated in its opinion:

> While confronting a defendant with the risk of more severe punishments clearly may have a "discouraging effect on the defendant's assertion of his trial rights, the imposition of these difficult choices is an inevitable"—and permissible—"attribute of any legitimate system which tolerates and encourages the negotiation of pleas." . . . It follows that, by tolerating and encouraging the negotiation of pleas, this Court has necessarily accepted as constitutionally legitimate the simple reality that the prosecutor's interest at the bargaining table is to persuade the defendant to forgo his right to plead not guilty.

Scott v. Illinois, 440 U.S. 367 (1979)

The U.S. Supreme Court limited the right to counsel by deciding that there is no entitlement to appointed counsel in criminal cases when the indigent defendant faces only a fine as punishment. The majority of justices based their decision, in part, on a concern about the financial costs that would be imposed on state and local governments if they had to provide attorneys for indigent defendants in every criminal case. According to the majority:

> We believe that the central premise of *Argersinger* [*v. Hamlin* 1972] "that actual imprisonment is a penalty different in kind from fines or the mere threat of im-

prisonment" is eminently sound and warrants adoption of actual imprisonment as the line defining the constitutional right to appointment of counsel. *Argersinger* has proved reasonably workable, whereas any extension would create confusion and impose unpredictable, but necessarily substantial, costs on 50 quite diverse States.

Heath v. Alabama, 474 U.S. 82 (1985)

A man hired two men to kidnap and kill his girlfriend. They abducted the woman in Alabama and took her to Georgia, where she was killed. When they were caught, the boyfriend pleaded guilty to murder charges in Georgia to gain a life sentence rather than risk the imposition of the death penalty. Later, Alabama also prosecuted him for kidnapping and murder. Alabama convicted him and sentenced him to death. He claimed that the Alabama conviction was invalid because it constituted illegal double jeopardy by trying him twice for the same crime. The U.S. Supreme Court declared that there was no double jeopardy violation because he was not charged twice for the same crime. Instead, he was charged with two different crimes in two different jurisdictions, which is permissible even when those charges arise out of the same series of acts. According to the Supreme Court:

> The dual sovereignty doctrine, as originally articulated and consistently applied by this Court, compels the conclusion that successive petitions by two States for the same conduct are not barred by the Double Jeopardy Clause. The dual sovereignty doctrine is founded on the common law conception of crime as an offense against the sovereignty of the government. . . . [The states'] power to undertake criminal prosecutions derives from separate and independent sources of power and authority originally belonging to them before admission to the Union and preserved to them by the Tenth Amendment.

Batson v. Kentucky, 476 U.S. 79 (1986)

During the process of selecting jurors prior to a trial, *challenges for cause* may be used to exclude potential jurors whose responses to questions by lawyers and the judge include overt expressions of bias. There is no limit to the number of challenges for cause that can be applied by each side's attorney because there is a desire to avoid placing people with overt biases on the jury. Other potential jurors can be excluded through the discretion or even whim of each side's attorney. The prosecution and defense each have a specific number of *peremptory challenges* that they can use to exclude people who they believe will be sympathetic to the other side but who have not made overt expressions of bias. Unfortunately, prosecutors in some locations began using the peremptory challenges to exclude African Americans from juries whenever there was an African-American defendant. In this case, the Supreme Court addressed the issue by declaring that race-based exclusions of jurors violate the constitutional rights of such individuals by using racial discrimination to deny them the opportunity to participate in judicial processes as jurors. In addition, the Court stated:

> The harm from discriminatory jury selection extends beyond that inflicted on the defendant and the excluded juror to touch the entire community. Selection procedures that purposefully exclude black persons from juries undermine public confidence in the fairness of our system of justice. . . . Discrimination within the judicial system is most pernicious because it is "a stimulant to that race prejudice which is an impediment to securing to [African Americans] that equal justice which the law aims to secure to all others."

Thus the Court said that if the defense attorney sees evidence of race-based exclusions occurring during jury selection, the attorney can raise the issue with the judge and the judge will ask the prosecutor for a nonrace-based explanation for the use of the peremptory challenges.

Moran v. Burbine, 475 U.S. 412 (1986)

A burglary suspect was to be questioned for an unsolved murder. Shortly after the suspect's arrest, his sister contacted an attorney who called the police station. The attorney informed the police that the suspect was represented by counsel and expressed a willingness to come to the station to be present for any questioning. The police assured the attorney that no questioning would occur until the following day. Instead, the suspect was questioned immediately without the attorney present. The suspect voluntarily agreed to talk to the police but was never told that an attorney was standing by to provide representation. After the suspect was convicted of the murder, he claimed that the police should have informed him that an attorney was already available to represent him during questioning. The Supreme Court declared that the police have no obligation to inform a suspect that he or she already has an attorney, even when the suspect is clearly not aware of that fact. Moreover, the Supreme Court majority did not object to the fact that the police misled the defense attorney about whether and when questioning would occur. As described by the Court's opinion:

> Events occurring outside of the presence of the suspect and entirely unknown to him surely can have no bearing on the capacity to comprehend and knowingly relinquish a constitutional right. . . . Nothing in our waiver decisions or in our understanding of the essential components of a valid waiver requires so incongruous a result. No doubt the additional information would have been useful to respondent; perhaps even it might have affected his decision to confess. But we have never read the Constitution to require that the police supply a suspect with a flow of information to help him calibrate his self-interest in deciding whether to speak or stand by his rights. . . . Once it is determined that a suspect's decision not to rely on his rights was uncoerced, that he at all times knew he could stand mute and request a lawyer, and that he was aware of the State's intention to use his statements to secure a conviction, the analysis is complete and the waiver is valid as a matter of law. . . . Although highly inappropriate, even deliberate deception of an attorney could not possibly affect a suspect's decision to waive his *Miranda* rights unless he were at least aware of the incident. . . . Granting that the "deliberate or reckless" withholding of information is objectionable as a matter of ethics, such conduct is only relevant to the constitutional validity of the waiver if it deprives a defendant of knowledge essential to his ability to understand the nature of his rights and consequences of

abandoning them. Because respondent's voluntary decision to speak was made with full awareness and comprehension of all the information *Miranda* requires the police to convey, the waivers were valid.

Taylor v. Illinois, 484 U.S. 400 (1988)

A criminal defense attorney violated court rules by attempting to spring a surprise witness on the prosecution during a trial. The attorneys were supposed to exchange witness lists prior to the trial, but the defense attorney claimed that he had discovered and located the new witness only after the trial had already started. The witness contradicted the attorney by telling the judge that he had spoken with the defense attorney two weeks prior to the start of the trial. As a consequence of failing to list the witness prior to trial, the judge refused to permit the witness to testify. The defendant claimed that this witness exclusion violated his Sixth Amendment right to compulsory process. This right is intended to enable defendants to present a case by giving them the authority to obtain documents and to require witnesses to appear in court. The U.S. Supreme Court disagreed, however. The justices declared that no rights were violated by the judge's decision to exclude the defense witness. According to the majority opinion:

> It is elementary, of course, that a trial court may not ignore the fundamental character of the defendant's right to offer the testimony of witnesses in his favor. But the mere invocation of that right cannot automatically and invariably outweigh countervailing public interests. The integrity of the adversary process, which depends on the presentation of reliable evidence and the rejection of unreliable evidence, the interest in the fair and efficient administration of justice, and the potential prejudice to the truth-determining function of the trial process must also weigh in the balance.

Maryland v. Craig, 497 U.S. 836 (1990)

The U.S. Supreme Court struggled with the question of whether the Sixth Amendment right to confrontation requires face-to-face confrontation in the courtroom between the criminal defendant and any witnesses providing evidence for the prosecution. Some analysts argued that the right should not be defined in a literal fashion because of the need to protect some categories of witnesses, especially child sex-abuse victims, from the trauma of facing their victimizers in the courtroom. These concerns led some states to experiment with mechanisms to protect certain victims. In *Coy v. Iowa* (1988), a divided Supreme Court ruled that a screen could not be placed in the courtroom between the witness stand and the defense table to keep the defendant and the sex-crime victims from viewing each other. In *Maryland v. Craig* (1990), by contrast, a divided court approved the use of closed-circuit television as a means to permit witness testimony that avoids psychological trauma for the witness. Through this mechanism, the defendant and others in the courtroom can watch the witness on television as he or she testifies, but the witness, located in another room, cannot see the defendant. The decision made it clear that the Sixth Amendment right to confrontation need not be interpreted literally in all cases. As summarized by the Supreme Court, "In sum, our precedents establish that 'the Confrontation Clause reflects a preference for face-to-face confrontation at trial,' . . . a preference that 'must occasionally give way to considerations of public policy and the necessities of the case.'"

Edmonson v. Leesville Concrete Co., 500 U.S. 614 (1991)

The Supreme Court expanded its prohibition on racial discrimination in jury selection to bar attorneys in civil trials from using their peremptory challenges to exclude potential jurors because of their race. According to the Supreme Court:

> Race discrimination within the courtroom raises serious questions as to the fairness of the proceedings conducted there. Racial bias mars the integrity of the judicial system, and prevents the idea of democratic government from becoming a reality. . . . To permit racial exclusion in this official forum compounds the racial insult inherent in judging a citizen by the color of his or her skin.

Georgia v. McCollum, 502 U.S. 1056 (1992)

The U.S. Supreme Court expanded the prohibition on the use of race-based exclusions of potential jurors through peremptory challenges. In this case, the Court said that criminal defense attorneys, like prosecutors, cannot engage in racial discrimination in jury selection. In the words of the majority opinion,

> This Court firmly has rejected the view that assumptions of partiality based on race provide a legitimate basis for disqualifying a person as an impartial juror. . . . We therefore reaffirm today that the exercise of a peremptory challenge must not be based on either the race of the juror or the racial stereotypes held by the party.

J.E.B. v. Alabama ex rel. T.B., 511 U.S. 127 (1994)

The U.S. Supreme Court further expanded the prohibition on discrimination in jury selection. In this case concerning an issue of paternity and child support, the Court declared that attorneys cannot engage in gender discrimination when using peremptory challenges to exclude potential jurors. The majority opinion made a strong statement against gender discrimination in the trial process:

> It denigrates the dignity of the excluded juror, and, for a woman, reinvokes a history of exclusion from political participation. The message it sends to all those in the courtroom, and all those who may later learn of the discriminatory act, is that certain individuals, for no reason other than gender, are presumed unqualified by state actors to decide important questions upon which reasonable persons would disagree.

Despite this strong statement against discrimination, the Court has not expanded its prohibition on discrimination beyond the categories of race and gender that receive the greatest protection under the Fourteenth Amendment's Equal Protection Clause.

Lewis v. United States, 518 U.S. 322 (1996)

A mail handler for the U.S. Postal Service was prosecuted for two criminal charges after allegedly opening other people's mail to look for money. Each charge carried a possible punishment of six months' imprisonment. The defendant requested a jury trial, but the request was denied. The judicial officer said that the right to a trial by jury applies only when the defendant faces the possibility of more than six months' imprisonment. Here, however, prior to the trial the judicial officer promised that the sentence would be no more than six months upon conviction, even if convicted on both charges. When the U.S. Supreme Court considered this issue about when the right to a jury applies, a majority of justices agreed with the trial judge. According to the justices, the right to trial by jury applies only when a defendant faces a charge carrying a possible punishment in excess of six months. The right does not apply to charges with lesser punishments, even when the defendant's total sentence could well exceed six months if sentenced to consecutive sentences upon conviction for multiple charges. The Sixth Amendment states, "In all criminal prosecutions, the accused shall enjoy the right to a speedy and public trial, by an impartial jury." Yet the Court applied the right to a jury trial to only some cases. According to the conclusion of the Court's slim majority,

> The Constitution's guarantee of the right to a jury trial extends only to serious offenses, and petitioner was not charged with a serious offense. That he was tried for two counts of a petty offense, and therefore faced an aggregate potential term of imprisonment of more than six months, does not change the fact that the legislature deemed this offense petty.

Martinez v. Court of Appeal of California, 528 U.S. 152 (2000)

Criminal defendants are permitted to waive their constitutional rights, including their right to counsel. Thus the Sixth Amendment right to counsel has been interpreted to mean that defendants are entitled to represent themselves at trial if that is what they wish to do. In this case, a defendant with years of professional experience as a paralegal sought to represent himself in his criminal appeal. However, the Supreme Court declared that the Sixth Amendment right to counsel does not apply to appeals. It applies only to the trial level. Thus the court could force him to be represented by an attorney in the appellate court. According to the Court's reasoning:

In light of our conclusion that the Sixth Amendment does not apply to appellate proceedings, any individual right to self-representation on appeal based on autonomy principles must be grounded in the Due Process Clause. Under the practices that prevail in the Nation today, however, we are entirely unpersuaded that the risk of either disloyalty or suspicion of disloyalty [by attorneys to their clients' interests] is a sufficient concern to conclude that a constitutional right of self-representation is a necessary component of a fair appellate proceeding. We have no doubt that instances of disloyal representation are rare. In both trials and appeals there are, without question, cases in which counsel's performance is ineffective. Even in those cases, however, it is reasonable to assume that counsel's performance is more effective than what the unskilled appellant could have provided for himself.

Data on Courts and Trials

This section provides illustrations on court structure, the nature of court caseloads, the prevalence of trials, and the duration of cases, including trials. Specific data on these issues will vary depending on the court system and individual courthouse. These data are drawn from examples in the United States.

Court Organization

Each government, whether federal, state, or local, can design its own court system. The organization of some court systems may be established in a national or state constitution. In other jurisdictions, the legislature or executive officials may have significant authority to design and alter the organization of courts. Streamlined court organizations often reflect centralization of administrative management and funding. Such is the case with the State of South Dakota in Table 5.2. The lack of an intermediate appellate court in South Dakota is made possible by the state's relatively small population and correspondingly small caseloads. By contrast, in the same figure, the court system for Georgia shows greater complexity, including a variety of limited jurisdiction trial

Table 5.2 Comparison of Complexity of Court Organization, Georgia and South Dakota

Types of Courts	Georgia	South Dakota
Court of last resort	Supreme	Supreme
Intermediate appellate court	Court of appeals	None
General jurisdiction trial court	Superior	Circuit court
Limited jurisdiction trial courts	State court	Magistrate court
	Juvenile court	
	Probate court	
	Magistrate court	
	Municipal court	

Source: David Rottman, Carol R. Flango, and R. Shedine Lockely. *State Court Organization 1993.* Washington, D.C.: U.S. Department of Justice, 1995, pp. 34–35, 40–41, 50–53, 64–65.

courts. The existence of multiple differentiated local courts often demonstrates the influence of local political power. Greater numbers of local courts also provide increased opportunities for political parties to gain judgeships and reward loyal partisans with jobs within the court.

The federal court system, illuminated in Table 5.3, was designed by Congress because only the U.S. Supreme Court is established by the U.S. Constitution. The national system has a streamlined design with one trial court (district courts), one intermediate appellate court (circuit courts of appeals), and one court of last resort (the Supreme Court). The complex aspect of the federal courts stems from the short list of specialized courts that handle particular kinds of legal issues. By removing these issues, many of which require special expertise, from the regular court system, the court system's capacity for efficient and consistent case processing is increased.

The Nature of Court Caseloads and the Prevalence of Trials

The disposition of state criminal cases with convictions is illustrated in Table 5.4. The data in the table highlight the fact that trials are relatively rare events. As indicated by the table, more than 90 percent of state criminal cases ending with convictions are terminated through the entry of a guilty plea. Jury trials conclude only 4 percent of cases with convictions, and bench trials, presided over by a judge, terminate only 5 percent of such cases. Similar data are shown for federal criminal cases in Table 5.5, which also includes data on cases of dismissals and acquittals.

Table 5.3 Organization of United States Federal Court System

U.S. Supreme Court (court of last resort)
U.S. Court of Appeals (intermediate appellate courts)
divided into 12 geographic circuits plus the Federal Circuit for patent and trade cases

1st Cir	2nd Cir	3rd Cir	4th Cir	5th Cir	6th Cir	7th Cir	8th Cir	9th Cir	10th Cir	11th Cir	D.C. Cir.
ME	CT	DE	MD	LA	KY	IL	AR	AK	CO	AL	DC
MA	NY	NJ	NC	MS	MI	IN	IA	AZ	KS	FL	federal
NH	VT	PA	SC	TX	OH	WI	MN	CA	NM	GA	government
PR		VI	SC		TN		MO	Guam	OK		
RI		WV					NE	HA	UT		
							ND	ID	WY		
							SD	MT			
								NV			
							Northern Mariana Islands				
							OR				
							WA				

U.S. District Courts (general jurisdiction trial courts states) and territories are divided into 94 districts

Special Courts with limited subject-matter jurisdiction:
   U.S. Court of Appeals of the Federal Circuit (patent and international trade case appeals)
   U.S. Court of Appeals for Veterans' Claims (appeals from denials of veterans' benefits)
   U.S. Court of Federal Claims (claims involving federal government)
   U.S. Court of International Trade (international trade cases)
   U.S. Tax Court (federal taxation cases)
Source: Table constructed by author based on information drawn from the Federal Judiciary web page,
http://www.uscourts.gov.

Both tables also indicate the nature of criminal caseloads, including the disproportionate numbers of property crimes and drug offenses among the total number of offenses prosecuted.

The data in Table 5.6 provide a glimpse of the general categories of civil cases in state courts by showing how many tort, contract, and real property cases went to trial in the seventy-five largest counties. Data for civil cases are collected and monitored less consistently at a national level because these cases are usually considered less important for purposes of policymaking than are criminal cases. Trends in crime rates and prosecutions are monitored closely to inform politicians and policymakers about the success of current laws and the need for reforms. A more complete picture of a court system's civil caseload is presented in Table 5.9, which illustrates the kinds of cases that make up federal courts' civil caseloads. Several categories of cases, such as social security and copyright, are unique to federal courts. State courts'

Table 5.4 Criminal Cases in State Courts: Felony Convictions by Offense Category and Method of Conviction, 1996 (by number and percent)

Most Serious Conviction Offense	Jury Trial	Bench Trial	Guilty Plea
All offenses	37,541 4%	54,474 5%	905,957 91%
Murder and manslaughter	4,519 40	780 7	6,133 54
Rape and sexual assault	3,414 11	2,154 7	24,489 81
Robbery	4,128 10	2,858 7	35,844 84
Aggravated assault	4,653 7	4,737 7	60,134 86
Other violent crimes	958 7	1,119 8	11,908 85
Burglary	2,705 3	4,577 5	85,915 2
Larceny and auto theft	2,155 2	5,172 4	115,874 4
Fraud, forgery, and embezzlement	676 1	4,095 5	77,462 94
Drug possession	2,908 2	9,321 7	123,040 91
Drug trafficking	6,935 3	9,424 4	196,145 92
Weapons offenses	1,217 4	1,663 5	30,456 91
Other nonviolent offenses	3,274 2	8,575 6	138,557 92

Source: Kathleen Maguire and Ann L. Pastore, eds., *Sourcebook of Criminal Justice Statistics 2000*. Washington, D.C.: U.S. Department of Justice, 2001, p. 457.

Table 5.5 Federal Criminal Cases Completed in U.S. District Courts, by Type of Disposition and Major Offense for a 12-month Period Ending September 30, 2001

	Total Defendants	Not Convicted		Convicted		
		Dismissed	Jury Trial Acquittal	Bench Trial Acquittal	Guilty Plea and No Contest	Jury Trial	Bench Trial
Total	75,650	7,017	423	479	64,148	2,294	1,035
Homicide	308	39	7	2	225	32	3
Robbery	1,581	65	8	2	1,460	53	3
Assault	612	165	10 8	396	27	6	
Burglary	75	10	0	1	62	1	1
Larceny/theft	3,395	730	25	13	2,521	82	24
Embezzlement	1,084	93	6 0	965	19	1	
Fraud	10,268	713	47	18	9,086	386	18
Auto theft	223	33	2	0	172	16	0
Forgery/counterfeiting	1,383	124	4	2	1,229	24	0
Sex offenses	901	70	12	0	767	47	5
Drugs	28,238	2,212	172	39	24,852	920	43
Other general offenses	12,667	1,931	78	357	9,587	478	236
Immigration	11,256	463	12	4	10,642	111	24
Liquor tax	7	0	0	0	5	2	0
Federal regulations	3,652	379	40	33	2,433	96	671

Source: Annual Report of the Director of the Administrative Office of U.S. Courts, 2001. Washington, D.C.: U.S. Government Printing Office, 2002, pp. 211–213.

Table 5.6 Trial Award Winners in Civil Trials in State Courts for Tort, Contract,
and Real Property Cases: Courts in 75 Largest Counties in the United States, 1996
(by total number and percentage of plaintiff wins)

Case Type	Jury Trials	Bench Trials	Other Trials (directed verdict, defaults)
Tort	8,751 47.5%	1,271 56.9%	237 25.4%
Contract	1,740 55.6%	2,955 67.8%	150 34.1%
Real Property	105 35.7%	399 30.5%	6 49.1%

Source: Carol J. DeFrances and Marika F.X. Litras. "Civil Trial Cases and Verdicts in Large Counties," 1996, Bureau of Justice Statistics Bulletin, September 1999, p. 6.

civil caseloads typically have less differentiation and are dominated by cases about torts, contracts, and real property.

Case Processing Time and Duration of Trials

The median length of time needed to process federal criminal cases is displayed in Table 5.7. Obviously, jury trials are more time-consuming than other mechanisms for termination, such as dismissals and guilty pleas. Jury trials require significant preparation and often take longer to schedule because of the many actors involved. As indicated in Table 5.8, the trials themselves are not always lengthy. Most trials are completed in one or two days. However, a small number of trials may last twenty days or longer.

Sentencing Guidelines

The federal government and many states have created sentencing guidelines to standardize sentences and reduce the inequitable and lenient aspects of judges' discretionary sentencing. Typically, the judge determines the sentence by identifying the offender's prior criminal record and severity of most recent offense. The judge then looks at the sentencing guidelines grid to see what sentence must be imposed for an individual with those particular factors. Table 5.10 shows the sentencing-guidelines grid for Massachusetts.

Table 5.7 Median Time Interval (in months) from Filing to Disposition of Federal Criminal Cases in U.S. District Courts, during 12-Month Period Ending September 30, 2001 (by total number and median)

Total Cases	Dismissed	Plea of Guilty	Jury Trial	Bench Trial
75,650	7,017	64,402	2,717	1,514
6.0	4.7	6.0	11.1	2.3

Source: Annual Report of the Director of the Administrative Office of U.S. Courts, 2001. Washington, D.C.: U.S. Government Printing Office, 2002, p. 218.

Table 5.8 Length (in days) of Civil and Criminal Federal Trials Completed in U.S. District Courts, during the 12-Month Period Ending September 30, 2001

Length	Civil Trials	Criminal Trials
1	2,675	3,657
2	1,022	1,173
3	869	794
4–9	1,665	1,154
10–13	249	201
20 or more days	33	66
Sub total	6,513	7,045
Total trials 13,558		

Source: Annual Report of the Director of the Administrative Office of U.S. Courts, 2001. Washington, DC: U.S. Government Printing Office, 2002, p. 166.

Table 5.9 Federal Civil Cases Commenced in U.S. District Courts (by nature of suit and party) during the 12-Month Period Ending September 30, 2001

	Cases with U.S. Government as a Party (63,324 total)	Cases with Other Parties (187,583)
Contract	14,029	29,119
Real property	4,364	2,926
Tort	2,718 (including personal injury)	29,950
Civil rights	3,032	37,878
Employment	0	995
Prisoner petitions	14,619 (state prisoners)	44,186
Forfeiture	1,938	0
Labor	500	14,695
Copyright/patent/trademark	0	8,282
Social security	17,074	0
Other	5,050	19,552
Total Civil Cases 250,907		

Source: Annual Report of the Director of the Administrative Office of U.S. Courts, 2001. Washington, D.C.: U.S. Government Printing Office, 2002, p. 137.

Table 5.10 Massachusetts Sentencing Guidelines (sentence lengths in months)

| Offense Severity | Prior Criminal Record | | | | |
	No/Minor	Moderate	Serious	Violent/ Repeat	Serious Violent
LEVEL 9 Murder	Life	Life	Life	Life	Life
LEVEL 8	96–144	108–162	120–180	144–216	204–306
Voluntary manslaughter					
Rape of a child with force					
Aggravated rape					
Armed burglary					
LEVEL 7	60–90	68–102	84–126	108–162	160–240
Armed robbery					
Rape					
LEVEL 6	40–60	45–67	50–75	60–90	80–120
Involuntary manslaughter					
Armed robbery (no gun)					
Assault (significant injury)					
LEVEL 5	12–36 or probation	24–36 o probation	36–54	48–72	60–90
Unarmed robbery					
Stalking-violation of order					
Unarmed burglary					
Larceny ($50,000 and over)					
LEVEL 4	0–24 or probation	3–30 or probation	6–30 or probation	20–30	24–36
Larceny from a person					
Assault (moderate injury)					
Breaking into a dwelling					
Larceny ($10,000–50,000)					
LEVEL 3	0–12 or probation/ or fine	0–15 or probation or fine	0–18 or probation or fine	0–24 or probation or fine	6–24 or probation or fine
Assault (minor injury)					
Breaking into nondwelling					
Larceny ($250–10,000)					
LEVEL 2	probation/fine	0–6 or probation or fine	0–6 or probation or fine	0–6 probation or fine	0–12 probation or fine
Assault (no battery)					
Larceny under $250					
LEVEL 1	probation or fine	probation or fine	probation or fine	0–3 probation or fine	0–6 probation or fine
Vandalism					
Disorderly conduct					
Driving with suspended license					

Source: "Massachusetts Sentencing Guidelines Grid," Massachusetts Court System Web Page, http://www.state.ma.us/courts/formsandguidelines/sentencing/grid.html

6

Agencies and Organizations

This chapter provides information about major organizations and institutions concerned with courts and trials, including information about individual courts and related administrative agencies. Because each state has its own court system, the organization of courts varies by jurisdiction. In some states, courts are part of a centralized organization. Frequently, the state supreme court and the state court administrator exert significant influence over judicial operations. By contrast, courts in some other states are semiautonomous entities under the administrative control of city or county governments and are overseen by one or more judges. As a result, court organizations are so numerous and varied that only a sample of state and federal entities is included in this chapter. Information about each individual state's court system can be found at the Findlaw website (http://www.findlaw.com).

Judicial processes and trials are also affected by the actors who work within courts. There are national and state organizations advancing the interests of judges, court administrators, prosecutors, and attorneys. In addition, there are many interest groups that use litigation processes to advance their policy goals and to shape the law. Other independent organizations are dedicated to improving court procedures and providing training for courts and judges.

Administrative Office of the U.S. Courts
Office of Public Affairs
Thurgood Marshall Federal Judiciary Building

One Columbus Circle, NE
Washington, DC 20544
(202) 502-2600
http://www.uscourts.gov

The Administrative Office (AO) of the United States Courts was established in 1939 to provide administrative support to the federal court system. The AO employs lawyers, public administrators, accountants, architects, statisticians, and other staff to monitor and plan budgets, personnel, facilities, and other management aspects of the federal courts. When a federal court needs to request additional resources, such as office equipment, staff, or computer systems, the AO must analyze the request and help to determine how resources will be distributed to courts throughout the country. The AO also keeps case processing records concerning courts around the country so that resource needs can be analyzed.

American Bar Association
541 N. Fairbanks Court
Chicago, IL 60611
(312) 988-5522
http://www.abanet.org

The American Bar Association (ABA) is the largest membership organization of lawyers in the United States. Because it has more than 400,000 members, it exerts significant influence over the legal profession and the governmental policies affecting courts. The ABA provides accreditation for law schools by examining whether schools offering postgraduate law degrees meet ABA standards for curriculum, facilities, and faculty credentials. Many states use ABA accreditation decisions to determine whether graduates of specific law schools will be permitted to become licensed attorneys. The ABA provides continuing legal education programs for attorneys and judges. The organization also sponsors public information programs, such as its annual nationwide Law Day, to educate the public about the law and to protect the image of lawyers and judges in the eyes of the public. Historically, the ABA has played a role in the selection of federal judges by evaluating and rating nominees and reporting those ratings to the president and U.S. Senate. The ratings of judicial candidates' qualifications became a source of controversy in the 1980s and 1990s, as the ABA committee was unable to reach a consensus about the fitness for judicial office of several nominees for the U.S. Supreme Court. One of the ABA's most important and influential activities is the adoption of policy positions on behalf of a large segment of the nation's lawyers. The ABA's House of Delegates debates proposals for policy positions that the organization might adopt. There are often deep divisions within the organization about whether to adopt a position on controversial issues such as abortion and capital punishment. When the ABA announces the adoption of a policy position, its position receives significant national publicity and is used by advocates for that position as an important source of support and legitimacy. If Congress receives proposals concerning court reform, the status of lawyers and judges, or other matters relevant to courts and trials, ABA representatives will frequently testify about the proposals, and the organization's position can be influential in determining court-related laws and policies. The organization's monthly magazine, *ABA Journal*, presents articles about legal developments and law office management.

American Civil Liberties Union
125 Broad Street, 18th Floor
New York, NY 10004
http://www.aclu.org

The American Civil Liberties Union (ACLU) is a nonprofit national organization with individual state chapters. Founded in 1920, it uses litigation as a means to protect individuals' constitutional rights. Individuals who believe that their constitutional rights have been violated contact state chapters with complaints. Because the organization has only limited resources and relies on volunteer attorneys to handle cases, it is very selective about which cases it accepts. It tries to accept cases that will have the broadest impact to protect rights within society. Frequently, it must decline to represent people with valid claims because it does not have enough money or volunteer attorneys to provide assistance. The organization traditionally emphasizes the protection of First Amendment rights to freedom of speech and religion as well as cases concerning race and gender discrimination and the right to privacy. The national office in New York sponsors litigation addressing specific issues of national interest, including opposition to the death penalty, support for women's right to make choices about abortions, and prisoners' rights. A national legislative office in Washington, D.C., lobbies Congress about civil rights and civil liberties issues. Officials at the state chapters also lobby their legislatures. Although the ACLU has a reputation as a politically liberal organization, its support for constitutional rights has led it to join with conservatives to oppose certain kinds of government interference with religious practices. The organization has also gone to court to protect the free speech rights of Ku Klux Klan members and Nazis; individuals whose political beliefs conflict with those of ACLU members but whose right to speak is supported by the organization. Because it draws upon the voluntary services of many prominent law professors and attorneys, the organization has a good reputation for providing thorough professional advocacy on behalf of its causes. It is not a legal services agency because it carefully picks and chooses which cases it will carry into court.

American Judges Association
P.O. Box 8798
Williamsburg, VA 23187-8798
(757) 259-1841
http://aja.ncsc.dni.us

The American Judges Association (AJA) is a membership organization of judges, magistrates, and court referees in North America. The purpose of the organization is to provide educational conferences and dissemination of information for judicial officers regarding issues relevant to the administration of justice. The AJA's House of Delegates determines the association's position on policy issues and thereby enables judges to educate the public and policymakers about problems facing court systems and recommended solutions for those problems.

American Judicature Society
180 N. Michigan Avenue, Suite 600
Chicago, IL 60601
(312) 558-6900
http://www.ajs.org

The American Judicature Society (AJS) is a nonpartisan membership organization of judges, lawyers, and law professors that seeks to improve the administration of justice. Since the mid–twentieth century, the organization has served as the leading advocate of merit-selection systems for choosing judges. AJS has published numerous books and articles on judicial selection. Other publications have focused on judicial independence, ethical standards for judges, effective involvement of citizens as jurors in court processes, and court administration. The organization's bimonthly journal, *Judicature,* publishes research and commentary on courts and judicial administration. AJS also prepares training materials and sponsors education programs for lawyers and court personnel.

Association of Trial Lawyers of America
Leonard M. Ring Law Center
1050 31st Street, NW
Washington, DC 20007
(800) 424-2725
http://www.atlanet.org

The Association of Trial Lawyers of America (ATLA) proclaims that it is an organization "dedicated to promoting and protecting consumer safety, the right to trial by jury, and America's civil justice system." As indicated by its statement of objectives, ATLA is a national membership organization for civil trial attorneys who represent plaintiffs in tort cases, such as medical malpractice, personal injury, products liability, and property damage. ATLA lobbies on behalf of trial lawyers and gives special attention to preventing legislative initiatives that would diminish opportunities for injured plaintiffs to use litigation to obtain remedies. Thus ATLA often finds itself in opposition to doctors' organizations, insurance companies, and manufacturing entities that seek legislation to place caps on jury awards in civil lawsuits. ATLA provides continuing education for trial attorneys as well as publications for attorneys to keep them up to date about developments in civil law, court procedures, and trial tactics. The organization's monthly magazine, *Trial,* presents articles about legal trends, law office technology, and other issues of interest to trial attorneys.

Australia, Federal Court of
Parkes Place
Canberra, Australian Capital Territory, 2600
61-2-6270 6811
http://www.fedcourt.gov.au (including related links)

The High Court of Australia is the country's court of last resort. It interprets and applies the country's law, including cases that challenge the constitutional validity of laws, as well as appeals from federal, state, and territorial courts. The Federal Court of Australia was created in 1976. It handles appeals from decisions by single judges of the federal court, by the supreme courts of Australian Capital Territory and Norfolk Island, by the Federal Magistrates Service in nonfamily law matters, and by Australian state supreme courts when they exercise federal jurisdiction. The family court attempts to help families resolve their disputes by agreement rather than resorting to formal judicial proceedings. The court has the power to grant divorces, and it handles child custody, child support, spousal maintenance, and distribution of property after divorce. Individual Australian states have their own court systems. The state supreme court has unlimited civil jurisdiction and handles the most serious criminal charges such as murder. Its judges also sit on the state court of appeals and the state court of criminal appeals, where they review decisions made by a single judge of the supreme court. The state district court handles many serious criminal charges. The district court also handles civil lawsuits over amounts up to $750,000. Local courts handle minor criminal matters, traffic offenses, juvenile matters, civil cases up to $40,000, and some family law issues. Magistrates preside over local courts.

Canadian Court System
Supreme Court of Canada
301 Wellington Street
Ottawa, ON K1A 0J1
(613) 995-4330
http://www.scc-csc.gc.ca (including links to descriptions
of various courts)

Courts within the Canadian court system have four levels. The Supreme Court of Canada sits at the top. It hears appeals from the federal court system and the provincial court system. Unlike the U.S. Supreme Court, which only hears federal issues, the Supreme Court of Canada can hear cases and serve as the ultimate authority for all legal issues arising in the country. Below the supreme court are the appeals division of the Federal Court of Canada, and the courts of appeals for each province. These courts hear appeals from trial courts. The top-level trial courts are the trial division of the federal court and the general jurisdiction trial courts of each province. The provincial trial courts do not merely handle matters concerning provincial legislation. They also handle matters related to federal legislation, such as criminal cases. The lowest level of the system is composed of limited jurisdiction provincial courts, such as traffic courts and small-claims courts. Judges in Canada are appointed from a pool of lawyers who submit applications.

Conference of Chief Justices
c/o National Center for State Courts
P.O. Box 8798
Williamsburg, VA 23187-8798
(757) 259-1841
http://ccj.ncsc.dni.us

The Conference of Chief Justices is an association of the chief justices of all state supreme courts throughout the United States. The conference provides an organizational entity through which chief justices can share information about problems, reform initiatives, and other issues affecting state court systems. The conference also enables the leaders of state court systems to increase their political influence by speaking with one voice on important policy issues affecting court systems. The conference issues reports and recommendations on matters of importance to state courts.

Conference of State Court Administrators
c/o National Center for State Courts
P.O. Box 8798
Williamsburg, VA 23187-8798
(757) 259-1841
http://cosca.ncsc.dni.us

The Conference of State Court Administrators was founded in 1953. Its mission is to encourage the improvement of state court systems. The conference is composed of the chief state court administrator from each state. The conference enables state court administrators to share information about problems and court reform initiatives. It also permits state court administrators to join together in publicizing important court management issues and in seeking resources and support from legislatures and judges. The conference issues policy statements and resolutions about issues of importance to courts.

England and Wales Court System
The Court Service
Southside
105 Victoria Street
London, UK SW1E 6QT
44+(0)20-7210-2266
http://www.courtservice.gov.uk

The court system in England and Wales is composed of several levels and kinds of courts. Civil cases are heard in county courts throughout the country as well as in the high court located in large cities. Crown courts handle serious criminal matters that are referred from magistrates courts or are on appeal from magistrates courts. Criminal jury trials take place in crown courts. Lesser criminal offenses are handled in local magistrates courts, where nonlawyer members of the public are appointed to serve as magistrates who make determinations of guilt and impose punishments. The Court of Appeals–Civil Division, composed of thirty-five justices, hears appeals in civil matters from the high court or from country courts. Criminal appeals are heard by the Court of Appeals–Criminal Division.

Federal Bar Association
2215 M Street, NW
Washington, DC 20037
(202) 785-1614
(202) 785-1568
http://www.fedbar.org

The Federal Bar Association is the membership organization of 15,000 private-practice attorneys, federal government lawyers, and federal judges whose work focuses on federal courts and law. The association sponsors conferences and training sessions for its members to keep them up to date on new developments in law. The association also produces publications on subjects related to federal law, including a monthly publication, the *Federal Lawyer*. The organization also communicates with Congress and the federal judiciary about proposed changes in law and procedure affecting federal courts.

Federal Judicial Center
Thurgood Marshall Federal Judiciary Building
One Columbus Circle, NE

Washington, DC 20002-8003
(202) 502-4153
http://www.fjc.gov

The Federal Judicial Center was established in 1967 as the research and education agency of the federal courts. The center sponsors research that evaluates aspects of federal court operations. Research studies are published and disseminated throughout the country. They are usually available in university libraries and many public libraries. In addition, the center organizes training programs for people who work within the federal courts, including judges, magistrate judges, and law clerks. The center operates the Federal Judicial Television Network, through which it offers live interactive and videotaped training programs via satellite downlinks at federal court locations throughout the country. Personnel at the center plan educational programs for judicial personnel and handle the video production and broadcasting processes.

Federal Public Defenders
Defender Services Division
Administrative Office of the U.S. Courts
One Columbus Circle, NE
Washington, DC 20544
(800) 788-9908
http://www.fd.org

See links to federal courts at http://www.uscourts.gov/links. html (e.g., Federal Public Defender for the District of Columbia: http://www.dcfpd.org).

Federal public defenders provide representation for indigent criminal defendants prosecuted in the federal courts. Congress provides funding for federal public defender offices that provide services in U.S. district courts throughout the country. Because federal public defender offices often lack the attorneys and resources necessary to represent all indigent defendants, private attorneys may also be appointed to represent defendants in some federal cases. The compensation for appointed attorneys is established by law, so they cannot determine their own fees as they would when hired privately by a paying client.

Hong Kong Court System
Judiciary Administrator
High Court Building

38 Queensway
Hong Kong
(852) 2530-4411
http://www.info.gov.hk/jud/intro/index.htm

The court system of the Hong Kong Special Administrative Region of the People's Republic of China reflects the region's history as a former British colony. At the top of the system is the Court of Final Appeal. It hears appeals for both civil and criminal matters. The high court is composed of the court of appeals and the court of first instance. The court of appeals hears appeals for civil and criminal matters from the court of first instance, the district court, and the land tribunal. The court of first instance hears appeals from criminal cases in the magistrates courts. It also is the trial court for serious criminal charges and has unlimited jurisdiction over all civil matters. The district court has jurisdiction over civil matters with disputes over money or property worth less than $600,000. The district court may handle indictable criminal offenses with the exception of murder, manslaughter, and rape, which are handled exclusively by the court of first instance. The magistrates courts handle minor criminal cases, including those subject to brief prison terms, as well as juvenile cases. There are also limited-jurisdiction courts, such as the small-claims court. Although Hong Kong left British control and became part of the People's Republic of China, its court system is modeled on the British system, and it maintains substantial independence from the court system of China.

Judicial Conference of the United States
Administrative Office of the U.S. Courts
Thurgood Marshall Federal Judiciary Building
One Columbus Circle, NE
Washington, DC 20544
(202) 502-2600
http://www.uscourts.gov

The Judicial Conference of the United States is a committee of federal judges that serves as the policymaking body for the federal judiciary. The predecessor organization, the Conference of Senior Circuit Judges, was created by Congress in 1922. Its name was changed to Judicial Conference by an act of Congress in 1948. Later, its membership was expanded to include U.S. district judges. With the Supreme Court's chief justice as its chairperson, the conference meets several times each year to discuss the needs and priorities of the federal court system. The conference makes recommendations to Congress about needed legislation, including budget requests and the creation of new judgeships. Subcommittees appointed by the chief justice handle special tasks, such as long-range planning.

Legal Aid Ontario
375 University Avenue
Toronto, ON M5G 2G1
(800) 668-8258
http://www.legalaid.on.ca

Legal Aid Ontario is the agency that provides legal services for low-income people in Canada's most populous province. Legislation established Legal Aid Ontario as an independent, publicly funded, nonprofit agency. Eligibility for representation is based on financial need and the type of case. If approved for assistance, the client will pay nothing or only a portion of the cost of legal aid, depending on the individual's financial situation. Poverty law services that help people gain access to social assistance benefits is provided through a network of local offices throughout the province. These offices assist qualified clients with the following types of issues: tenant rights; welfare and job training; disability payments; government pensions; workplace safety and insurance; unemployment benefits; crime victim compensation; and employment rights. For other kinds of cases, the agency provides certificates that low-income people use to hire private attorneys for representation in specific kinds of cases. The attorneys use the certificates to obtain payment from the agency. For these cases, the lawyers must accept compensation rates established by the agency. The certificates can be used for several kinds of legal services. Family law services focus on cases involving child custody, visitation, and child support. Immigration and refugee law services are for matters related to refugee hearings, deportation, and detention. Criminal law services are for representation when defendants are charged with jailable offenses. The agency also provides duty counsel—attorneys at courthouses who provide advice to poor people who arrive at court without any representation.

Legal Aid Society of New York
90 Church Street
New York, NY 10007

(212) 577-3346
http://www.legal-aid.org

Founded in 1876, the Legal Aid Society of New York provides representation for poor people in criminal and civil cases in New York City. As the largest and oldest provider of legal services for indigent people, the Legal Aid Society's 900 attorneys handle more than 200,000 criminal cases each year and represent 38,000 individuals and families in civil cases. The organization handles a wide array of cases. The criminal division handles criminal appeals as well as trials and legal actions by prisoners. The civil division handles cases involving consumer protection, landlord-tenant matters, and legal protections for people who are unemployed, disabled, victimized by domestic violence, immigrants, or subjected to discrimination because of medical conditions such as AIDS. The juvenile rights division represents 90 percent of the children appearing in New York City courts for such matters as juvenile delinquency and victimization through child abuse or neglect. The organization receives government funding but also raises several million dollars from private contributions. The organization also provides opportunities for private-practice attorneys to volunteer their time for public service legal work.

Legal Services Corporation
750 First Street, NE
Washington, DC 20002-4250
(202) 336-8800
http://www.lsc.gov

The Legal Services Corporation (LSC) is a private nonprofit corporation established by Congress in 1974 to provide legal representation for poor people in certain kinds of civil cases. Its board of directors is appointed by the president of the United States. It receives funding from the federal government and provides services through a network of 179 offices across the country. Because of political controversies about the success of LSC attorneys in winning significant lawsuits against corporations and state government, limitations were placed on the kinds of cases that could be handled by LSC-funded attorneys. LSC attorneys can represent individual clients only if they meet eligibility criteria based on low income in specific categories of civil cases. LSC attorneys are not permitted to handle any civil cases, such as personal injuries, that would otherwise be handled by private attorneys on a contingency-fee basis. LSC attorneys are prohibited from filing the following activities: class-action lawsuits; challenges to welfare reform laws and regulations; lawsuits seeking to collect attorneys' fees in civil rights and other cases; lobbying for or against legislation or executive agency rules; lawsuits on behalf of prisoners; representation of tenants who have been evicted from public housing for drug-related activities by themselves or their relatives; and representation of certain categories of noncitizens. Local offices are independent agencies that are governed by their own boards of directors. They must adhere to the rules and restrictions of LSC to receive funding from the national headquarters of LSC in Washington, D.C.

Los Angeles County District Attorney's Office
210 West Temple Street
Los Angeles, CA 90012-3210
(213) 974-3512
http://da.co.la.ca.us

The Los Angeles County District Attorney's Office is responsible for prosecuting all felonies in Los Angeles County as well as all misdemeanors in unincorporated areas of the county. City prosecutors handle misdemeanors within their jurisdictions. The office has a staff of 1,035 prosecutors and 280 investigators. The office emphasizes a variety of crime-related matters in addition to the usual street crimes such as robbery and theft. These special emphases include: truancy; insurance and other fraud; crimes against law enforcement officers; child abduction; child abuse; consumer protection; election codes; environmental crimes; family violence; gangs; hate crimes; narcotics; nursing home abuse; organized crime; and police misconduct. Like many other local prosecutors' offices, this agency also has a program to assist and support crime victims and witnesses. The office is headed by the elected district attorney, who serves for a four-year term before facing the voters again if seeking reelection.

Mexican American Legal Defense and Education Fund
634 South Spring Street
Los Angeles, CA 90014
(213) 629-2512
http://www.maldef.org

The Mexican American Legal Defense and Education Fund was

founded in 1968 as a nonprofit organization to undertake litigation, advocacy, and public education, including employment discrimination and voting rights, on behalf of issues affecting Latinos. The organization also concentrates its efforts on education, immigration, and equity in distribution of public resources. The organization employs twenty-two staff attorneys. It is headquartered in Los Angeles and has regional offices in Atlanta, San Antonio, Chicago, and Washington, D.C.

NAACP Legal Defense and Education Fund
99 Hudson Street, Suite 1600
New York, NY 10013
(212) 965-2202
http://www.naacpldf.org

The NAACP Legal Defense and Education Fund (LDF) describes itself as the nation's premier civil rights law firm. It was founded in 1940 under the leadership of future U.S. Supreme Court Justice Thurgood Marshall with the purpose of pursuing a litigation strategy to fight racial discrimination in education, civil participation, and other sectors of society. The LDF has been involved in more U.S. Supreme Court cases than any other legal organization, except for the U.S. Department of Justice. The organization has won many important civil rights cases, including *Brown v. Board of Education* (1954). The organization is supported by contributions from members of the public. Its current legal cases focus on seeking the abolition of the death penalty, equal education opportunity, affirmative action, fair housing opportunities, and other issues related to racial discrimination and economic justice. The LDF was originally associated with the National Association for the Advancement of Colored People, the long-standing lobbying and political action group for African Americans. However, the LDF became a completely independent entity in 1957.

National Asian Pacific American Legal Consortium
1140 Connecticut Avenue, NW, Suite 1200
Washington, DC 20036
(202) 296-2300
http://www.napalc.org

The National Asian Pacific American Legal Consortium is a nonprofit organization founded in 1991 to advance the legal and civil rights of Asian and Pacific Americans through litigation, public education, and policy advocacy. The consortium coordinates the efforts and enhances the effectiveness of three older affiliate organizations that engaged in independent litigation and public education efforts for the same cause: Asian Pacific American Legal Center in Los Angeles; Asian Law Caucus in San Francisco; and Asian American Legal Defense and Education Fund in New York City. The consortium works on issues such as immigration, hate crimes, affirmative action, voting rights, language rights, and welfare reform.

National Association for Court Management
c/o National Center for State Courts
P.O. Box 8798
Williamsburg, VA 23187-8798
(757) 259-1841
http://www.nacmnet.org

The National Association for Court Management (NACM) is a membership organization composed of court administrators, judges, lawyers, and scholars who are interested in improving court administration. The NACM sponsors national and regional conferences to provide opportunities for members to learn about recent research, utilize training programs, and share ideas about management problems facing courts. The association's quarterly publications, *Court Manager* and *Court Communique,* disseminate information about research and court management initiatives.

National Association of Criminal Defense Lawyers
1025 Connecticut Avenue, NW, Suite 901
Washington, DC 20036
(202) 872-8600
http://www.nacdl.org

The National Association of Criminal Defense Lawyers, founded in 1958, represents some 10,000 public defenders, private criminal defense lawyers, law professors, and judges. The organization lobbies legislatures on behalf of issues important to litigators who represent criminal defendants, such as statutes affecting court procedures and individual rights in criminal justice. The organization also sponsors education and training programs to assist defense lawyers in staying up to date on recent developments in law and in enhancing their skills as courtroom advocates. The organization is also a source of information for its members about new developments concerning programs to represent indigent defendants, capital punishment, and programs to use scientific testing of old evidence to establish that people have been wrongly convicted of crimes.

National Association of Women Judges
1112 16th Street, NW, Suite 520
Washington, DC 20036
(202) 393-0222
http://www.nawj.org

The National Association of Women Judges is a membership organization that includes female and male judicial officers who are committed to the organization's goal of ending gender bias in the selection of judges and other aspects of the legal system. The association sponsors an annual conference to disseminate information about issues relevant to its members. It also develops and disseminates training materials and publications on related issues such as elder abuse, family violence, sentencing of pregnant substance abusers, and battered women's syndrome as a defense to criminal offenses.

National Bar Association
1225 11th Street, NW
Washington, DC 20001
(202) 842-3900
http://www.nationalbar.org

Because racial discrimination led to the exclusion of African Americans from professions and their organizations, the National Bar Association (NBA) was founded in 1925 to provide organizational support for African-American attorneys. The organization continued to exist and pursue its historic objectives of advancing equal justice under law even after the American Bar Association and other professional legal organizations changed their policies and admitted African Americans as members in the mid–twentieth century. It has 84 affiliate chapters and 20,000 members, including affiliate chapters in Canada, the United Kingdom, Africa, and the Caribbean. The organization sponsors conferences, seminars, awards, and other professional activities for its members. In addition, it participates in litigation and engages in legislative lobbying on issues relevant to its historic goals for the advancement of equal justice. The NBA has filed appellate briefs in cases concerning employment discrimination, affirmative action, voting rights, and other legal issues of interest to its membership. The organization's publications include directories of African-American attorneys and judges.

National Center for Juvenile Justice
710 Fifth Avenue, Suite 3000
Pittsburgh, PA 15219
(412) 227-6950
http://www.ncjj.org

The National Center for Juvenile Justice is the research division of the National Council of Juvenile and Family Court Judges. It conducts research and produces publications that are intended to improve the operation of courts addressing legal issues affecting juveniles and families, including substance abuse, domestic violence, and delinquency.

National Center for State Courts
300 Newport Avenue
Williamsburg, VA 23185
(800) 616-6164
(757) 220-0449
http://www.ncsconline.org

The National Center for State Courts (NCSC) is a nonprofit organization dedicated to the improvement of the administration of justice. The NCSC conducts studies and publishes research about case management, court reform innovations, and other topics to help guide state court systems in making decisions about how to improve their policies and practices. The NCSC was founded in 1971 at the urging of Chief Justice Warren Burger, who had a special interest in developing resources to improve court administration throughout the United States. The NCSC has published research on improving jury trial procedures, incorporating technology into court processes, judicial personnel issues, and other matters of importance for court administration. The NCSC's Institute for Court Management provides training programs for judges, court administrators, and other court personnel.

National Council of Juvenile and Family Court Judges
P.O. Box 8970
Reno, NV 89507

(775) 784-6012

http://www.ncjfcj.unr.edu/index.html

The National Council of Juvenile and Family Court Judges is an organization dedicated to improving courts that handle legal matters affecting juveniles and families. The organization focuses its efforts on research, training, and the establishment of standards for performance. Specific departments within the organization focus on the following areas: alcohol and substance abuse; continuing judicial education; family violence; permanency planning for children; and victim advocacy. Its research department is the National Center for Juvenile Justice, located in Pittsburgh, Pennsylvania.

National District Attorneys Association
99 Canal Center Plaza, Suite 510
Alexandria, VA 22314
(703) 549-9222
http://www.ndaa.org

The National District Attorneys Association is the national organization of prosecuting attorneys. It lobbies legislatures regarding issues of importance to prosecutors, including matters affecting evidentiary rules and court procedures. The organization also disseminates information about anticrime programs and prosecution tactics. It sponsors conferences at which prosecutors can gain additional information and training. An affiliated institution, the American Prosecutors Research Institute, provides research, training, and technical assistance for prosecutors throughout the United States.

National Lawyers Guild
126 University Place, 5th Floor
New York, NY 10003
(212) 627-2656
http://www.nlg.org

The National Lawyers Guild (NLG) is a membership organization of activist lawyers who are, in the words of the organization, "dedicated to the need for basic change in the structure of our political and economic system. . . . to the end that human rights shall be more sacred than property rights." The organization was founded in 1937 as a racially integrated alternative to the segregated American Bar Association. In its early years, it worked to support the labor union movement. The NLG provides resources, coordination, and contacts for attorneys who see themselves as pursuing litigation to end racism and sexism; advance the welfare and safety of minimum wage workers; protect the interests of poor people; and guard individuals' civil rights and liberties. National projects supported by the NLG are aimed at such issues as preventing abusive behavior by police, protecting immigrants from unfair treatment by the U.S. government, and preserving constitutional rights in the face of governmental efforts to increase security measures against terrorism. NLG members attempt to use public education, political protests, and other forms of mobilization in addition to litigation to achieve their objectives. The NLG has committees focused on specific issues, such as the prohibition of capital punishment and the advancement of economic justice for poor people, as well as individual chapters in most states and student chapters at many law schools.

Nigerian Court System
Federal Ministry of Justice
New Federal Secretariat Complex, 10th Floor
Wing IB, Block One
Shehu Shagari Way
Abuja, Nigeria 09-5235194
http://www.nigeria-law.org

In Nigeria's court system, the Supreme Court of Nigeria is the court of last resort. It hears appeals from the court of appeals. The court of appeals is divided into eleven districts throughout the country, each with three to five judges hearing appeals brought from the trial courts. Civil and criminal trials are held in the high court.

Pacific Legal Foundation
10360 Old Placerville Road, Suite 100
Sacramento, CA 95827
(916) 362-2833
http://www.pacificlegal.org

The Pacific Legal Foundation (PLF) is a nonprofit legal foundation supported by contributions. It was founded in 1973 with the mission of litigating cases to support the free enterprise system, private property rights, and a reduction in government regulation of business and property. It lawyers frequently square off in court against government agencies and environmental groups. For example, the PLF has fought against endangered species designations for birds and other wildlife, which, under federal and state laws, can prevent landowners and lumber companies from using rural land for logging, mining, recreation, and other profitable activities. The PLF uses litigation and public education to advance a number of policy objectives: the elimination of affirmative action; reduction in government spending on welfare; advancement of crime victims' rights; an end to rent-control laws that limit landlords' ability to raise rents; limits on lawsuits over products liability; and public funding for students who attend charter schools and other institutions instead of regular public schools. Many of the PLF's positions are shared by conservative political interests and business, and the PLF receives financial contributions from such people who support their efforts to use litigation to advance their specific policy goals.

Southern Poverty Law Center
400 Washington Avenue
Montgomery, AL 36104
(334) 956-8200
http://www.splcenter.org/splc.html

The Southern Poverty Law Center (SPLC) is a nonprofit organization supported by donations that uses litigation and public education to combat racial hatred and discrimination. Founded in 1971 by Alabama attorneys Morris Dees and Joseph Levin, the center gained success in filing civil lawsuits against hate groups that commit acts of violence. The SPLC sues on behalf of victims of this violence and has put several groups out of business by forcing them to turn over their property and other assets to victims. The SPLC also files cases concerning racial discrimination and rights violations experienced by poor people, prisoners, and others who lack political power and resources. The organization sponsors a project to monitor the activities of hate groups throughout the United States and another project to provide educational materials for teachers who want to teach their students about racial tolerance and the value of diversity.

State Attorneys General
See individual state websites at http://www.findlaw.com (e.g., Massachusetts Attorney General: http://www.ago.state.ma.us). State attorneys general are the chief legal officers for state gov-

ernment. They are elected through statewide elections. They are responsible for representing the state in legal matters concerning such issues as consumer protection, civil rights, environmental regulation, taxation, and workplace safety. Criminal prosecution in most states is handled by county- or city-level prosecutors who are elected separately and are not under the supervision or control of the state attorney general. Most state attorneys general have offices dedicated to defending the state against civil rights lawsuits by prisoners, and many also represent the state against appeals filed by convicted offenders. As elected officials, attorneys general usually establish the state's priorities for matters that will be pursued through litigation. Although most attorneys general have dozens of lawyers who work in their offices, they have limited resources and must decide which issues deserve the greatest attention. Thus the actual patterns of litigation for attorneys general will vary by state, depending on each state's particular needs and problems.

State and Local Bar Associations–United States
See individual state websites (e.g., Iowa Bar Association: http://www.iowabar.org).

In the United States, organizations that advance lawyers' interests and establish guidelines for their behavior are called bar associations. The American Bar Association (see entry above) is the largest national organization of lawyers. There are also bar associations at the state, county, and civil levels. Bar associations typically provide conference and training opportunities for attorneys so that they can keep up to date on the law and enhance their lawyering skills. Bar associations also adopt policy positions on behalf of attorneys and attempt to lobby state supreme courts and legislatures to implement rules about courts and legal processes that are preferred by practitioners. Bar associations may also cooperate with state supreme courts in developing procedures for bar exams, attorney licensing, and ethical rules and disciplinary procedures for lawyers. In many locations, bar associations establish lawyer referral services so that people in need of legal representation can be referred to licensed attorneys who specialize in an area of law relevant to their legal problems.

State Court Systems–United States
See links to state governments at http://www.findlaw.com (e.g., Washington State Courts at http://www.courts.wa.gov).

State court systems in the United States handle the vast majority of legal cases filed each year. Each state has the authority to design its own state court system. Some states have streamlined systems with central administration and only two or three levels of trial and appellate courts. Other states have myriad trial courts with different jurisdictions that are administered by political subunits, such as counties, cities, or villages. The websites for individual state court systems typically describe the organization of the courts, provide descriptions of related organizational entities, such as sentencing commissions, and provide links to recent court decisions.

Supreme Court of Appeal of South Africa
P.O. Box 258
Bloemfontein, South Africa 9300
(051) 447-2769
http://wwwserver.law.wits.ac.za/sca/about.html

The Supreme Court of Appeal of South Africa is one of the country's two courts of last resort. The constitutional court handles constitutional law cases. The supreme court of appeals handles final appeals on all other legal matters. The chief justice and other judges on the supreme court of appeals are appointed by the president with the advice of the Judicial Service Commission. The decisions of the supreme court of appeals are binding on the high court and the magistrates' courts throughout the country.

Trinidad and Tobago Court System
Department of Court Administration
Hall of Justice
Knox Street
Port of Spain, Trinidad
(868) 623-7969
http://www.ttlawcourts.org

The Supreme Court of Judicature for Trinidad and Tobago is the court of last resort created by that country's constitution. The supreme court comprises the high court and the court of appeals. The court of appeals hears appeals from the high court, which hears indictable criminal matters, family cases, and civil cases worth more than $15,000. The supreme court sits in four locations. Magistrates courts are divided into thirteen districts. These courts handle minor civil and criminal matters without the use of juries.

**United States Court of Appeals for the
Seventh Circuit (Illinois, Indiana, Wisconsin)**
219 S. Dearborn Street
Chicago, IL 60604
(312) 435-5850
http://www.ca7.uscourts.gov (links to other federal courts can
be found at: http://www.uscourts.gov/links.html).

United States Courts of Appeals hear appeals from decisions of
U.S. district courts, the trial courts of the federal system. Jurisdiction is divided into circuits, each of which represents a specific geographical area of the country. For example, the U.S. Court of Appeals for the Seventh Circuit handles appeals from decisions in federal trial courts in Illinois, Indiana, and Wisconsin. Appeals must be filed in a specified time period after the conclusion of a trial. Appeals must allege specific errors of law or procedure in the processing of a case in the district court. Appeals courts do not hear evidence, conduct trials, or determine the guilt of defendants. Their function is to examine allegations about trial court errors, determine if errors occurred, and then decide whether any errors were sufficiently serious to warrant a reversal of the district court decision or an order for a new trial in the district court. Appeals are heard by three-judge panels.

United States Department of Justice
950 Pennsylvania Avenue, NW
Washington, DC 20530-0001
(202) 353-1555
http://www.usdoj.gov

The U.S. Department of Justice provides legal services for the U.S. government. The department is headed by the U.S. Attorney General, a member of the president's cabinet. The president appoints U.S. attorneys to serve as the federal prosecutor in U.S. district courts. These federal prosecutors work under the direction and supervision of the U.S. Attorney General. The central office in Washington, D.C., houses divisions that specialize in enforcing specific federal criminal laws, civil rights laws, and federal regulations. These divisions include a civil rights division that enforces laws against discrimination, an antitrust division that enforces federal law regulating corporations, and a tax division that enforces federal taxation laws. The department also contains many of the federal government's important criminal justice agencies, including: the Federal Bureau of Investigation, which investigates federal crimes; the U.S. Marshals Service, which provides security at federal courthouses and tracks down fugitives from the law; the Drug Enforcement Administration, which enforces federal drug laws; and the Bureau of Prisons, which administers the federal prison system. One of the top officials in the Department of Justice is the solicitor general, the lawyer who represents the U.S. government in cases before the Supreme Court.

United States District Court for the Northern District of Ohio (Cleveland, Akron, Youngstown, Toledo)
210 Superior Avenue
Cleveland, OH 44114
(216) 522-4355
http://www.ohnd.uscourts.gov (links to other federal courts can be found at: http://www.uscourts.gov/links.html).

U.S. district courts are the trial courts of the federal judicial system. The United States is divided into ninety-four districts, each with its own U.S. district court. Some districts encompass entire states (e.g., if the states are relatively small, such as Massachusetts and Connecticut). Other states are divided into multiple districts (e.g., Ohio, which is divided into a northern district and a southern district). Within each district there may be multiple courthouses. For example, there are four courthouse locations in the northern district of Ohio: Cleveland, Akron, Toledo, and Youngstown. There may be multiple district judges in each courthouse, although smaller courthouses tend to have one courtroom and a single judge. Criminal and civil cases concerning federal law are filed and processed in U.S. district courts. In these courts, federal judges preside over jury trials that determine the guilt of defendants charged with federal offenses or the verdicts in civil cases when lawsuits are filed under federal law or involve litigants who are residents of different states in disputes worth more than $75,000.

United States Sentencing Commission
One Columbus Circle, NE
Washington, DC 20002-8002
(202) 502-4500
http://www.ussc.gov

The U.S. Sentencing Commission was created by act of Congress in 1984. The agency is responsible for developing sentencing guidelines to be used by federal judges in imposing punishments on people convicted of federal crimes. The sentencing guidelines were intended to equalize sentences so that similarly situated offenders would receive similar sentences. In the process of seeking to equalize sentences, the guidelines also made sentences more severe and significantly reduced judges' discretion to look at individual situations in developing appropriate punishments. Under sentencing guidelines, punishments are based on a combination of two factors: the seriousness of the offense, and the offender's criminal history. The U.S. Sentencing Commission is composed of federal judges and attorneys. It is required to undertake studies of the implementation and consequences of sentencing guidelines to suggest adjustments in the mandated punishments that are to be imposed in federal cases.

United States Supreme Court
Public Information Office
One First Street, NE
Washington, DC 20543
(202) 479-3211
http://www.supremecourtus.gov

The United States Supreme Court is the only court explicitly created by the U.S. Constitution. The Court is composed of nine justices who are appointed by the president, confirmed by the U.S. Senate, and serve during good behavior, which effectively means lifetime appointment. Over the course of history, several justices have served on the Court for more than thirty years. It is not unusual for justices to continue serving when they are in their seventies, and some justices have remained on the Court past the age of 80. The Court controls its own docket by selecting only 75–85 cases each year from among the 6,000–7,000 petitions filed annually seeking reviews of decisions by state supreme courts and U.S. courts of appeals. The justices decide cases concerning federal constitutional and statutory law issues and, in a few cases, disputes between different states or between residents of different states. If a case concerns only an issue of state law, then the relevant state supreme court, rather than the U.S. Supreme Court, is the final authority over the issue. After selecting cases for hearing, the Court schedules oral arguments from October through May.

The oral arguments are open to the public, but they are not televised. Justices read written arguments, listen to hour-long oral arguments, and then discuss and vote on the cases in private conferences. A five-member majority can determine the outcome of a case. Because the Supreme Court is the highest court in the federal system and the ultimate authority over the interpretation of the U.S. Constitution, its decisions set precedents that must be followed by lower courts throughout the country. During the twentieth century, the Court's interpretations of the Constitution shaped many important public policy issues, including abortion, affirmative action, school desegregation, rights of criminal defendants, and capital punishment.

Vera Institute of Justice
233 Broadway, 12th Floor
New York, NY 10279
(212) 334-1300
http://www.vera.org

The Vera Institute of Justice is a nonprofit organization that develops innovative reforms for problems in the criminal justice system and then works with agencies to implement and evaluate them. The institute first became nationally famous for developing a bail reform initiative that helped poor people gain release prior to trial and then provided them with advice and assistance to assure that they would return to court. The program demonstrated that innovative approaches to pretrial release could alleviate the problem of poor suspects sitting needlessly in jail while awaiting the processing of their cases. The institute is involved in a variety of projects concerning courts. For example, it advises a national demonstration project in three states to use closer judicial supervision of domestic violence cases. It developed an online tutorial for managers of public defender organizations. It helped to develop and guide justice assistance centers in Russia and South Africa that are intended to improve the effectiveness of courts and justice processes.

Washington Legal Foundation
2009 Massachusetts Avenue, NW
Washington, DC 20036
(202) 588-0302
http://www.wlf.org

The Washington Legal Foundation (WLF) is an independent organization that litigates cases to advance its goals for "individual freedom, limited government, free market economy, and a strong national security and defense." The WLF litigates cases concerning "business civil liberties," including businesses' ability to advertise and provide information to the public without undue interference from governmental regulation. The WLF has gone to court to oppose efforts by other interest groups to limit the defense and international relations powers of the president and executive agencies. The WLF has also presented arguments in court to oppose the use of environmental regulations to limit military training exercises, to support deportation of aliens with criminal records, and to support the application of the death penalty to people convicted of spying on behalf of foreign governments. The WLF has also supported tort reform that would limit product-liability and personal-injury lawsuits against corporations and government. The organization has also monitored and opposed the Food and Drug Administration for actions that it perceives as impeding the success of U.S. companies that manufacture medicines. The WLF is supported by donations. It also pursues its goals through public education and the publication of materials on topics of interest.

7

Print Resources

Books and other materials about courts and trials focus on a variety of topics. Some materials provide overviews of court systems, including organizations and processes. Because nations and subdivisions of nations, such as states, can have their own individual court systems, such materials are usually specific to a particular setting and not necessarily common to other contexts. Other books and articles present research studies about how courts work and the consequences of court processes. These materials often focus on such factors as the volume of cases processed by courts, costs associated with trials and other forms of case processing, and the nature of outcomes of cases. Other books and articles provide real-life accounts of specific trials or the lives of particular judges and lawyers. These accounts often best convey the sense of drama and human emotion that can be central elements of court proceedings that will have a significant impact.

Books

Abraham, Henry J. *The Judicial Process*, 6th ed. New York: Oxford University Press, 1993.

Written by one of the most prominent judicial scholars in the United States, this book provides detailed descriptions of the structure of courts, the personnel who work within courts, trial processes, and the legal authority of courts. Unlike most books that focus solely on a single country, this book provides a comparative perspective by also examining the courts of England and France.

The comparative material provides insights about the U.S. court system, which is the primary subject of the book.

Adler, Stephen J. *The Jury: Disorder in the Court.* New York: Doubleday, 1994.

Juries are mysterious entities because they operate behind closed doors and produce their decisions without explanation. This book sheds light on jury processes by using interviews with jurors, lawyers, and judges to reconstruct the trials and jury deliberations in a set of specific cases. The book reveals that jury trials are uncertain human processes that can be shaped by reactions and emotions as jurors attempt with the utmost seriousness to understand and analyze complex and difficult cases presented through adversarial trial proceedings. Each trial is presented in story form with the jurors' thoughts and discussions reconstructed from interviews. Thus the reader is placed inside the jury and given an unparalleled opportunity to hear and feel the thinking and emotions that determined the fates of specific individuals called before the court.

Baum, Lawrence. *The Puzzle of Judicial Behavior.* Ann Arbor: University of Michigan Press, 1997.

There are many theories about why judges decide cases as they do. Legal studies scholars often study judges' decisions to determine their causes and effects because these decisions are especially important in determining the fates of people drawn into the legal system. This book reviews the studies of judicial decision-making to organize the current state of knowledge about how and why judges make decisions. The book examines the effect of judges' attitudes, values, and policy preferences. Judges are also influenced by their role orientation, which is their conception of what judges ought to do. In addition, interactions between judges can influence appellate decisions as judges persuade each other about the best course of action. The book documents how decisions produced by courts are genuinely human decisions made by imperfect people. Formal rules of law influence decisions, but they do not determine the outcomes of cases. Civil litigants, criminal defendants, and appellants have their fates significantly determined by the decisions of human beings who possess official authority within the system.

Belli, Melvin. *My Life on Trial.* New York: William Morrow, 1976.

The autobiography of a prominent twentieth-century lawyer. Belli became famous for representing prominent people and for taking controversial cases. He handled criminal defense as well as tort cases on behalf of individual clients. He represented Jack Ruby, the man who shot Lee Harvey Oswald, the alleged assassin of President John F. Kennedy. He also represented African-American prisoners noted for their 1960s political activism who were killed by California prison guards. Other famous cases included representation of boxing champion George Foreman and tennis star Maureen Connolly in civil lawsuits. The cases described by Belli are not typical cases in the U.S. court system, but his book conveys the importance and prominence of legal processes in addressing issues of public controversy.

Black, Roy. *Black's Law: A Criminal Lawyer Reveals His Defense Strategies in Four Cliffhanger Cases.* New York: Simon and Schuster, 1999.

In this book, one of the most prominent criminal defense lawyers in the United States describes in detail his strategies and struggles to advance his clients' interests in difficult, controversial cases. In one case, there are political pressures and risks of a race riot as the lawyer defends a police officer who is charged with killing a troubled youth. Another case concerns efforts to save a mentally ill client who is facing the death penalty. The other cases involve the difficulties in persuading jurors when there is strong evidence to support the prosecution. This book helps readers to see how a lawyer thinks, as it also illuminates the difficult decisions and controversies that arise in court cases.

Bodenhamer, David J. *Fair Trial: Rights of the Accused in U.S. History.* New York: Oxford University Press, 1992.

In this brief, readable volume, a historian traces the history of rights in criminal trials. The book discusses criminal trials and associated protections for defendants in the colonial era and changes that began to occur during the period of revolution and independence. A chapter describes trial processes in the period prior to the ratification of the Fourteenth Amendment after the conclusion of the Civil War. The Fourteenth Amendment was the first constitutional amendment to provide individuals with explicit legal protections against the actions of state and local governments as well as against the federal government. After the Fourteenth Amendment became law, the Supreme Court went through a gradual process of taking rights applicable in federal trials and making them applicable to state trials. The process did not come to its conclusion until the 1960s. Afterward, the composition of the U.S. Supreme Court became more conservative, and new judicial decisions refined and reduced legal protections throughout the remaining years of the twentieth century.

Canon, Bradley C., and Charles A. Johnson. *Judicial Policies: Implementation and Impact*, 2nd ed. Washington, DC: Congressional Quarterly Press, 1999.

U.S. courts have affected public policy by interpreting the U.S. Constitution and statutes in ways that instruct governmental officials about what they must and must not do. Judicial decisions have affected policies on abortion, school desegregation, and other issues. This book provides a description of courts' policymaking influence with special attention to the implementation and impact of those policies. The book is especially useful in describing and analyzing the impediments to successful implementation of court decisions. Because judges' decisions are not self-effectuating, the actual implementation of those decisions depends on the understanding and cooperation of lower level judges, police officers, and others who must make sure that the decisions are carried out as intended. In actuality, these actors often fail to implement policies as intended. These failures are sometimes intentional, but in other cases they stem from flaws in the process for communicating decisions or a lack of resources that impedes complete implementation. The book provides a readable and thorough picture of the weaknesses in courts' roles as policymaking institutions.

Choper, Jesse, ed. *The Supreme Court and Its Justices*, 2nd ed. Chicago: American Bar Association, 2001.

This volume brings together edited versions of fifty articles on the U.S. Supreme Court that appeared in the *ABA Journal*. The volume includes twenty-five articles analyzing individual justice who have served on the Supreme Court. Other articles discuss the selection of justices, lawyers' performances in presenting cases to the Court, and the Court's internal processes. Because the volume includes the work of authors who have diverse perspectives, the articles convey many of the debates among lawyers and scholars about the nature and importance of the Court's role and operations.

Cole, George F., Stanislaw J. Frankowski, and Marc G. Gertz. *Major Criminal Justice Systems: A Comparative Study,* 2nd ed. Newbury Park, CA: Sage, 1987.

This volume contains detailed descriptions of different countries' criminal justice systems, including their courts and trials. The articles about each country are written by lawyers and scholars from those countries who have training and experience with the system that they are describing and analyzing. The countries covered in the book include the United States, England, Nigeria, Germany, Sweden, Japan, and the old socialist systems of the Soviet Union and Poland. The book provides an excellent resource for gaining an understanding of similarities and differences among legal systems.

Cooper, Phillip J. *Hard Judicial Choices.* New York: Oxford University Press, 1988.

Policymaking by U.S. courts is a controversial subject because many observers believe that it leads judges to use powers that are reserved to officials in the legislative and executive branches. This book sheds light on the use of litigation to shape public policy by examining the decisions of federal trial court judges who have been presented with cases raising significant public policy issues. The book provides detailed examinations of court cases concerning racial discrimination in housing and education, access to public mental health facilities, prison reform, and police practices. These are among the most difficult issues that courts have faced. When presented in the form of litigation, such issues challenge judges to use law in innovative ways to achieve societal goals. Because judges are not experts on policy subjects and the litigation process does not always provide the best mechanism for illuminating information about policy issues, cases about major societal controversies place courts in a difficult position. This book demonstrates the challenges facing trial judges in litigation raising policy issues and reinforces concerns about the effectiveness of judicial policymaking.

Dees, Morris. *A Season for Justice.* New York: Scribner, 1991.

This is the autobiography of the activist civil rights lawyer who founded the Southern Poverty Law Center. Morris Dees, a white

Southerner, grew up on a farm in Alabama and attended the University of Alabama. In college, law school, and the years following law school, he focused on his successful business interests. Eventually, he had a change of heart about the kind of work to which he should dedicate his life. He sold his business and began to file lawsuits against racial discrimination and inequality. Dees tells the story of his transformation as a civil rights lawyer, including his development of the litigation strategy of filing civil liability lawsuits against hate groups that injure or kill people through acts of violence. Through this strategy, Dees was able to take property and financial assets from these groups and thereby render them less effective in their efforts to advance racial hatred and discrimination. This book became the basis for a made-for-TV movie.

Dershowitz, Alan M. *The Best Defense.* New York: Random House, 1982.

Harvard law professor Alan Dershowitz is one of America's best-known and most outspoken lawyers. In this book, he tells the inside story of several of his most famous cases. The cases range from a politically motivated bombing to the defense of people charged with obscenity offenses based on their involvement with pornographic films. In the course of discussing his strategies in the cases, Dershowitz also analyzes important issues of constitutional rights and flaws in the judicial system.

Eisenstein, James, Roy B. Flemming, and Peter F. Nardulli. *The Contours of Justice: Communities and Their Courts.* Boston: Little, Brown, 1988.

This book presents results from one of the most fascinating and famous studies of local courts and their trial processes. For each of the following states, Pennsylvania, Michigan, and Illinois, the authors selected three counties for study. Within each state, one county was an urban county, another was rural, and the third was suburban. Through extensive interviews with lawyers and judges as well as analysis of case-processing information, the authors present an illuminating description and analysis of how cases are really processed within the lower state courts that handle the vast majority of legal matters within the United States. The authors found that a county's courthouse community, composed of lawyers, judges, and other courthouse workers, developed informal practices and relationships based on local values and political influence. These informal practices and relationships were largely responsible for determining how cases were processed within each courthouse because discretionary decisions by judges and lawyers are the primary determinants of case outcomes. The study provided further proof that cases are not determined by formal principles of law but rather by myriad discretionary decisions and negotiations that occur outside of public view. This book is especially readable and interesting because the authors use so many quoted descriptions and comments from lawyers and judges who are actually deciding cases within the nine counties studied.

Epstein, Lee, and Joseph Kobylka. *The Supreme Court and Legal Change.* Chapel Hill: University of North Carolina Press, 1992.

By focusing on the issues of capital punishment and abortion, the authors show how interest groups use litigation to attempt to influence judicial policymaking. It is well known that interest groups use litigation strategies through which they sponsor or adopt cases that they believe may advance their policy goals. Less well understood is how interest groups formulate their actual arguments and how these arguments may influence courts' decisions. This book sheds light on these issues through a careful examination of the actual arguments presented by interest groups, showing how those arguments affected judicial opinions.

Feeley, Malcolm. *Court Reform on Trial.* New York: Basic Books, 1984.

This book reports on studies of several different court reforms and provides an analysis to explain why it is so difficult to reform courts and their procedures. Courts are difficult institutions to reform. Frequently, observers make suggestions about how courts could be changed to improve their efficiency and effectiveness. These reforms are seldom adopted, and even if they are implemented, they often fail to fulfill their objectives. The reforms examined include bail reform, mandatory sentencing, and speedy trial laws. In each case, the success of the reform was hindered by institutional characteristics. Courts are fragmented institutions that are typically controlled at the county or city level. They are not under the effective supervision and control of a centralized authority, such as a state government. Thus individual judges are the primary sources of power within courthouses, and they possess the power to determine whether reforms will be implemented fully. In addition, many reform proposals are based on ideal conceptions of courts and do not adequately consider the role of discretionary decisionmaking in determining case outcomes. Moreover, the evaluation of court reform programs is frequently in the hands of advocates who are unwilling to fully recognize and admit that their own ideas have fallen short of original objectives. This book provides an insightful analysis of courts and their institutional characteristics. Its information conveys an understanding of why courts are more independent, autonomous, and difficult to change than many other government agencies and institutions.

Forer, Lois G. *Money and Justice: Who Owns the Courts?* New York: W. W. Norton, 1984.

Lois Forer was a trial judge in the Philadelphia court system. She uses her experiences to provide firsthand examples of the disadvantages imposed on poor people who are drawn into the legal system. She examines criminal, civil, and family matters. Her analyses also consider the organization of courts and the self-interested actions of the legal professionals who decide the fates of citizens. Judge Forer concludes the book with thought-provoking suggestions to reform courts and judicial processes to increase accessibility, fairness, and equal treatment for less affluent people.

Giles, Robert, and Robert W. Snyder, eds. *Covering the Courts: Free Press, Fair Trials, and Journalistic Performance.* New Brunswick, NJ: Transaction, 1999.

This volume contains a series of articles examining media access to court proceedings and the public's access to information about trials. The articles focus on a number of topics. Several articles examine the case of Timothy McVeigh, the man convicted and executed for bombing the federal building in Oklahoma City. Other articles examine whether trials should be televised. Other articles contain interviews with lawyers and judges, as well as commentary from judges about the role and impact of the news media in trial processes.

Glick, Henry R. *Courts, Politics, and Justice,* 2nd ed. New York: McGraw-Hill, 1988.

This volume is a general work that describes courts and their processes. Various chapters discuss the structure of courts, the role of lawyers, the selection of judges, civil litigation, criminal prosecution, trials, and judicial policymaking.

Goodman, James. *Stories of Scottsboro.* New York: Vintage, 1994.

In this book, a historian presents a detailed account of one of the most famous legal cases in U.S. history. In 1931 several unemployed African-American youths got into an altercation with several similarly situated white men as both groups hitched a ride on a freight train crossing Alabama. They were all looking for work during the Great Depression. When the train stopped at a station near Scottsboro, Alabama, the African-American youths were accused of attempting to murder the white men and, more significantly, raping two white women who were also on the train. The defendants were quickly convicted, without being represented by attorneys, and they were sentenced to death. Their case became highly publicized and led to protest marches in the North, especially after one of the white women recanted and said that she had not been raped. Eventually, the U.S. Supreme Court ruled that the defendants were entitled to a new trial because poor people must be represented by a defense attorney when facing capital charges. The book details the alleged crime and places the events, including the trial, in the context of the segregated South during the 1930s. The book provides a revealing picture of the U.S. justice system, as well as its glaring contradictions and deficiencies when issues of race arose in criminal cases during the early part of the twentieth century.

Harr, Jonathan. *A Civil Action.* New York: Vintage, 1995.

The author spent many months following an attorney through each step of a complex civil lawsuit concerning children's cancer deaths in a community in which manufacturing enterprises had polluted the groundwater. The step-by-step descriptions of lawyers' meetings, encounters with clients, and courtroom action provide unparalleled insights into the workings of the civil justice process. The lawyer in the case faced many obstacles, including the difficulties involved in proving which corporations were responsible for the pollution, establishing connections between the pollution and abnormal cancer rates in the community, and fending off large corporations that had unlimited funds at their disposal to defend themselves in court. The book does an excellent job of demonstrating the difficult decisions that lawyers face in trying to determine whether their clients' interests would be best served by taking a case all the way to trial or by negotiating a settlement. For those who have idealistic beliefs in the U.S. legal system's effectiveness in achieving justice, the book raises disturbing questions. The details of the case are so vivid that the book reads like a novel rather than a description of an actual case. When it was published in 1995, the book received the National Book Critics Circle Award, and it was later made into a major motion picture.

Heumann, Milton. *Plea Bargaining: The Experiences of Prosecutors, Judges, and Defense Attorneys.* Chicago: University of Chicago Press, 1977.

Based on detailed interviews with judges and lawyers involved in criminal cases, the author examines how courtroom actors learn about and adapt to plea bargaining when they begin their careers in criminal court. More than 90 percent of all criminal convictions are obtained through negotiated agreements rather than trials. Predictions about probable trial verdicts shape the nature of the negotiated outcomes that are the basis of agreements among prosecutors, defense attorneys, and judges. Like members of the public, some legal professionals initially believe that plea bargaining somehow undercuts the ends of justice and that cases should really go through the trial process. As they interact with others in the courthouse and come to understand the nature of criminal cases, however, they learn the benefits of plea bargaining, and they adapt their expectations and performance to participate in negotiating outcomes. The book is especially interesting for lay readers because it contains so many descriptions of the plea-bargaining process through the eyes of legal professionals who learned how to participate in it.

Irons, Peter. *The Courage of Their Convictions: Sixteen Americans Who Fought Their Way to the Supreme Court.* New York: Free Press, 1988.

When the U.S. Supreme Court decides a case, its decision usually shapes law and policy while triggering debates about whether the decision was proper. The individual people whose cases are being decided by the Supreme Court are often ignored amid the debates about their cases as public policy issues. This book lets those individuals speak for themselves. It contains first-person accounts by the actual people who were drawn into the justice system and subsequently pushed their cases all the way to the nation's highest court, often at substantial cost to themselves, both financially and personally. The book provides fascinating details about the human-interest stories that underlie major court cases. The book includes cases about freedom of speech, the right to privacy, discrimination, and other issues. Not all of these individuals won their cases. However, they all demonstrated a remarkable commitment to the idea that courts, law, and trial processes should advance the truth and provide protections for the rights of individuals.

Jacob, Herbert, et al. *Courts, Law, and Politics in Comparative Perspective.* New Haven, CT: Yale University Press, 1996.

This book contains detailed descriptions of several countries' legal systems. One chapter is about the United States, another focuses on England, and the others cover Germany, France, and Japan. Each chapter provides descriptions and analyses of the organization of courts and procedures used in trials. The book points out differences in judges' roles, rules of courtroom procedure and evidence, and opportunities for verdicts by juries. Often, one can gain new insights into the justice system in one's own country by comparing it to systems elsewhere. The use of detailed comparisons provides a basis for considering how specific kinds of court reforms may alter the nature of case processing and, perhaps, better advance the goal of achieving equal justice, fair outcomes, and accurate decisions.

Lazarus, Edward. *Closed Chambers.* New York: Times Books, 1998.

The Supreme Court maintains such secrecy that justices and their law clerks consistently refuse to comment publicly on what transpired in the process of deciding specific cases. If law clerks speak to the news media or others, they know that they will be fired and probably harm their job prospects for life for violating the Court's sacred tradition of secrecy. Thus *Closed Chambers* created a minor splash upon publication, because it is the first insider's account of the conflicts, interactions, and processes that shape the high court's decisions. The author was a law clerk for Justice Harry

Blackmun during a year in which there were many controversial cases that divided the justices, such as cases concerning capital punishment. The author claims to use interviews with law clerks to reconstruct the internal battles within the Court while attempting to avoid accusations that he has violated his own pledge to avoid revealing confidential information. The book provides fascinating insights into the personalities of the justices, the political battles among liberal and conservative law clerks, and the strategic interactions by law clerks and justices that seek to influence the outcomes of cases.

Levine, James P. *Juries and Politics.* Pacific Grove, CA: Brooks/Cole, 1992.

Juries play an important role in American trial processes. This volume is one of the few that focuses comprehensively on juries and their role in trials. With a focus on the United States, the book reviews the history of juries. It describes jury-selection procedures that, in the eyes of the lawyers, provide the critical moment in which cases are won or lost. Lawyers often believe that cases are determined by who is selected to serve on the jury because their preferences and biases will determine how the evidence is perceived. The book discusses research on jury decisionmaking, including juror biases and interactions among jurors during deliberations. There is also a chapter on jury nullification (the power of U.S. juries to go against the principles of law to achieve their own sense of justice). The book is relatively brief, readable, and comprehensive.

Mays, G. Larry, and Peter R. Gregware, eds. *Courts and Justice: A Reader.* Prospect Heights, IL: Waveland, 1995.

This volume contains twenty-nine articles on various aspects of courts and their operations, including topics that are not typically covered in other books on courts. The articles are written by leading scholars and thereby present original, insightful analyses. In addition to presenting articles about juries, prosecutors, and defense attorneys, the volume also addresses such neglected subjects as alternative dispute resolution, alternative sentences, and secret trials in Colombia. The book's breadth of coverage provides good information about the operation of courts, as well as comparative topics with perspectives on alternative approaches in other countries.

McCoy, Candace. *Politics and Plea Bargaining.* Philadelphia: University of Pennsylvania Press, 1993.

The public often perceives plea bargaining as subverting the trial process and defeating the goal of achieving justice. Plea bargaining is perceived as giving defendants lighter punishments than they truly deserve. This book examines the role of plea bargaining in state trial courts by discussing a California initiative through which voters abolished plea bargaining in the state's superior courts. The book provides a marvelous review of research on plea bargaining that gives a fuller picture of the benefits for the system as well as the justice that is produced by negotiated outcomes. In addition, the book illustrates the power of discretion, revealing that the prohibition on plea bargaining in superior courts was defeated by moving plea negotiations to an earlier pretrial phase in the district and municipal courts. Moreover, some judges and lawyers disobeyed the ban and acted informally to seek agreements that would spare the system the time and expense of trials while also imposing appropriate punishments. The book illuminates the inevitable influence of informal processes and discretionary decisions in courts.

Morgan, Charles. *One Man, One Voice.* New York: Holt, Rinehart and Winston, 1979.

The author, a prominent civil rights lawyer, presents his autobiography, with particular attention to his most prominent cases. Morgan was forced to leave Alabama after receiving death threats when he spoke out about racial injustice in the aftermath of a church bombing that killed four young African-American girls in 1963. A year later he went to Atlanta to establish the southern regional office of the American Civil Liberties Union (ACLU). Later, he served as the director of the ACLU's national legislative office in Washington, D.C. During his years as a lawyer, he handled many important cases, including *Reynolds v. Sims* (1964), in which the Supreme Court ordered states to reapportion legislative districts to give equal representation to all constituents, urban and rural. He handled cases to combat racial segregation in jury selection and prisons. He also represented boxer Muhammad Ali in his successful legal fight for religious freedom and conscientious-objector status during the Vietnam War. He also represented civil rights leader Julian Bond in his struggle to gain his rightful place in the Georgia legislature after other legislators refused to seat him because of his opposition to the Vietnam War. Later, Morgan led the legal effort for the impeachment of President Richard Nixon. The book provides an especially illuminating picture of a period in U.S. history—the 1960s and 1970s—when litigation played an important role in addressing social controversies concerning civil rights, the antiwar movement, and government accountability.

Nolan, James L. Jr., ed. *Drug Courts in Theory and in Practice.* Hawthorne, NY: Aldine de Gruyter, 2002.

This book presents studies and assessments of the drug court innovation implemented in many judicial systems. Individual chapters examine how drug courts have worked in specific cities. Other chapters assess how the drug court setting changes the roles of courtroom actors as they focus on diverting offenders to treatment and supervision rather than merely punishment.

O'Brien, David M., ed. *Judges on Judging: Views from the Bench.* Chatham, NJ: Chatham House, 1997.

This volume presents writings by judges about court processes and their roles as judicial officers. Topics of articles range from the trial judge's role in the adversary process to U.S. Supreme Court justices' discussions of their approaches to constitutional interpretation. Most of the judges represented in the volume are appellate judges, so trial processes receive significantly less coverage. Overall, the articles provide an insightful picture of judges' views of themselves and how they carry out their responsibilities.

Perry, H. W. Jr. *Deciding to Decide: Agenda Setting in the United States Supreme Court.* Cambridge: Harvard University Press, 1991.

This award-winning book examines the unseen internal processes within the U.S. Supreme Court for deciding which cases to accept for hearing. The Supreme Court gives full consideration and decisions to only 75–85 cases from among the 6,000–7,000 presented to it each year. The author is one of the few people ever to have the opportunity to interview Supreme Court justices about how the highest court in the United States really operates. Normally, Supreme Court justices refuse to discuss court operations to protect the image and secrecy that are important components of the high court's legitimacy. The study documents the important role and influence of law clerks, who are recent law school graduates responsible for reviewing and summarizing the petitions sent to the Court for consideration. The book presents an especially interesting and important description of the hidden processes within appellate courts that help to determine which cases will receive judicial attention and which cases will never have the opportunity to be reexamined by the nation's top court.

Polenberg, Richard. *Fighting Faiths: The Abrams Case, the Supreme Court, and Free Speech.* New York: Penguin, 1987.

The author uses a famous World War I–era legal case concerning freedom of speech to illustrate issues of political conflict and civil liberties that faced the United States early in the twentieth century. In the *Abrams* case, political radicals were prosecuted for passing out leaflets urging people to oppose U.S. intervention in the Russian Revolution. The defendants were convicted and sentenced to prison as a result of a famous Supreme Court decision that defined the right to free speech very narrowly. Indeed, the meaning of free speech became so much broader in the 1960s and thereafter that the defendants would not have been prosecuted if they had committed the same acts later in the century. This award-winning book shows the links between constitutional litigation and social history so that the role of courts and trials can be recognized as more important than decisionmaking processes that merely affect specific individuals.

Provine, Doris Marie. *Judging Credentials: Nonlawyer Judges and the Politics of Professionalism.* Chicago: University of Chicago Press, 1986.

This book examines the performance of nonlawyer judges in courts in the United States. Nonlawyer judges are familiar in England and the former British colonies that use magistrates courts to decide minor criminal and civil matters. In the United States, however, there is often a mistaken assumption that people must be trained as lawyers before they can become judges. This is true for most courts, but not for the lowest level (limited-jurisdiction courts in rural areas). Provine's book examines the history of nonlawyer judges and compares their performance to that of judges who have training in law. The book makes a provocative case for pushing aside prevailing assumptions that judges must have legal training. Moreover, the book argues that the emphasis on law-trained judges stems more from protecting the interests of the legal profession than from ensuring valuable service to society in the performance of judging.

Rehnquist, William H. *The Supreme Court: How It Was, How It Is.* New York: William Morrow, 1987.

A history and description of the U.S. Supreme Court written by the person who has served as an associate justice since 1972 and as chief justice since 1986. Rehnquist begins his story with his experiences as a law clerk at the Supreme Court in the 1950s. He discusses several of the Court's monumental cases before tracing the complete history of the Court. He ends with a description of the Court's current processes for making decisions but does not include any revealing information that might diminish the Court's image and reinforce critics' claims about the political influences that shape judicial decisions.

Rosenberg, Gerald N. *The Hollow Hope: Can Courts Bring about Social Change?* Chicago: University of Chicago Press, 1991.

The influence of courts over public policy is well recognized. Many interest groups plan litigation strategies in an effort to persuade judges to decide legal issues that will shape public policy concerning such issues as affirmative action, criminal justice, abortion, and the environment. This important and controversial book calls into question the effectiveness of courts in effecting social change. The legacy of the U.S. Supreme Court's decision on school segregation in *Brown v. Board of Education* (1954) led many observers to conclude that courts are powerful policymaking institutions. Instead, this book argues that many court decisions are largely symbolic statements that have only a modest impact on the actual policies implemented in society that determine the behavior of government officials. The author presents evidence showing gaps between judicial pronouncements and the actual policies affecting society.

Schwartz, Bernard. *Decision: How the Supreme Court Decides Cases.* New York: Oxford University Press, 1996.

The U.S. Supreme Court is the most visible and powerful court in the United States. However, the processes of deciding individual cases are hidden behind closed doors. This book examines the processes used by the Supreme Court in deciding important cases that set legal precedents and shape public policy. The author used the papers of former Supreme Court justices, some of which were publicly available in research libraries and others of which were made available to the author privately, to reconstruct the steps in the decisionmaking processes for key cases. Because the author had access to memoranda that were written by and circulated among the justices as stepping stones toward the ultimate decisions, it is possible to learn how specific decisions were shaped. Moreover, at a general level, one can see how the justices' interactive processes helped to persuade particular members to shift their views on particular issues. The book reveals a human process that is guided by the boundaries of law.

Simenhoff, Mark, ed. *My First Year as a Lawyer.* New York: Penguin, 1994.

How do inexperienced lawyers make the transition from law student to attorney? This book uses the first-person accounts of eighteen lawyers to describe actual personal experiences that shaped people's legal careers. The accounts include difficult situations in which lawyers must help people cope with crises, including the deaths of family members and the stress of facing criminal charges. These accounts illuminate how the court system works as these lawyers recall their first learning experiences, as well as missteps, in attempting to perform properly on behalf of their clients. Because the material is presented as first-person accounts by experienced attorneys who now can give perspective to their initial encounters with the court system, the book provides useful insights into courts and trials.

Smith, Christopher E. *Courts and the Poor.* Chicago: Nelson-Hall, 1991.

This book reviews the impact of courts and judicial processes on low-income people by summarizing research about the disadvantages experienced by the poor in their contacts with the court system. Additional coverage analyzes the impact of constitutional law on the poor, including the lack of any equal protection right to prevent the government from enacting laws that treat the poor less favorably than middle-class and affluent people. Chapters cover such topics as the criminal justice system, civil litigation, constitutional law, legal processes in administrative agencies, and comparisons with court systems in European countries.

————. *Courts and Public Policy.* Chicago: Nelson-Hall, 1993.

Court decisions can have a significant impact on public policy. In the United States, courts' influence over public policy is the source of controversy because judicial action is often perceived as clashing with democratic governing processes. This book analyzes the legitimacy and capacity of courts for making effective public policy through litigation processes. It analyzes competing arguments about courts' actions and impact. Chapters focus on judicial action affecting specific policy issues, including abortion, school desegregation, school finance reform, and prison reform. One chapter examines the influence of civil liability lawsuits and how tort law shapes various public policy by affecting the behavior of government agencies and businesses.

————. *Courts, Politics, and the Judicial Process,* 2d ed. Chicago: Nelson-Hall, 1997.

This is a general work and discusses the organization and processes in the federal and state court systems in the United States. Chapters discuss criminal case processing and civil lawsuits. The book also discusses the selection of judges, the legal profession, and judicial policymaking and compares aspects of the U.S. legal system to those of other countries.

Stern, Gerald. *The Buffalo Creek Disaster: How the Survivors of One of the Worst Disasters in Coal-Mining History Brought Suit Against the Coal Company—and Won.* New York: Random House, 1977.

This book tells the story of a lawsuit filed by working people in West Virginia against a major coal company as the result of a flood that killed dozens of people and destroyed hundreds of homes when the company's dam broke. The book is written by the attorney who handled the case, and it conveys the difficulties faced in attempting to litigate against a wealthy entity within a jurisdiction where that entity has political influence. The book also shows how settlement negotiations between opposing sides serve a central function in shaping civil litigation.

Stolzenberg, Lisa, and Stewart J. D'Allesio, eds. *Criminal Courts for the 21st Century.* Upper Saddle River, NJ: Prentice-Hall, 1999.

This volume contains twenty articles about various aspects of case processing in criminal courts. The first section includes articles that examine the roles of prosecutors and defense attorneys as well as the use of diversion programs that send offenders into treatment or other alternatives to adjudication and punishment. The second section covers bail reform, plea bargaining, and issues related to evidence, including DNA testing and eyewitness identifications. The third section focuses on jury trials plus the use of cameras in the courtroom. The final section considers punishment, including three-strikes laws, victim participation in sentencing, the death penalty, and proposals for corporal punishment. Many of the articles are written by prominent scholars providing the most up-to-date arguments and evidence. The topics selected for inclusion in the book are all matters of controversy and debate; the book is more interesting than works that merely describe criminal trials and other court processes.

Stone, Irving. *Clarence Darrow for the Defense.* New York: Doubleday, 1989.

Clarence Darrow was one of the most famous lawyers of the twentieth century. He represented many individuals who lacked political power and were under scrutiny and attack from powerful interests in society. He also tackled controversial issues. This excellent biography tells the story of Darrow and his legal cases. Darrow is famous for successfully defending Bill Haywood, a labor leader accused of planning the assassination of the former governor of Idaho during violent conflicts between labor unions and corporate interests. He succeeded in getting prison sentences (instead of death penalties) for Nathan Leopold and Richard Loeb, wealthy, gifted University of Chicago students who were guilty of a thrill-killing in the carefully planned perfect-crime murder of a Chicago teenager. Darrow's arguments against capital punishment in the case continue to be quoted in debates about the subject. One of his most famous cases was the Scopes monkey trial, in which a Tennessee high school biology teacher was prosecuted for teaching evolution. Darrow's cross-examination of former presidential candidate William Jennings Bryan about the purported infallibility of the Bible became the basis for a popular theatrical production, *Inherit the Wind.* This book provides a detailed, insightful picture of one of America's greatest trial lawyers and shows the connections between court cases, societal developments, and political controversies.

Stumpf, Harry, and John H. Culver. *The Politics of State Courts.* New York: Longman, 1992.

This book describes the organization of state courts and the influence of local politics on the structure and processes within such courts. Each state has its own political culture and historical traditions, elements that are often reflected in the design and operation of court systems. The book includes coverage of the selection of judges, civil litigation, and criminal case processing.

Swanson, Wayne R. *The Christ Child Goes to Court.* Philadelphia: Temple University Press, 1990.

This book tells the story of a local dispute about religious liberty that worked its way through the entire system to reach the U.S. Supreme Court. The American Civil Liberties Union (ACLU) challenged the city of Pawtucket, Rhode Island, for putting up its city-owned nativity scene as part of its December holiday displays. The ACLU alleged that the public display of a government-owned religious symbol violated the First Amendment prohibition on establishment of religion by embodying inappropriate support for a particular religious orientation, namely, Christianity. The book traces the case's path through the court system, including its consideration by the Supreme Court. The book provides a good example of how cases work their way through the length of the court system and how litigation shapes public controversies.

Tucker, John C. *May God Have Mercy: A True Story of Crime and Punishment.* New York: W. W. Norton, 1997.

Years after a murder trial that led to the conviction and execution of a man with a prior criminal record, a writer who previously practiced law went back to investigate the crime and interview the participants in the case. In writing this book about the findings of his reinvestigation, the author raises troubling questions about the operation of the legal system in this case and, by implication, other cases that are determined by the same processes. A terrible rape-murder occurred in a small Virginia town. The police immediately focused their investigative attentions on the victim's brother-in-law, a man who had previously served a term in prison. Through an examination of witnesses' inconsistent statements and faulty memories, the book raises serious questions about facts that the police apparently missed during the investigation. In addition, the defendant's inexperienced attorneys may not have been as effective as they needed to be to overcome the prosecution's case. Later, the defendant forfeited his opportunity to have his case reviewed by state appellate courts or the federal courts. The U.S. Supreme Court decided that he had forfeited his opportunities for postconviction review when his attorneys missed a deadline for filing court papers. As a result, he was executed without ever having any court fully review the errors and problems in the prosecution's case and the trial proceedings. The most disturbing aspect of the book is the evidence uncovered by the author that points strongly to other suspects. The book presents a detailed examination of a criminal case from the police investigation, through the court proceedings, to the execution of the man convicted of murder despite strong questions about his guilt.

Wice, Paul. *Judges and Lawyers: The Human Side of Justice.* New York: HarperCollins, 1991.

This book provides a detailed examination of the working lives and roles of judges and lawyers. The author presents descriptive overviews of the legal profession and the judiciary. In addition, the author discusses the details of such subjects as lawyers' relationships with clients, different legal specializations, and the tasks undertaken by lawyers during the course of a trial. Similarly, there is description and analysis of judges' responsibilities and the actions of judges in processing cases by working together with other actors inside the courthouse. The book pays special attention to ethical standards and issues for lawyers and judges.

Wishman, Seymour. *Anatomy of a Jury.* New York: Time Books, 1986.

A fascinating account of a murder trial written by an experienced attorney who has worked as both a prosecutor and criminal defense attorney. The author focuses on the role of the jury and its reaction. Although the book includes details about the history of the jury and constitutional law concerning jury trials, the focus of the book is the riveting account of a single murder trial. It incorporates elements from a few other cases to create, in effect, a composite trial that illustrates the broader aspects of the jury trial process. The author walks through the attorneys' arguments, the evidence, and the jury's deliberations with descriptions worthy of any novel. The book demonstrates how trials are a very human process, tinged with uncertainty and the risk of error.

————. *Confessions of a Criminal Lawyer.* New York: Viking, 1982.

This book contains a riveting first-person account of a criminal defense lawyer's experiences in representing defendants in Newark, New Jersey. The book provides details that help the reader understand the daily lives of defense lawyers; it also gives perspectives on how and why lawyers defend guilty people. The book also illuminates the ethical tensions and dilemmas that confront those who work in the environment of courts.

Woodward, Bob, and Scott Armstrong. *The Brethren.* New York: Simon and Schuster, 1979.

This book was considered a blockbuster when it was published because it purported to provide the first inside look at the decisionmaking processes of the U.S. Supreme Court. Written by reporters for the *Washington Post*, the descriptions of interactions among the justices came from interviews with court personnel, although the authors do not identify these individuals. At the time of its publication, fewer people recognized and understood the human elements of judicial decisionmaking, and there was wider belief in the ideal of court outcomes determined by formal principles of law. This book gave examples that placed a very human face on the Supreme Court and its processes. It remains one of the few books that attempts to provide a scene-by-scene reconstruction of the processes that lead to decisions in controversial cases.

Journals, Magazines, and Newsletters

ABA Journal (American Bar Association Journal)
American Bar Association
541 N. Fairbanks Court
Chicago, IL 60611
(800) 285-2221
http://www.abanet.org/journal/subscribe.html

The monthly magazine of the American Bar Association (ABA), the largest lawyers' organization in the United States; contains articles about courts, law office management, the legal profession, judges, and new developments in law. The articles are written by professional writers, lawyers, and professors. They are written for an audience of lawyers rather than exclusively for scholars. The magazine also contains many advertisements for lawyers about legal research resources, expert witnesses, and new technologies. In addition, the magazine keeps ABA members up to date on the organization's activities and member benefits.

The American Lawyer
Subscription Department
345 Park Avenue South
New York, NY 10010
http://www.americanlawyer.com

This monthly magazine focuses on the U.S. legal profession. Its articles analyze current developments within law firms, including personnel changes, mergers, and major cases. It focuses primarily on large law firms and prominent litigators. As indicated by the high price of its subscriptions, it is aimed at successful attorneys who want to keep abreast of developments affecting their profession.

Criminal Justice
ABA Publication Orders
P.O. Box 10892
Chicago, IL 60610-0892
(800) 285-2221
http://www.abanet.org/crimjust/cjmag/info.html

This magazine is the official publication of the criminal justice section of the American Bar Association. It contains articles of interest to prosecutors, defense attorneys, judges, and scholars who are interested in criminal law and the processing of criminal cases. The magazine solicits articles from lawyers and scholars who seek to share their insights and expertise on issues related to criminal cases.

Family Advocate
Family Law Section
American Bar Association
750 N. Lake Shore Drive
Chicago, IL 60611
(800) 285-2221
http://www.abanet.org/family/subscription.html

Family Advocate is the quarterly magazine of the family law section of the American Bar Association. It is intended to provide useful information that will assist attorneys, judges, and mental health professionals in handling family law cases concerning such issues as divorce, child custody, domestic violence, and adoption.

Judges' Journal
Judicial Division
American Bar Association
541 N. Fairbanks Court
Chicago, IL 60611
(312) 988-5705
http://www.ornl.gov/hgmis/publicat/judges/judgetoc.html

This magazine provides information for judges about trial management, caseload monitoring, courthouse personnel, and other issues of concern to judges as well as to scholars who study the courts. It is published by the judicial division of the American Bar Association.

Judicature
American Judicature Society
180 N. Michigan Avenue, Suite 600
Chicago, IL 60601
(312) 558-6900
http://www.ajs.org/ajs/publications/ajs_judicature.asp

A bimonthly publication of articles on courts and judging. Most articles are written by professors of law, political science, and criminal justice. Many articles present research on courts, but others present commentary and essays on related subjects. The journal also has editorials concerning the organization's goal of improving judicial administration and advocating merit selection of judges. Book reviews are also published.

Justice System Journal
National Center for State Courts
Fulfillment Department
P.O. Box 580
Williston, VT 05495-0580
(888) 228-6272
http://www.ncsc.dni.us

A scholarly journal that publishes research on courts, this publication is aimed at judges, court administrators, and scholars who study courts. The journal regularly has special issues in which all articles are devoted to specific topics, such as state courts and trial court management. The journal also publishes book reviews and management notes.

Juvenile and Family Court Journal
National Council of Juvenile and Family Court Judges
P.O. Box 8970
Reno, NV 89507
(775) 784-6012
http://www.ncjfcj.unr.edu/pub/pub_home.html

This quarterly journal publishes articles on topics of concern to personnel in juvenile and family courts. Occasional issues are devoted to a single topic, such as child abuse or domestic violence.

Legal Times
1730 M Street, NW, Suite 802
Washington, DC 20036
(202) 457-0686
http://www.legaltimes.biz

Legal Times is a Washington, D.C.–based and capital-focused weekly publication with articles about law firms, lobbying firms, federal courts, and federal government agencies. The publication has significant coverage of the legal community in Washington, D.C., but it also has a national readership because of its attention to federal laws and regulations.

National Law Journal
Litigation Services Network
105 Madison Avenue
New York, NY 10016
(800) 537-2128
http://www.nlj.com/

This is the most widely disseminated weekly publication about lawyers, courts, and legal cases. *National Law Journal* reports on notable judicial decisions throughout the United States. It also focuses on the most significant jury verdicts produced around the country. It publishes a detailed annual review of the decisions by the U.S. Supreme Court. Its articles are written by staff writers, attorneys, and scholars.

Third Branch
Administrative Office of the U.S. Courts
Office of Public Affairs
One Columbus Circle, NE
Washington, DC 20544
(202) 502-2600
http://www.uscourts.gov

Third Branch is the monthly newsletter of the federal courts. It contains articles about recent developments in the federal judiciary, including the implementation of new technology, current caseload statistics, and interviews with federal judges who head various committees within the judicial branch. The publication prints the annual year-in-review statement of the chief justice of the U.S. Supreme Court. Its articles also give extensive coverage to issues concerning funding for the courts from Congress and issues affecting salary and benefits for federal judges.

Trial
Association of Trial Lawyers of America
1050 31st Street, NW
Washington, DC 20007
(800) 424-2725
http://www.atlanet.org

This monthly magazine provides articles of interest for civil trial attorneys, judges, and scholars. The articles focus on the latest trends in civil litigation, including emerging legal issues and courtroom strategies. The magazine also contains articles on law office technology as well as book reviews. It is published by the Association of Trial Lawyers of America.

Government Documents and Agency Publications

American Civil Liberties Union. **Unequal, Unfair, and Irreversible: The Death Penalty in Virginia** (2000). Available for order at: http://www.aclu.org

A report that examines judicial processing, prosecutorial discretion, racial discrimination, and the quality of defense counsel in capital punishment cases.

Bureau of Justice Statistics (BJS)

The Bureau of Justice Statistics is the federal government agency responsible for gathering, analyzing, and disseminating data about the justice system, including courts. It produces many publications each year that are available online as well as in printed versions available through its website: http://www.ojp.usdoj. gov/bjs/.

The following is a partial listing of BJS publications concerning courts and trials:

Civil Trial Cases and Verdicts in Large Counties, 1996. September 1999. NCJ 173426.

Defense Counsel in Criminal Cases. November 2000. NCJ 179023.

Federal Criminal Appeals, 1999, with Trends 1985–1999. April 2001. NCJ 185055.

Federal Pretrial Release and Detention, 1996. February 1999. NCJ 168635.

Federal Tort Trials and Verdicts, 1996–1997. March 1999. NCJ 172855.

Felony Defendants in Large Urban Counties, 1996. October 1999. NCJ 176981.

Indigent Defense Services in Large Counties, 1999. November 2000. NCJ 184932.

Juvenile Felony Defendants in Criminal Courts. September 1998. NCJ 165815

State Court Organization, 1998. June 2000. NCJ 178932.

State Court Sentencing of Convicted Felons, 1996. March 2000. NCJ 175708

State-Funded Indigent Defense Services, 1999. September 2001. NCJ 188464.

Chapper, Joy, and Roger Hanson. *Intermediate Appellate Courts: Improving Case Processing.* Williamsburg, VA: National Center for State Courts, 1990.

This volume presents a study of intermediate appellate courts' case processing, including the length of time required to complete cases. The authors include suggestions for improving case processing, organization, and management issues in the appeals process.

Clarke, Cait, and Christopher Stone. **Bolder Management for the Public Defense: Leadership in Three Dimensions**. Washington, DC: U.S. Bureau of Justice Assistance, 2001.

This report discusses how managers of public defender agencies are expanding the roles of their agencies beyond simply representing individual indigent defendants. Instead, innovative leadership in these agencies is facilitating a broader view of criminal defense attorneys' roles in developing court innovations and helping to shape crime policy.

Federal Judicial Center (FJC)

The Federal Judicial Center is the research agency for the federal judiciary. Through the work of its staff and visiting scholars, it evaluates court reform innovations in the federal courts. Many of its publications are available online as well as in print form from its website: http://www.fjc.gov.

The following is a partial listing of FJC publications:

ADR and Settlement Programs in the Federal District Courts: A Sourcebook for Judges and Lawyers (1996).

Case Management Procedures in the Federal Courts of Appeals (2000).

The Civil Justice Reform Act Expense and Delay Reduction Plans: A Sourcebook (1995).

Court-Annexed Arbitration in Ten District Courts (1990).

Effective Use of Courtroom Technology: A Judge's Guide to Pretrial and Trial (2001).

Electronic Media Coverage of Federal Civil Proceedings: An Evaluation (1994).

Expert Testimony in Federal Civil Trials: A Preliminary Analysis (2000).

Stalking the Increase in the Rate of Federal Civil Appeals (1995).

The U.S. Sentencing Guidelines: Results of the Federal Judicial Center's 1996 Survey (1997).

Voluntary Arbitration in Eight Federal District Courts: An Evaluation (1994).

Fluellen, Reginald, and Jennifer Trone. **Do Drug Courts Save Jail and Prison Bed Space?** New York: Vera Institute of Justice, 2000.

This report examines the innovation of using separate drug courts to address intensively the issue of drug offenders. Drug courts provide close monitoring, access to treatment programs, and an effort to avoid filling corrections institutions with offenders who might be better treated through monitoring and therapeutic approaches.

Hanson, Roger, et al. *Indigent Defenders: Get the Job Done and Done Well*. Williamsburg, VA: National Center for State Courts, 1992.

This volume presents a study of criminal defense attorneys, both public defenders and appointed counsel, who represent indigent defendants in nine jurisdictions, including large cities and small towns. The book highlights the difficulties in attempting to analyze indigent defense in different contexts. The study also found indications that defense attorneys for the indigent perform well with respect to timeliness and case outcomes when compared to private defense attorneys in these jurisdictions.

Munsterman, G. Thomas, Paula L. Hannaford, and G. Marc Whitehead, eds. *Jury Trial Innovations*. Williamsburg, VA: National Center for State Courts, 1997.

This book contains a detailed discussion of the advantages and disadvantages of many proposed reforms in the jury trial process. The book examines such initiatives as public education campaigns to inform citizens about the importance of jury service, simplifying instructions given by the judge to the jury, and debriefing sessions to alleviate juror stress after trials. The book is structured to describe each proposal clearly and then to provide clearly organized statements of the pros and cons. This book provides excellent insights into the practical problems with jury trials that are perceived by lawyers and other experts who work with this court process.

National Center for Juvenile Justice

The National Center for Juvenile Justice, the research division of the National Council of Juvenile and Family Court Judges, produces a variety of publications about courts. They are available for order at: http://brendan.ncjfcj.unr.edu/homepage/ncjj/.

These publications include:

Advocating for the Child's Best Interest in Family Court (2001).

Delinquency Cases in Juvenile Courts, 1998 (2001).

Delinquency Cases Waived to Criminal Court, 1988–1997 (2000).

Drug Offense Cases in Juvenile Court, 1989–1998 (2001).

Family Courts in the United States (2000).

Juvenile Justice With Eyes Open (2001).

Prosecuting Attorney in Dependency Proceedings in Juvenile Court (2001).

Steelman, David C., James E. McMillan, and John A. Goerdt. *Caseflow Management: The Heart of Court Management in the New Millennium.* Williamsburg, VA: National Center for State Courts, 2000.

This book discusses the basic methods of case-flow management. The process of monitoring and controlling the progress of cases is a central element of effective court administration and a key feature that affects litigants' experiences in court. The volume is primarily aimed at judges and court administrators.

8

Nonprint Resources

N onprint resources on courts and trials include films and websites. Trials are a favorite subject of filmmakers and TV pro-
ducers. TV shows and films about trials often focus solely on
the courtroom drama and fail to give viewers an adequate understanding of the weeks of preparation that absorb lawyers'
lives in the pretrial process. The trial is used as a mechanism for
portraying the drama, but the intent of the film is not to ensure
that the trial is realistic. In many classic films, there are significant
questions about the accuracy of the portrayal of the trial even
though the underlying dramatic point is well presented. In *To Kill
a Mockingbird*, the famous dramatic film in which an African-
American defendant is framed for sexual assault, the trial clearly
demonstrates the oppressive racism of the Southern justice system in the early twentieth century, but few poor defendants
would receive such outstanding (albeit hopeless) representation
from the attorney as portrayed by Gregory Peck. In another example, Henry Fonda portrays a holdout juror in *Twelve Angry
Men;* jury deliberations provide the device to create the dramatic
scene, but the deliberations themselves do not purport to be
drawn from reality.

Dramatic presentations often fail to convey the extent to
which negotiated agreements guide court processes and usually
determine the outcomes of cases. In addition, dramatic produc-
tions focus disproportionately on murder cases that lead to
drawn-out trial proceedings, when in fact murder cases compose
only a very small portion of the total caseload. The typical criminal case concerns a misdemeanor that is processed through a

quick guilty plea. Such cases are not considered sufficiently en-
tertaining to be the focus of a film or TV script. In addition, civil
cases tend to receive reduced attention in entertainment produc-
tions. Despite these limitations, there are a few films about courts
and trials produced by entertainment companies that provide
useful insights about aspects of judicial processes. These films can
convey the uncertainty and ambiguity produced through the
process of presenting evidence in the courtroom and thereby illuminate that trial processes are flawed human endeavors that
carry an inevitable risk of error and injustice. For the most part,
however, dramatic films are excluded from the sample of films
listed in this chapter.

Films

The Case for Innocence
Date: 2000
Media: VHS
Length: 90 minutes
Price: $49.95
Source: PBS Home Video
             P.O. Box 751089
             Charlotte, NC 28275
             Phone: (877) 727-7467
             http://www.pbs.org

This film examines what happened when new DNA testing techniques made it possible to reexamine evidence that had been used
to convict offenders in early cases. Through an examination of
several cases, the film shows that the court system has not handled adequately the resources of new technologies. Instead, prosecutorial obstinacy and political considerations block the examination of evidence, even though the new tests could have
indicated that an innocent person has been sent to prison. In
Texas, Virginia, and Louisiana cases, the new tests indicate that
the offenders were likely innocent, yet the prosecutors and judges
resist freeing the men.

A Civil Action
Date: 1998
Media: DVD and VHS
Length: 115 minutes

Price: $15.98
Source: Walt Disney Video
Barnes & Noble.com
6000 Freeport Avenue
Memphis, TN 38141
Phone: (800) 843-2665
http://www.bn.com

This is the Hollywood film version of an award-winning book on a civil lawsuit about children's cancer deaths in a community with water contaminated by industrial pollution. The film stars John Travolta as the lawyer for the children's families and Robert Duvall as the attorney for a corporation being sued. The film illuminates the complexity and cost of civil litigation, including the costs of scientific testing and expert witnesses. The film also shows the disadvantages experienced by average people who become courtroom adversaries with corporate entities that have significant legal resources. In addition, the story illustrates the uncertainty about whether litigation processes are capable of bringing forward the truth and achieving the ends of justice.

Criminal Justice
Date: 1986
Media: VHS
Length: 58 minutes
Price: $195 purchase; $90 rental
Source: Cinema Guild
130 Madison Avenue
New York, NY 10016-7038
Phone: (212) 685-6242
http://www.cinemaguild.com

This documentary provides a behind-the-scenes look at three criminal cases. The film follows the activities of the prosecutors, defense attorneys, police officers, and defendants. It includes comments from the officials involved in the processing of criminal cases about the flaws in the system as well as suggestions for reform.

Criminal Justice
Date: 1990
Media: VHS
Length: 92 minutes

Price: $9.98
Source: HBO Films
           Barnes & Noble.com
           6000 Freeport Avenue
           Memphis, TN 38141
           Phone: (800) 843-2665
           http://www.bn.com

Fictional film dramatization of a criminal case in New York City. The films stars Forest Whitaker as the suspect, Rosie Perez as the crime victim, Jennifer Grey as the prosecutor, and Anthony La-Paglia. The film is used in many law school classes because it effectively conveys the gritty context of local criminal courts and the assembly-line processing of cases. The film also captures the difficult decision faced by suspects who are offered the opportunity to accept a guilty plea even though they insist that they are innocent. The film shows the plea-bargaining process as well as the preparations for the trial process, including jury selection. As in many actual cases, the audience has good reason to keep asking itself, "Did he do it or not?"

Evidence of Guilt
Date: 1997
Media: VHS
Length: 45 minutes
Price: $129.95 purchase; $75 rental
Source: Films for the Humanities & Sciences
           P.O. Box 2053
           Princeton, NJ 08543-2053
           Phone: (800) 257-5126
           http://www.films.com

This CBS News presentation focuses on criminal trials in which there are questions about the evidence of guilt. In a murder case, there is no definitive cause of death. In a rape case, the victim did not see her assailant. The film includes interviews with key actors in the cases as well as footage of the actual courtroom action during the trial.

Gideon's Trumpet: The Poor Man and the Law
Date: 1964
Media: VHS (B&W)
Length: 51 minutes

Price: $89.95
Source: Films for the Humanities & Sciences
             P.O. Box 2053
             Princeton, NJ 08543-2053
             Phone: (800) 257-5126
             http://www.films.com

In the aftermath of the U.S. Supreme Court's landmark decision in *Gideon v. Wainwright* (1963), CBS News examined the case's path to the Supreme Court as it set a precedent for providing defense attorneys for indigent defendants. The film includes interviews with participants in the case, including Clarence Gideon, who filed the handwritten petition to the Supreme Court from his prison cell; his attorney, Abe Fortas; and Supreme Court Justice Arthur Goldberg.

Innocent Until Proven Guilty
Date: 1999
Media: VHS
Length: 64 minutes
Price: $295 purchase; $75 rental
Source: Filmakers Library
            124 East 40th Street
            New York, NY 10016
            Phone: (212) 808-4980
            http://www.filmakers.com

This documentary examines the life of a public defender in Washington, D.C., who represents indigent people charged with criminal offenses. In addition, the attorney founded an alternative high school for former juvenile offenders. The film highlights issues of race, poverty, and the operation of the criminal justice system.

Inside the Jury
Date: 1997
Media: VHS
Length: 45 minutes
Price: $129.95 purchase; $75 rental
Source: Films for the Humanities & Sciences
            P.O. Box 2053
            Princeton, NJ 08543-2053
            Phone: (800) 257-5126
            http://www.films.com

This documentary follows jurors through an armed robbery case. It goes behind the scenes in a jury room as jurors decide a criminal trial. It is one of the few times in U.S. history that cameras have been permitted to record the deliberations of a jury. The film conveys the challenges facing jurors in sorting out the evidence and interacting with each other.

Juvenile Justice
Date: 2001
Media: VHS
Length: 90 minutes
Price: $19.98
Source: PBS Home Video
              P.O. Box 751089
              Charlotte, NC 28275
              Phone: (877) 727-7467
              http://www.pbs.org

This film examines the question of whether teens who commit serious crimes should be tried in adult courts and face adult punishments. The filmmakers follow the cases of four youths in California. Two of the youths are Hispanic, one is white, and the other is African-American. Their stories illuminate the operations of courts, including legal factors and discretionary decisions, that determine whether young offenders are placed in rehabilitative settings or treated as adults.

Real Justice
Date: 2000
Media: VHS
Length: 180 minutes
Price: $29.98
Source: PBS Home Video
              P.O. Box 751089
              Charlotte, NC 28275
              Phone: (877) 727-7467
              http://www.pbs.org

This documentary follows the daily interactions and decisions of prosecutors, defense attorneys, and judges in Boston's criminal courts. The filmmakers examine the frantic pace of processing lesser offenses as well as the general jurisdiction trial court in which serious offenses are prosecuted. The film conveys a picture of the steps in the criminal case process and the negotiated arrangements that determine the outcomes in many cases.

Requiem for Frank Lee Smith

Date:	2002
Media:	VHS
Length:	60 minutes
Price:	$29.98
Source:	PBS Home Video
	P.O. Box 751089
	Charlotte, NC 28275
	Phone: (877) 727-7467
	http://www.pbs.org

Frank Lee Smith was convicted of murder and sentenced to death in Florida. Only after he had died of cancer while awaiting execution was DNA evidence tested that proved his innocence. The film traces Smith's case and examines the series of steps and errors that led to the conviction of an innocent man. Among the aspects of court processes examined in the film are unreliable eyewitness testimony based on a photo identification, as well as court procedures that hinder the examination of newly developed evidence. The film raises questions about the effectiveness and fairness of criminal court procedures.

The Trial Lawyer: Five Courtroom Champions Speak

Date:	1968
Media:	VHS (B&W)
Length:	52 minutes
Price:	$89.95
Source:	Films for the Humanities & Sciences
	P.O. Box 2053
	Princeton, NJ 08543-2053
	Phone: (800) 257-5126
	http://www.films.com

Through interviews and news footage, this documentary examines five of the most legendary trial lawyers of the twentieth century: F. Lee Bailey; Melvin Belli; Percy Foreman; Louis Nizer; and Edward Bennett Williams. These giants among trial attorneys discuss jury selection, the use of evidence, and other issues concerning trial processes.

White Justice
Date: 1987
Media: VHS
Length: 57 minutes
Price: $295 purchase; $95 rental
Source: Cinema Guild
             130 Madison Avenue
             New York, NY 10016-7038
             Phone: (212) 685-6242
             http://www.cinemaguild.com

This documentary examines the impact of the Canadian justice system on Inuit peoples in Quebec. The film shows behind-the-scenes activities and interactions as people are drawn into the court system. Fundamentally, the film seeks to raise questions about how a justice system externally imposed upon people with their own values and culture leads to conflict and the risk of injustice.

Who Killed Vincent Chin?
Date: 1988
Media: VHS
Length: 82 minutes
Price: $395 purchase; $75 rental
Source: Filmakers Library
             124 East 40th Street
             New York, NY 10016
             Phone: (212) 808-4980
             http://www.filmakers.com

This documentary examines the case of an Asian-American man in Detroit who was beaten to death with a baseball bat by autoworkers in an atmosphere of hostility toward Japanese auto companies when U.S. autoworkers feared for their jobs as their employers suffered financial declines. Although the film focuses on racism and cultural differences within the United States, it also raises questions about the links between courts and local politics, because the killer was initially given only a suspended sentence and a small fine for the homicide.

Internet Addresses

Author's note: See Chapters 6 and 7 for other Internet addresses. Many of the most useful and important websites are associated with the agencies and organizations listed in Chapter 6 and with the publications listed in Chapter 7.

Cornell Law School's Legal Information Institute
http://www.law.cornell.edu

The Cornell Law School website permits searches for U.S. Supreme Court decisions as well as links to other federal courts and New York state courts. In addition, it highlights important lower-court decisions from around the country. The site provides one of the best sources to find U.S. Supreme Court decisions immediately after they are announced by the Court.

Courts.Net
http://www.courts.net

This website ("the nation's courts directory") provides links to court systems throughout the United States. It also provides links to other websites containing information about courts.

Emory University School of Law
http://www.law.emory.edu/FEDCTS/

During the 1990s Emory University School of Law gathered federal appellate court opinions on its website. Many of these opinions predate the posting of opinions on the federal courts' own websites. However, when federal courts began posting opinions at their own sites, Emory ceased to continue what would have been a duplicative effort. Instead, Emory also provides links to each federal appellate court's own website to facilitate searches for specific judicial opinions and information about each court.

Findlaw.Com
http://www.findlaw.com

Findlaw is the most comprehensive website for links to information about law and courts. The site provides links to the official websites of all U.S. state court systems as well as to the U.S. federal court system. The site also provides links to all states' statutes and judicial decisions, including those concerning the organization of courts and mandated court procedures. In addition, there is a search engine to conduct full text searches of federal legal cases.

Law.Com

http://www.law.com

Law.com provides a comprehensive website with news stories about courts and legal issues, opportunities for lawyers to gain on-line continuing legal education credits, as well as search mechanisms to find legal jobs and law firms and to conduct legal research.

LawCommerce.Com

http://www.lawcommerce.com

A website that seeks to enhance the business and practice of law through web-based services and technology for lawyers. The site is a source of information about lawyers and new developments in the legal profession.

Northwestern University's Medill School of Journalism

http://www.medill.northwestern.edu/docket/

On the Docket provides useful information about pending U.S. Supreme Court cases. Northwestern students post summaries of the cases accepted for argument by the Court, including opposing arguments and the names of the attorneys in the case. This site provides an especially useful source of information about the issues that the Supreme Court will be addressing in the coming year.

Prosecutor Information

http://www.co.eaton.mi.us/ecpa/proslist.htm

The county prosecutor's office in Eaton County, Michigan, has created a website that serves as a directory for prosecutors' offices in the United States and in many countries throughout the world. The site has links to prosecutors' offices as well as to prosecutors' associations.

Glossary

adversary system The trial process in which the truth is presumed to be best revealed through the clash of skilled advocates in the courtroom. In the adversary system, opposing attorneys present evidence and arguments. Because both sides have incentives to present all of the evidence that will help prove their arguments, the system presumes that the decisionmaker (or fact finder), whether judge or jury, will have the best opportunity to consider all available evidence to determine what actually happened in the case. In the adversary system, the judge is relatively passive, much like a referee at a sporting event. The judge enforces rules of court procedure and evidence but does not actively participate in ways that might advance the interests of either side. As a result, there is a risk that the outcome will be determined by the effectiveness and persuasiveness of the attorneys rather than by a complete and objective examination of all available facts. If one side has an ineffective attorney, the case may be lost even if a thorough presentation of facts would have resulted otherwise. This system is used in the United States and other countries that follow British legal traditions.

alternative dispute resolution (ADR) Methods for processing disputes that provide alternatives to litigation and trials. Examples include arbitration, mediation, and summary jury trials. Many U.S. court systems have begun to incorporate ADR mechanisms into their processes in an effort to resolve cases by mutual agreement of the parties while avoiding the expense and delays of litigation and trials.

appellate briefs Written arguments submitted to appellate courts by lawyers for each side in a case. These detailed arguments are sometimes the basis for appellate court decisions if the judges do not believe that oral arguments are necessary. When oral arguments are held, the appellate briefs serve to give the judges detailed background information and arguments before they listen to the attorneys' presentations in court.

appointed counsel A method for providing defense attorneys for indigent criminal defendants. This includes attorneys in private practice who agree to accept criminal cases assigned by the court and who receive modest compensation from the government for their services. The appointed counsel system raises questions about whether the attorneys involved are always sufficiently knowledgeable and dedicated to providing the best possible representation for their clients.

arbitration An alternative dispute resolution mechanism in which an arbitrator listens to presentations from both sides in a civil lawsuit and then issues a decision about how the case should be resolved. In nonbinding arbitration, the arbitrator's decision serves to facilitate settlement by informing both sides about how their respective arguments and evidence have been evaluated by an objective decisionmaker. In binding arbitration, both parties have agreed to abide by the arbitrator's decision.

bench trial A trial conducted without a jury in which the judge is the decisionmaker. Approximately half of the trials that are conducted in U.S. courts each year are bench trials.

challenge for cause A mechanism used by attorneys to remove potential jurors from the jury pool if there are indications that these potential jurors are biased. As potential jurors respond to questions from the attorneys and judge prior to a trial, attorneys may ask the judge to exclude those jurors who make statements indicating that they will favor one side in the case. Frequently these exclusions occur because the potential juror has been a crime victim or expresses an unwillingness to consider that an accused person may be innocent. If the judge agrees that the statements indicate bias, the potential juror is excluded.

change of venue If an attorney believes that excessive pretrial publicity has made it impossible for the court to find unbiased jurors within a community, the attorney may request that the trial be moved to a different community, one where the crime was not committed and there have been fewer news reports about the case. The jurors are then drawn from people in the community that lacks a connection to the case. Because of the legal requirement that prosecutions typically occur in the location where the crime was committed, judges will order a change of venue only under compelling circumstances.

contingency fees A mechanism prevalent in the United States for compensating attorneys in civil cases; it enables even poor people to hire attorneys because the attorneys will receive a percentage, typically 30 percent, of any settlement or verdict award. Many other countries do not permit contingency fees because they fear that attorneys will seek to advance their own interests by soliciting clients and initiating unfounded lawsuits.

contract counsel A method for providing defense attorneys for indigent criminal defendants. Under a contract counsel system, an attorney or a law firm submits a bid to handle all of the cases of indigent defendants over the course of the year for a specific price.

courts of last resort The highest level of court in a court system. Courts of last resort typically are the final authority over legal issues presented in judicial proceedings. In the United States, the U.S. Supreme Court and state supreme courts are courts of last resort. They usually have discretion to select the cases that they wish to decide from among the many petitions for review they receive each year. In a few small U.S. states, the court of last resort is the only appellate court and therefore handles appeals from trial court decisions.

defendant The individual or corporation facing prosecution in a criminal case or being sued in a civil case for allegedly causing harm by violating a statute, contract, or legal duty.

discovery The pretrial process in which attorneys for opposing sides request information from each other and exchange documents and lists of witnesses. Discovery can sometimes produce disputes that must be decided by a judge when one side requests information that the opposing side believes it is entitled to keep confidential.

dissenting opinion Judicial opinion in an appellate case expressing the conclusions and reasoning of the minority of judges who disagree with the court's decision issued by the majority of judges on the appellate court. Dissenting opinions may bring forward ideas that will be accepted by a majority of judges in later years or decades.

double jeopardy The protection contained in the Fifth Amendment of the U.S. Constitution that forbids the pursuit of a second prosecution on the same charges and in the same court in which a defendant was acquitted of those charges in an initial trial. The right is intended to prevent the government from continually prosecuting an individual as a means of harassment.

dual court system Parallel court systems of state and national governments that operate simultaneously in the same geographic areas but have authority over different kinds of legal cases. The United States has a dual court system because it has state systems as well as a federal court system.

exclusionary rule Legal rule applied by the U.S. Supreme Court requiring that improperly obtained evidence of criminal wrongdoing be barred from use in prosecution in order to deter police officers from violating people's constitutional rights. The original rule barring all improperly obtained evidence was later modified to permit the use of evidence in certain situations, such as when it was obtained in a context in which the public's safety was at risk.

family courts State courts that are designed to consolidate all matters related to families, such as adoptions, child custody disputes, and divorces, under the authority of one court.

federalism Principle of the governing system in the United States that permits states to exercise significant authority over many of their own affairs while the federal government handles specific aspects of law and policy. As a result of federalism, the United States has a dual court system with simultaneously operating state and federal courts in cities and states throughout the country.

habeas corpus Traditional process under Anglo-American legal traditions for people held in government custody to challenge the legality of their detention. This legal process is usually used by convicted offenders being held in prison, but it can also be used by pretrial detainees in jail or by people confined to mental hospitals and other governmental institutions. In the criminal process in the United States, habeas corpus petitions are filed after all appeals have been exhausted. The petition must assert that a federal constitutional right was violated by the police or prosecutor in the course of the investigation and prosecution of a case that led to an individual's confinement in jail or prison. A federal statute permits prisoners in state prisons to initiate habeas corpus petitions in federal court so that federal judges can examine the actions of state and local criminal justice officials to see if a constitutional right was violated.

inquisitorial system The trial process that involves active participation of judges who are responsible for ensuring that all of the facts are revealed and that an accurate decision is rendered. This system is used in continental Europe and in countries that do not follow British traditions. In the inquisitorial process, judges become actively involved in questioning witnesses and examining evidence.

intermediate appellate courts The first level of appeals courts that handle appeals from trial court decisions. The intermediate appellate courts handle the majority of appeals in the federal court system, as well as in those states that maintain such courts.

peremptory challenge The traditional mechanism used by attorneys to exclude potential jurors without providing any reason for the exclusion. Each side in a civil or criminal case has a specific number of peremptory challenges to employ. The number varies according to each state's laws. The attorneys use hunches to exclude jurors whom they suspect of being susceptible to arguments by the opposing side. Although attorneys traditionally had complete discretion to use these challenges, in the 1980s and 1990s, the U.S. Supreme Court declared that attorneys could not use them in order to exclude potential jurors because of their race or gender.

plaintiff The individual or corporation who files a civil lawsuit seeking a remedy for a harm allegedly caused by another individual or corporation. The plaintiff bears the burden of showing by a preponderance of evidence that the defendant is legally responsible for harms caused in contract violations, automobile collisions, and other kinds of civil cases.

pro bono work Legal services provided free of charge by private attorneys in order to provide a public service or in order to fulfill state bar association requirements of donating time to serve poor individuals or nonprofit agencies. American attorneys typically donate very few hours of service to poor individuals and therefore pro bono work does not solve the problems faced by poor people in seeking to make use of courts.

probable cause The standard of evidence that must be fulfilled in order to justify the issuance of a search warrant or arrest warrant, or to justify any arrest made without a warrant. The Fourth Amendment of the U.S. Constitution requires that police and prosecutors provide evidence to judges that shows that it is likely that criminal evidence will be found in a specific location or that a specific individual committed a crime in order to justify search warrants and arrests.

magistrates courts Limited-jurisdiction courts in England and Wales in which citizens chosen from the community serve as judicial officers despite their lack of legal training and qualifications.

mandatory sentences A sentencing reform undertaken to reduce judges' discretionary authority in sentencing. Legislatures pass mandatory sentencing plans that require judges to impose specific sentences for offenders who commit specific offenses. Such laws are typically enacted when legislatures perceive that some judges are too lenient in sentencing criminal offenders. Judges complain that these laws lead to injustices because judges are no longer able to take into consideration the individual circumstances of each case in designing an appropriate sentence.

mediation An alternative dispute resolution mechanism used by some courts in which an individual mediator or a panel of attorneys discusses a civil case with both parties and attempts to facilitate a negotiated settlement.

merit selection A method for selecting judges that emphasizes the identification of candidates with the most outstanding qualifications for judicial office. This method was developed in an effort to change the traditional reliance on political considerations for the choice of judges within the United States. Merit selection does not eliminate the influence of politics, however, because merit-selection committees make recommendations to an appointing authority, usually the governor. The governor's final decision may incorporate political considerations. In addition, interest groups may lobby the governor for inclusion of their representatives on the merit-selection committee.

public defender system A method of providing defense attorneys for indigent criminal defendants. Public defenders are full-time salaried attorneys on the government payroll who represent indigent defendants. Although public defenders are typically knowledgeable about criminal law, they may lack the resources to mount the strongest possible defense for each client. They may also be burdened by excessively large caseloads.

sentencing guidelines A mandatory sentencing scheme first used by Minnesota and later developed for use by the federal government and other states. Under sentencing guidelines, a commission develops an elaborate grid specifying sentence ranges that are determined by the seriousness of the offender's crime and the extent of the offender's prior criminal record. Sentencing guidelines were developed to create consistency in sentencing within a specific jurisdiction, but critics claim that the scheme improperly deprives judges of discretionary authority to design sentences that fit specific circumstances.

summary jury trial An alternative dispute resolution mechanism used in some federal courts to facilitate negotiated settlements. Actual jurors hear a condensed, one-day presentation of arguments and evidence in civil lawsuits and then issue nonbinding verdicts. These advisory verdicts inform attorneys about how an actual jury might react to their presentations in a real trial. As a result, many attorneys realize that their evidence is less persuasive than they believed and thus become more willing to engage in serious settlement negotiations.

three-strikes laws Mandatory sentencing laws that impose very long sentences, typically 25 years to life, for offenders convicted of three felonies. Some states require the third felony to be a violent crime before the severe mandatory sentence applies. In California, controversy arose because the third conviction that generates a long sentence could be merely a theft offense.

tort reform Legislative efforts in the United States to enact legislation that will limit jury awards in civil lawsuits or otherwise protect product manufacturers, medical doctors, and insurance companies from significant liability in the litigation process. Advocates of tort reform often argue that juries go too far in making awards against corporations and individuals perceived as having deep pockets. As a result, advocates claim that companies are driven out of business and doctors are no longer able to afford skyrocketing insurance premiums.

trial courts of general jurisdiction Trial courts in which cases are initiated and processed concerning the full range of civil and criminal matters without regard to the severity of the criminal offense or the amount in controversy in the civil lawsuit.

trial courts of limited jurisdiction The lowest level of courts. Trial courts of limited jurisdiction handle specific kinds of civil cases involving disputes over small amounts of money or criminal cases concerning traffic offenses and misdemeanors.

waiver (juvenile justice) The decision to send juveniles accused of crimes out of the juvenile court system and into the regular court system, where they will face the same sentences and punishments imposed on adult offenders. During the 1990s states increasingly altered their laws to create more opportunities to send juveniles into the regular courts. The waiver decision is usually made by a judge, but prosecutors have significant authority over determining which young defendants will be placed in the waiver process. Juveniles are usually waived into adult courts because they are charged with committing the most serious offenses, such as homicides, but sometimes prosecutors steer repeat offenders into the process even if their crimes are not as serious.

Index

ABA Journal, 208, 226–227
Abortion, 1, 7, 208, 211, 222
Abrahamson, Shirley S., biographical
    sketch of, 107–108
Access, 33, 34, 56–62
    controversy over, 68–69
    governmental priorities and, 61–62
    for indigent people, 59–61
    information, 68–73
    limitations on, 18
Accountability, 35, 36, 68, 104
    effectiveness of, 69
    government, 218
Accusers, confronting, 19
ACLU. *See* American Civil Liberties
    Union
Adams, John, 82, 83, 84
Adams, John Quincy, 85
Administrative Office of the U.S.
    Courts, 91, 177–178
ADR. *See* Alternative dispute
    resolution
Adversary system, 28–29, 31, 33, 245
    attorneys and, 41
    in Canada, 48–49
    commitment to, 49
    and inquisitorial system compared,
        40–45
    jury trials and, 44
    secret trials and, 73
    truth and, 48
African Americans
    jury service and, 86
    trial of, 84–85
Ali, Muhammad, 217
Allen, Florence, 91
    biographical sketch of, 108–109
Allred, Gloria, biographical sketch of,
    109–110
Alternative dispute resolution (ADR),
    60, 99–100, 216, 245
    court-annexed, 65–68

in Florida, 139
    recognition of, 98
    in Sweden, 66
American Bar Association, 178–179
American Civil Liberties Union
    (ACLU), 179–180, 217, 224
American Judges Association, 180
American Judicature Society, 180–181
American Lawyer, The, 227
American Tort Reform Association, 63
Amistad (film), 85
Anthony, Susan B., voting rights and,
    85–86
Anti-Riot Act, 94
Apodaca v. Oregon (1972), 95
    synopsis of, 156–157
Appeals, 231
    secret trials and, 73
Appellate briefs, 14, 245
Appellate courts, 13–15, 19, 29, 30, 37,
    86, 87
    hidden processes of, 219
    intermediate, 13, 15, 231, 248
Appellate judges, 39, 86–87
    appointment of, 37, 38, 96–97
Appointments, 40, 96–97
    politics of, 36–38
Arbitration, 66, 246
    ADR and, 67
    binding, 68
    court-annexed, 67
    nonbinding, 67
Argersinger v. Hamlin (1972), 15, 46
    synopsis of, 157–158
Article III, 99, 132–133
Articles of Confederation, 82
Ashcroft, John, electronic surveillance
    and, 24
Assassination, 8, 97–98
Association of Trial Lawyers of
    America, 181
Attorney-client communications, 24

Attorneys
  adversary system and, 41
  appointed, 47, 233, 245–246
  in Canada, 49
  civil cases and, 57, 99
  civil rights, 93, 209–210, 217
  contract, 47–48, 247
  criminal defendants and, 47, 49
  effectiveness of, 42
  ethical standards for, 225
  hiring, 45
  licensing of, 9
  private-practice, 48, 233
  questioning and, 21
  right to, 15, 17, 45, 46–47, 93
  tort reform and, 64
  See also Defense attorneys
Attorneys' fees, 57, 61, 67

Bail hearings, 21–22, 49
Bail reform, 98, 211, 223
Bail Reform Act (1984), 98
Bailey, F. Lee, biographical sketch of,
  110
Bailiffs, 62
Baldwin, Roger, 85
Bankruptcy, 9, 10, 99
Barker v. Wingo (1972), 18
  synopsis of, 155–156
Barron v. Baltimore (1833), 84
Batson v. Kentucky (1986), 99
  synopsis of, 162–163
Belli, Melvin, 207
Bench trials, 26, 62, 246
Benton v. Maryland (1969), synopsis of,
  154
Bill of Rights, 83, 84, 89, 92
Birth defects, suing for, 59
BJS. *See* Bureau of Justice Statistics
Black Panther Party, 94
Blackmun, Harry, 215–216
Bond, Julian, 217
Bordenkircher v. Hayes (1978), synopsis
  of, 160–161
Boston massacre, 82
Bradwell, Myra, biographical sketch
  of, 110–111
Brady, Jim, 97
Brady rule, 24
Brady v. Maryland (1963), 24
Breathalyzer tests, 49
Brown v. Board of Education (1954), 220
Bryan, William Jennings, 89, 223
Buffalo Creek, disaster at, 222
Bureau of Justice Statistics (BJS),
  publications by, 231

Burger, Warren, 93–94
  biographical sketch of, 111–113
Burr, Aaron, 84
Bush, George W.
  Gore and, 102–103
  secret trials and, 73
  terrorism and, 72

Cabranes, Jose, biographical sketch of,
  113
Cameras
  courtroom, 70–72, 140–142, 223
  North Dakota rules on, 140–142
Canadian Court System, 182–183
Capital punishment. *See* Death
  penalty cases
Carter, Jimmy, 39
  merit selection and, 40
  nominating commission and,
  96
Case for Innocence, The (video), 236
Case processing, 210, 211, 215, 231
  time for, 173–175, 174 (table)
Case-flow management,
  monitoring/controlling, 234
Caseloads, 97, 169
  nature of, 170–171, 173
Cases, 223
  controversial, 226
  high-profile, 70
  information about, 34, 68–73
  terminating, 48
  See also Criminal cases
Challenges
  for cause, 25, 246
  peremptory, 25, 99, 101, 249
Change of venue, 19, 246
Chicago Seven, 94
Chief justices, 83
Circuit courts of appeal, 37, 86, 87
  appointment to, 38
Citizenship, privileges/immunities of,
  85
Citizenship tests, 86
Civil Action, A (video), 236–237
Civil cases, 8, 30, 33, 55, 95, 98, 171,
  206
  ADR mechanisms for, 66
  assuming risks for, 61
  attorneys for, 99
  in British Empire, 52
  courts for, 9–11
  federal, 174 (table)
  jury trials in, 53
  liability in, 12, 52
  right to counsel for, 57

Civil injuries/disputes, remedies for, 46
Civil Justice Reform Act (1990), 99–100
Civil lawsuits, 1, 3, 6, 10, 12, 19, 29, 98, 213
  filing, 56, 66, 210
  manufacturers and, 63, 64
  negotiated resolutions for, 67
  participants in, 65
  processing, 62, 222
  See also Lawsuits
Civil liberties, 88, 219
Civil litigation, 14, 43, 44, 55, 62, 213, 221, 224
  binding arbitration and, 68
  profits from, 64
  rights and, 19
Civil rights activists, tort reform and, 64
Civil rights law, 17, 100, 102
Civil service, 38
  judges and, 40, 44
Civil trials, 29–30
  award winners in, 173 (table)
Closing statements, 28
Compensatory damages, 102
Compulsion (film), 88
Compulsory process, 19, 93
Conference of Chief Justices, 183
Conference of State Court Administrators, 183
Confrontation, right to, 19
Connolly, Maureen, 207
Constitutional Convention, 82
Consumer advocates, tort reform and, 64
Contingency fees, 58–59, 246–247
Contract cases, 171
  award winners in, 173 (table)
Contracts, reading, 68
Convictions, 21, 23, 24
Counsel. *See* Attorneys
Court costs, paying, 56–57, 58, 61
Court of Claims, Court of Customs and Patent Appeals and, 97
Court of Veterans Appeals, 99
Court referees, 57
Court reform, 31–32, 34, 76, 211, 212
Court reporters, 26, 62, 71
Court systems, 9, 33, 221
  issues for, 34
  organization of, 8, 169–170, 170 (table), 171 (table), 224
Court TV, trials on, 70
Courts
  appellate, 13–15, 19, 29, 30, 37, 38,

86, 219, 231, 248
  bankruptcy, 10
  characteristics of, 1, 2–16, 30, 31, 76, 205, 212, 221
  civil, 33, 56–62
  connection between, 101
  cyber, 64–65, 103–104, 142
  development of, 79
  district, 12
  drug, 218, 233
  in England/Wales, 10–11
  effectiveness of, 35, 73
  family, 11, 212, 248
  federal, 82
  of general jurisdiction, 12–13, 251
  juvenile, 11, 87
  of limited jurisdiction, 9–11, 219, 251
  lower-level, 2, 15
  politics and, 224
  public policies and, 7, 30, 209
  shire, 79
  small-claims, 57–58, 61
  state, 14–15, 31, 224
  supreme, 14–15, 31, 146–147
  trial, 9–14, 251
Courts.Net, 243
Criminal cases, 9, 10, 13, 29, 30, 33, 46, 80, 170, 171, 213, 221
  in British Empire, 52
  convictions in, 23
  defense attorneys and, 24
  examination of, 225
  federal, 174 (table)
  guilt in, 12
  investigation of, 31
  jurors and, 54
  pretrial stage of, 19–20
  processing, 174 (table), 222, 224
  public defenders and, 48
  in state courts, 172 (table)
  in U.S. District Courts, 172 (table)
Criminal Justice (magazine), 227
Criminal Justice (video), 237–238
Criminal justice systems, 11, 209, 221
Criminal law, 4, 8, 47, 48, 212
Criminal records, 50, 173
Criminal trials, 19–29, 41, 102, 213, 223
  change of venue for, 19
  counsel for, 46
  defendants in, 45
  federal, 173
  history of, 207–208
  shaping of, 16
  state, 92
  time limit on, 18
Crown Courts, 11

Culpability, 27, 75
Customs House, 82
Cyber court, 64–65, 103–104, 142

Darrow, Clarence, 87, 223
  biographical sketch of, 113–115
  Leopold/Loeb and, 88
  Scopes monkey trial and, 89
  Sweet and, 90
Death penalty cases, 7, 12, 13, 21, 73,
  88, 207, 213, 216
  Darrow and, 223
  defense counsel quality in, 230
  judicial policymaking and, 211
  victim participation in, 223
Decisionmaking, 25, 27, 30, 40–44,
  49–56, 62, 65, 76, 219, 221
  authoritative, 6
  discretionary, 211, 212, 217
  distinctive, 2–3
  fair, 33
  government, 55
  human element of, 226
  judges and, 50, 52
  jurors and, 54, 56
  law and, 5–6
  nature of, 31, 55–56
  openness of, 69
  outcomes and, 42
  politics and, 220
  process of, 3
  rules and, 55
  unbiased, 50
Dees, Morris, 209–210
  biographical sketch of, 115–116
Defendants, 3, 14, 25, 29, 46, 53, 247
  affluent, 23
  appointed, 233
  attorneys and, 47, 49
  in Canada, 48–49
  cases by, 27
  fair trials and, 69
  guilt/innocence of, 28, 50–52
  high-profile, 70
  indigent, 17, 23, 212, 231
  middle-class, 23
  prosecutors and, 16
  rights of, 44, 73
  secret trials and, 73
Defense attorneys, 100, 213, 216
  appointing, 15, 46, 47
  case types and, 24
  criminal, 43, 48, 99, 207, 226, 232,
  233
  grandstanding by, 71
  indigent clients and, 17, 45, 47

murder and, 41–42
prosecutors and, 7, 22, 24, 25, 26, 44
  quality of, 48, 230
  questioning by, 26–27
  role of, 27, 223, 232
  See also Attorneys
Delays, 18
Democratic National Convention
  (1968), 94
Dershowitz, Alan, 210
Desegregation, 7, 208
Discrimination, 86, 215
  gender, 16
  immigrant, 88
  racial, 8–9, 16, 17, 90, 210, 230
Dismissals, 170, 173
Dispute processing, 5–6, 30, 56–62
Dissenting opinions, 14, 247
Divorces, 7, 57
DNA testing, 26, 54, 223
Double jeopardy, 29, 30, 100, 247
  freedom from, 16–17
Douglas, William O., and Rosenbergs,
  92
Douglas v. California (1963), synopsis
  of, 149–150
Drug courts, 218, 233
Drug dealers, guilty pleas by, 75
Drug felonies, sentences for, 74
Drug trafficking, 72, 76
Dual court system, 8–9, 247
Due Process Clause, 85, 89
Duncan v. Louisiana (1968), 53
  Sixth Amendment and, 93
  synopsis of, 153–154

Edmonson v. Leesville Concrete Co.
  (1991), synopsis of, 166
Edward III, 80
Eighth Amendment, 92
  bail and, 22
  text of, 134–135
Eisenhower, Dwight, 92
Emory University School of Law, 243
England and Wales Court System, 184
Enslen, Richard A., biographical
  sketch of, 116–117
Equal protection, 49, 221
Equal Protection Clause, 9, 86, 103
Erlenborn, John, testimony of,
  144–145
Escobedo v. Illinois (1965), synopsis of,
  151
Evidence, 29, 215, 223
  favorable, 48
  gathering, 14, 20, 25

hiding, 43
improper, 62
incriminating, 21
insufficient, 21
jurors and, 54
physical, 23
presentation of, 12, 24, 26, 27, 28, 41
rules of, 3, 42, 62
Evidence of Guilt (video), 238
Exclusionary rule, 20, 248
Executions, 51, 73, 225

Family Advocate, 227–228
Family courts, 11, 212, 248
Federal Bar Association, 184
Federal Bureau of Investigation (FBI),
    surveillance by, 104
Federal Court of Australia, 181–182
Federal Courts Improvement Act
    (1982), 97
Federal Judicial Center (FJC), 93,
    184–185
    publications by, 232
Federal Magistrates Act (1968), 93
Federal Magistrates Act (1979), 96, 97
Federal Public Defenders, 185
Federal Rules of Civil Procedure, 98
Federalism, 8, 248
Felonies, 10, 12, 25, 97
    committing, 51
    juveniles and, 11
    punishment for, 73, 74
Fifth Amendment, 83, 89
    criminal trials and, 16–17
    defendant's rights and, 44
    double jeopardy and, 29, 100
    self-incrimination and, 20, 93
    text of, 133
    trial rights in, 84
    violation of, 20
Findlaw.com, 243
First Amendment, 89, 224
    limitations on, 69
Force, use of/threat of, 21
Foreman, John, 207
Forer, Lois, 212
Foster, Jodie, 97–98
Fourteenth Amendment, 85, 89, 207,
    208
    text of, 135
    violation of, 9, 86
Fourth Amendment,
    searches/seizures and, 20
Freedom of speech, 215, 219

Gag orders, 70

Gender
    discrimination, 16
    peremptory challenges and, 101
Georgia v. McCollum (1992), synopsis
    of, 166–167
Gideon v. Wainwright (1963), 46, 93
    synopsis of, 148–149
*Gideon's Trumpet: The Poor Man and the
    Law* (video), 238–239
Ginsburg, Ruth Bader, biographical
    sketch of, 117–118
Gitlow v. New York (1925), 89
Gore, Al, Bush and, 102–103
Grand jury, 13
Gregg v. Georgia (1976), synopsis of,
    159–160
Grey, Horace, 86
Griffin v. Illinois (1956), synopsis of,
    147–148
Guilt, 12, 28, 50–52
    criminal, 40, 45
    determining, 50
    God and, 50–51
Guilty pleas, 10, 13, 26, 47, 74, 75, 173

Habeas corpus, 46, 248
Habitual offenders, 10, 23, 74
Hamilton, Alexander, Zenger and, 81
Hastie, William H., biographical
    sketch of, 118–119
Hauptman, Bruno, 91
Haywood, Bill, Darrow and, 87, 223
Hearings, 13
    bail, 21–22, 49
    pretrial, 18
Heath v. Alabama (1985), synopsis of,
    162
Henry I, 79
Henry II, ordeals/battles and, 51
Hinckley, John, Jr., trial of, 97–98
Hoffman, Abie, 94
Hoffman, Julius, 94
Hong Kong Court System, 185–186
Houston, Charles Hamilton,
    biographical sketch of, 119–120

Incarceration, 17, 47, 75
Indigent defendants, 23, 212, 231
    courts and, 60–61
    defense attorneys for, 17, 45, 47
    in Europe, 59–61
    representation for, 33, 45–49, 221
Information, public access to, 34,
    68–73
Inherit the Wind (play), Darrow and,
    223

Innocent III, Pope, 51, 80
Innocent Until Proven Guilty (video),
 239
Inquisitorial system, 31, 33, 48, 248
 and adversarial system compared,
 40–45
 judges and, 41, 43
Insanity defense, 54, 98
Inside the Jury (video), 239–240
Insurance companies, 59, 61, 63
Interest groups, judges and, 39
Internet, 65, 71
Investigations, 20, 31, 47, 49

J.E.B. v. Alabama ex rel. T.B. (1994), 101
 synopsis of, 167
Jefferson, Thomas, 83, 84
John I, Magna Carta and, 79–80
Johnson, Lyndon B., Marshall and, 93
Johnson v. Zerbst (1938), synopsis of,
 147
Judges, 1, 4, 14, 30, 170
 African American, 93
 appellate, 37, 39, 86–87, 96–97
 appointing, 37, 39, 40
 circuit, 85, 86–87
 decisionmaking by, 27, 42, 50, 52,
 69, 206, 211
 district, 93, 96
 ethical standards for, 225
 European, 38
 federal, 39, 40, 88, 91, 93, 96
 higher-court, 38
 inquisitorial system and, 41, 43
 law-trained, 220
 lower-court, 38
 nonlawyer, 219–220
 panels of, 41
 performance of, 220
 politics and, 35–36
 prosecutors and, 11
 public policy and, 7, 40
 responsibilities of, 42, 218
 role of, 41, 225
 sentences and, 73
 unqualified/incompetent, 36, 37, 43
 women, 91
Judges' Bill (1925), 89
Judges' Journal, 228
Judicature (journal), 228
Judicial Conference of the United
 States, 88, 186–187
Judicial elections, 35–36, 37
Judicial selection, 33, 34–40, 45, 82,
 213, 224
 in Missouri, 136–138

 in New Mexico, 138–139
 politics and, 40
Judiciary Act (1789), 83
Judiciary Act (1801), 83, 84
Juries, 30, 42, 102
 English, 53
 grand, 13
 hung, 29
 judges and, 41
 lay, 41
 mixed, 41
 selecting, 216
 size/unanimity rules for, 53–54
 trial processes and, 216
 women on, 96
Jurors
 capacity of, 33, 49–56
 criminal cases and, 54
 decisionmaking by, 50, 54, 56
 dissenting, 53
 evidence and, 54
 neutral/objective, 54, 216
 potential, 70
 prosecutors and, 55
 summons for, 25
 unbiased, 73
Jury deliberations, 28, 55
Jury instructions, 28, 54–55
Jury nullification, 216
Jury trials, 79, 170, 173, 206, 223, 225
 adversary system and, 44
 in British Empire, 51–52
 in civil cases, 29, 53
 history of, 50–51
 right to, 26, 53, 93
 summary, 67, 250
 in U.S., 52–54
Justice, 76, 213
 achieving, 58, 214, 215
 media and, 70–72
 neutral principles of, 3
 portrayals of, 7
 reform, 33, 62–68
 second-class, 60
 secret trials and, 73
 self-help, 5
Justice System Journal, 228–229
Juvenile and Family Court Journal, 229
Juvenile courts, 11, 87
Juvenile Justice (video), 240

Kennedy, John F., 207
King, Rodney, 100
Klopfer v. North Carolina (1967)
 Sixth Amendment and, 93
 synopsis of, 152–153

Ku Klux Klan, 89
Kunstler, William, 94
  biographical sketch of, 120–121

Lambros, Thomas D., biographical
  sketch of, 121
Landlord-tenant disputes, 57, 60
Law, 46, 215
  civil, 9, 212
  constitutional, 8–9, 219, 221, 225
  criminal, 4, 8, 47, 48, 212
  decisionmaking and, 5–6
  equal treatment, 56
  interpretation of, 62
  neutral principles of, 81
  overriding, 56
  politics and, 35
  self-defense under, 56
  setting up, 81
  state, 8–9
Law clerks, 62, 86, 215–216, 219
Law.com, 244
LawCommerce.com, 244
Laws and Liberties of Massachusetts,
  publication of, 80–81
Lawsuits, 12, 19, 59
  credit card agreements and, 68
  deterring, 59
  filing, 6, 29, 61
  frivolous, 63–64
  malpractice, 63
  See also Civil lawsuits
Lee, Charles, 84
Legal Aid Ontario, 187
Legal Aid Society of New York,
  187–188
Legal assistance, entitlement to, 49,
  60, 143–144
Legal Information Institute (Cornell
  Law School), 243
Legal protections, 208
Legal Services Corporation, 143–144,
  188–189
  poverty guidelines by, 144 (table)
  presidential testimony from,
  144–145
Legal Times, 229
Leopold, Nathan, 88, 223
Lewis v. United States (1996), 17, 53
  synopsis of, 167–168
Liability, 12, 52, 55
  basis for, 59
  civil, 40, 45, 210
  imposing, 54
  manufacturer, 63
Life sentences, 13, 74

Lindbergh, Charles, 91
Literacy tests, 86
Litigation
  civil, 14, 19, 43, 44, 55, 62, 64, 68,
    213, 221, 224
  constitutional, 219
  costs of, 56–59, 61–63
  policy shaping and, 209
  processes of, 64, 66
  public controversies and, 224
  resolving disputes with, 62, 222
  strategies for, 220
  technology and, 64–65
  unnecessary, 59
  value of, 62
Loeb, Richard, 88, 223
Los Angeles County District
  Attorney's Office, 189

Magistrate Courts, 10–11, 249
Magna Carta, 79–80
Malloy v. Hogan (1964), Fifth
  Amendment and, 93
Management issues, 139, 232
Mandatory sentences, 74, 75, 211,
  249
Mansfield, Arabella, 85
  biographical sketch of, 121–122
Marbury v. Madison (1802), 83–84
Marshall, John, 84
Marshall, Thurgood, 93
  biographical sketch of, 122–123
Martin, Luther, 84
Martinez v. Court of Appeal of California
  (2000), synopsis of, 168–169
Maryland v. Craig (1990), 19
  synopsis of, 165–166
McVeigh, Timothy, 70, 102, 212
Media
  court proceedings and, 212
  fines for, 69
  justice and, 70–72
  limitations on, 19
  Lindbergh kidnapping and, 91
  McVeigh trial and, 70
  military trials and, 72–73
  Simpson trial and, 101
  victims and, 70
  voluntary cooperation by, 70
Mediation, 60, 66–67, 250
Medill School of Journalism
  (Northwestern University), 244
Merit selection, 38–40, 91, 250
  in Missouri, 136–138
Mexican American Legal Defense and
  Education Fund, 189–190

Military tribunals, media and, 72–73
Minnesota Sentencing Guidelines
　Commission, 96
Miranda v. Arizona (1966), 21, 49
　synopsis of, 151–152
Misdemeanors, 10, 12
Mixed systems, 52
Moran v. Burbine (1986), synopsis of,
　163–165
Morgan, Charles, 217
Murder trials, 41–42, 225, 242–245
Murphy, Frank, 90

NAACP Legal Defense and Education
　Fund, 190
National Asian Pacific American
　Legal Consortium, 190–191
National Association for Court
　Management, 191
National Association of Criminal
　Defense Lawyers, 191–192
National Association of Women
　Judges, 192
National Bar Association, 192–193
National Center for Juvenile Justice,
　193
　publications by, 233–234
National Center for State Courts, 193
National Council of Juvenile and
　Family Court Judges, 193–194
National District Attorneys
　Association, 194
National Law Journal, 229
National Lawyers Guild, 194–195
New York v. Quarles (1984), 21
Nichols, Terry, 102
Nigerian Court System, 195
Nineteenth Amendment, 86
Nixon, Richard M., 93–94, 218
Nominations, 37, 38, 39
Norm enforcement, 4, 5, 7, 30
Normans, 79
Note-taking, 142–143

O'Connor, Sandra Day, 97
　biographical sketch of, 123–124
Ombudsman, 66
Omnibus Judgeship Act (1978), 96–97
Opening statements, 26, 28
Oswald, Lee Harvey, 207
Outcomes, 33, 67, 211
　decisionmakers and, 42
　determining, 52
　equal, 31, 76
　negotiated, 214

Pacific Legal Foundation, 195–196
Personal injuries, 6, 7
Physicians, insurance and, 63
Plaintiffs, 29, 249
Plea bargains, 10, 13, 22, 47, 69, 214,
　223
　indigent and, 23
　role of, 217
Pointer v. Texas (1965), 93
　synopsis of, 150
Police brutality, 101
Policy
　court decisions and, 7, 30, 209, 220,
　　222
　judicial, 7, 40, 211, 213
　shaping, 7, 30, 69, 71, 80, 209
Political dissidents,
　imprisonment/execution of, 73
Politics, 3, 223
　civil liberties and, 219
　courts and, 224
　judicial decisions and, 220
　judicial selection and, 38, 40
　law and, 35
Pound, Roscoe, biographical sketch
　of, 124
Powell v. Alabama (1932), 90
　synopsis of, 146–147
Precedents, public policy and, 221
Pretrial hearings, 18
Pretrial publicity, 69
Prison conditions, 7
Prison Litigation Reform Act (1996),
　102
Prison reform, 222
Prisoners, civil rights lawsuits and,
　102
Private property, 81
Pro bono work, 60, 249
Probable cause, 21, 249
Probation, 10, 75
Procedure, 6, 31, 215, 223
　civil lawsuit, 62
　technical rules of, 3
　time-consuming, 60
　violation of, 42
Proceedings, 31, 41, 81, 212
　early, 79
　efficiency in, 76
　public access to, 68–73
Processes, 93
　case, 173–175, 174 (table), 210, 211,
　　215, 231
　connection between, 101
　criminal, 16–19
　developing, 41

dispute, 5–6, 30, 56–57, 61, 62
  fair, 6
  informal, 217
  judicial, 33, 76, 80, 82, 206, 221, 230
  juries and, 216
  nonjudicial, 60, 61
  reviewing, 225
  trial, 16–30, 68, 101, 205, 210,
    214–217, 225, 233
Prosecutor Information, 244
Prosecutors, 10, 29, 30, 43, 171, 216,
  230
  challenges by, 99
  civil service, 22, 25
  criminal cases and, 13, 16, 22
  defense attorneys and, 7, 22, 24, 25,
    26, 44
  discretionary authority of, 74
  grandstanding by, 71
  judges and, 11
  jurors and, 55
  murder and, 41
  plea negotiations and, 23
  political influence of, 22–23
  role of, 44, 223
  testimony and, 27
Public controversies, 68–69
  litigation and, 224
Public defenders, 43, 232, 233, 250
  criminal cases and, 48
Public trials, right to, 17, 18–19
Punishment, 9, 13, 50, 76, 96, 98–99
  alternatives to, 223
  corporal, 223
  criminal, 15, 102
  imposing, 11, 74, 75
  increase in, 23
  sentences and, 73
  statutes defining, 74
Punitive damages, 63
Pursuit driving, 64

Questioning, 21
Quincy, Josiah, 82

Racism, 8–9, 16, 17, 90, 101, 102, 210,
  230
Randolph, Edmund, 84
Rape, 90–91
Reagan, Ronald
  appointments by, 40, 97
  attempted assassination of, 97–98
  judicial selection process and, 96
Real Justice (video), 240–241
Real property cases, 171
  award winners in, 173 (table)

Reasonable doubt, 26, 27, 29, 43
  secret trials and, 72
Red scare, 88
Rehabilitation, 11, 74, 75
Rehnquist, William Hubbs, Jr., 220
  biographical sketch of, 124–125
Religion, 5
  freedom of, 16, 224
Representation, 33, 45–49, 221
Requiem for Frank Lee Smith (video),
  241
Reynolds v. Sims (1964), 217
Rights, 44, 73
  citizens', 16
  civil, 94, 218
  civil litigation and, 19
  to confrontation, 19
  constitutional, 19, 103, 210
  to counsel, 15, 17, 45, 46–47, 57, 93
  defendant's, 44
  deprivation of, 6, 208
  individual, 215
  investigations and, 20
  privacy, 215
  role of, 16–30
  self-incrimination, 16, 21, 44
  trial, 17, 18–19, 26, 53, 84, 93
  voting, 85–86
Robinson v. California (1962), 92
Roe v. Wade (1973), 7
Roosevelt, Franklin D., 91
Rosenberg, Ethel and Julius, 92
Ross v. Moffitt (1974), 17
  synopsis of, 158–159
Ruby, Jack, and Belli, 207
Rules, 6, 27, 42, 60, 62
  decisionmaking and, 55

Saboteurs, trials/sentences for, 72
Sacco and Vanzetti trial, 87–88
Sanity, testimony about, 54, 98
School finance reform, 222
Scientific tests, 26, 54, 223
Scopes monkey trial, 88–89, 223
Scott v. Illinois (1979), 15, 17, 46
  synopsis of, 161–162
Scottsboro trials, 90–91, 213
Seale, Bobby, 94
Searches, 16, 20, 42
Secret trials, 18, 72, 73, 216
Security, 8, 72–73
  military trials and, 72
  oversight/accountability for, 104
Seditious libels, 81
Segregation, 213, 217, 222
Self-defense, law and, 56

Self-incrimination, 20, 93
  right against, 16, 21, 44
  See also Testimony
Sentencing
  alternative, 216
  discretionary, 173
  mandatory, 74, 75, 211, 249
  recommended, 31
  reform of, 34, 73–76, 173
  severe, 49, 74, 75
  victim participation in, 223
Sentencing guidelines, 74–76, 96, 173,
  250
  in Massachusetts, 175 (table)
  in Minnesota, 74–75, 139–140
Sentencing Reform Act (1984), 98–99
Settlements, 10, 59, 67
  negotiated, 67, 222
Seventh Amendment, text of, 134
Sex-offense cases, 26, 53
  access and, 18
  victims of, 70
Simpson, O. J., trial of, 71, 101–102
Sixth Amendment, 12, 44, 72, 83, 89
  compulsory process and, 93
  criminal trials and, 16, 17
  jury trials and, 52, 53, 93
  right to counsel and, 45, 46–47, 57,
    93
  text of, 133–134
  trial rights in, 68, 84, 93
Slave revolt, trial for, 84–85
Small-claims courts, 57–58, 61
Social Security, 8, 171
Southern Poverty Law Center, 196,
  209
Speedy Trial Act (1974), 95
Speedy trials, 17, 18, 93, 211
Spence, Gerry, biographical sketch of,
  125–126
Stamp Act (1735), 81–82
State and Local Bar Associations-
  United States, 197
State Attorneys General, 196–197
State Court Systems-United States,
  197–198
Strauder v. West Virginia (1880), 86
  synopsis of, 146
Supreme Court of Appeal of South
  Africa, 198
Supreme courts, state, 14–15, 31
Surveillance, electronic, 104
Sweet, Dr., 89, 90
Sweet, Henry, 90

Taxation, 8, 9, 79, 82

Taylor v. Illinois (1988), synopsis of,
  165
Taylor v. Louisiana (1975), 95–96
Technology, 104
  litigation and, 64–65
Terrorism, 9, 24
  threat of, 72, 103, 104
Testimony, 23, 26, 27, 54
  closed-circuit, 19
  emotional, 54
  reviewing, 28, 71
  See also Self-incrimination
Theft, sentences for, 74
Third Branch, 230
Three-strikes law, 74, 223, 250–251
Tort cases, 171
  award winners in, 173 (table)
Tort reform, 63–64, 251
Treatment programs, 233
Trial (magazine), 230
Trial courts, 9, 14
  in England/Wales, 10–11
  of general jurisdiction, 12–13, 251
  of limited jurisdiction, 9–11, 251
*Trial Lawyer: Five Courtroom Champions
    Speak, The* (video), 241
Trials
  access to, 68–73
  duration of, 66, 173–175, 174 (table)
  early, 50–51
  fair, 69, 73
  insights of, 221
  murder, 41–42, 225, 242–245
  preparation for, 22
  prevalence of, 170–171, 173
  secret, 68, 72, 73, 216
  speedy, 17, 18, 93, 211
  supervising, 62
  Supreme Court decisions on,
    146–147
  televised, 70–72
  witch, 81
  See also Jury trials
Trials by ordeal, 50–51, 80
Trinidad and Tobago Court System,
  198
Truth seeking, 43, 45, 48

United States Attorney General, 22
United States Circuit Judge
  Nominating Commission, 96
United States Constitution, 12, 15, 44,
  52, 83, 85
  Article III of, 99, 132–133
  courts and, 2
  drafting of, 82

selected provisions of, 132–135
state laws and, 8–9
Supreme Court and, 170
United States Court of Appeals for the
    Eleventh Circuit, 97
United States Court of Appeals for the
    Federal Circuit, 97
United States Court of Appeals for the
    Fifth Circuit, 97
United States Court of Appeals for the
    Second Circuit, and Marshall, 93
United States Court of Appeals for the
    Seventh Circuit, 199
United States Court of Appeals for the
    Sixth Circuit, Allen and, 91
United States Court of Military
    Appeals, 91 92
United States Department of Justice,
    22, 40, 199 200
United States District Court for the
    Northern District of Ohio, 200
United States Foreign Intelligence
    Court, surveillance and, 104
United States House of
    Representatives, 37
United States Sentencing
    Commission, 75, 98, 200–201
United States Supreme Court, 90,
    201–202, 213
    appeals to, 14, 15, 46
    creation of, 82, 83, 170
    decisions by, 83–84, 214–215, 226
    double jeopardy and, 17
    King, Rodney and, 100
    literacy/citizenship tests and, 86
    processes of, 218–219
    Rehnquist on, 220
    reviews by, 225
    rights taking by, 208
    role of, 218
    secrecy of, 215–216, 220–221
    slave revolt and, 85
    speedy trials and, 18
Use of force, 64

Vanderbilt, Arthur T., biographical

sketch of, 126–127
Vera Institute of Justice, 202
Verdicts
    negotiated outcomes and, 214
    nonbinding, 67
    nonunanimous, 53
    reaching, 29
    trial, 67
Victims, 56
    child, 70
    media and, 70
    participation by, 223
    sex-abuse, 19
Video conferencing, 65, 103–104
Violent crime, 11, 49
Voir dire, 25–26

Warren, Earl, 92, 94
    biographical sketch of, 127 129
Washington Legal Foundation,
    202–203
Weinglass, Leonard, 94
Western Federation of Miners, 87
White Justice (video), 242
Who Killed Vincent Chin (video),
    242
William the Conqueror, 79
Williams v. Florida (1970), 53, 95
    synopsis of, 155
Wiretaps, 24, 104
Wirt, William, 84
Witch trials, 81
Witnesses, 100, 223
    credibility of, 27
    delays and, 18
    expert, 27, 47
    inconsistent, 224
    obtaining, 17
    questioning, 24, 26–27, 42, 43
    rebuttal, 28
Women's suffrage, 85–86

Youth International Party (Yippies),
    94

Zenger, John Peter, 81

About the Author

Christopher E. Smith, professor of criminal justice at Michigan State University, is a lawyer and social scientist who has written twenty books and more than eighty scholarly articles on courts, law, and criminal justice. He holds degrees from Harvard University, the University of Bristol (England), the University of Tennessee College of Law, and the University of Connecticut.